W9-ASH-055

DEATH

The End of Self-Improvement

Joan Tollifson

NEW SARUM PRESS

UNITED KINGDOM

DEATH: THE END OF SELF-IMPROVEMENT

First edition published November 2019 by New Sarum Press

Parts of this book have appeared previously in *Noumenon Journal, Inquiring Mind, InZicht*, in Leo Hartong's Newsletter, on Facebook, and in the SAND anthology, *On the Mystery of Being*.

Cover drawing, self-portrait by the author
Author photo by Rosanna Durham
Cover design and interior layout, Julian Noyce

© Joan Tollifson 2019
© New Sarum Press 2019

Joan Tollifson has asserted her right under the Copyright, Designs and Patents Act, 1988, to be identified as author of this work.

www.joantollifson.com

All rights reserved.

No part of this book may be reproduced or utilised in any form or by any means, electronic or mechanical, without prior permission in writing from the Publisher.

NEW SARUM PRESS | 6 Folkestone Road | Salisbury | SP2 8JP |United Kingdom
ISBN: 978-1-9162903-0-3
www.newsarumpress.com

Practice is not about overcoming human problems. It's not about becoming serene and transcendent. It's about embracing our lives as they really are, and understanding at every point how deep and profound and gorgeous everything is—even the suffering, even the difficulty. So we forgive ourselves for our limitations, and we forgive this world for its pain. We don't say, "That's not pain." It is pain. You don't say, "It's not difficulty." It is difficult. But when we embrace the difficulty... we see this is exactly the difficulty we need, and this difficulty is the most beautiful and poignant thing in this world.

— Zoketsu Norman Fischer

Don't grieve.
Anything you lose comes round
in another form...

God's joy moves from unmarked box
to unmarked box, from cell to cell.
As rainwater, down into flowerbed.
As roses, up from ground.
Now it looks like a plate of rice and fish,
now a cliff covered with vines,
now a horse being saddled.
It hides within these, till one day
it cracks them open.

—Rumi

TABLE of CONTENTS

Note to the reader: *A few of the names in some of the personal stories contained in this book were changed to protect privacy, and in a few cases, chronologies were condensed or slightly altered to simplify the narrative and improve the overall readability of the book. All these stories reflect my experience of what happened; others may remember the same events differently—in no case should they be heard as an objective report on reality, nor should this be taken as a comprehensive autobiography of everything that happened in my life during these years—many people and events have been left out for one reason or another.*

Joan Tollifson
Ashland, Oregon
October 8, 2019

Dissolving

I shall soon be quite dead at last in spite of all.

—opening line of *Malone Dies* by Samuel Beckett

I began writing this book in Chicago almost two decades ago. When I was in my fifties, I moved back to the city where I was born to be with my mother, then in her nineties, in her final years. I stayed on for several more years after she died to be with my mother's oldest friend in her final years.

During my eight years in Chicago, I went through menopause and began to experience my own aging in a new and more visceral way. Several close friends died, two went into nursing homes, all were growing noticeably older. Eventually, the year I turned sixty, I moved to Oregon. One of my Zen teachers, Joko Beck—one of the clearest, sharpest people I'd ever met—slipped into what seemed to many to be some form of dementia, behaved in strange and unexpected ways, and eventually died. My main teacher, Toni Packer, suffered a more than decade-long, painful, debilitating illness culminating in death. My first lover from college died. I got cancer. I turned seventy. On a global scale, there was talk of the sixth mass extinction being underway, and humanity itself seemed to be flirting with death in the form of climate change or nuclear holocaust. And so, rather naturally, I found myself writing about aging and dying, that time of life when everything falls apart. Paradoxically, I found that what I was really writing about was living—being alive now.

I also began to notice that aging and dying share much in common with spiritual awakening. Both involve a dissolving of old identities, the disappearance of future time, the end of the known, and letting go of absolutely everything. Aging and dying, like awakening, are a great stripping process, a process of subtraction. Everything we have identified with gradually disintegrates—our bodies, cognitive skills, memory, ability to function independently. Eventually, everything perceivable and conceivable disappears.

Am I saying that *nothing* survives death? Actually, I'm suggesting that there are no separate and persisting "things" to begin with, either to be born or to die. All apparent forms—people, tables, chairs, atoms, quarks, planets, dogs, cats, consciousness, energy—are mental concepts reified and abstracted out of a seamless and boundless actuality that does not begin or end, for it is ever-present Here-Now. And whatever this boundless actuality is, it seems to have infinite viewpoints from which it can be seen, and infinite layers of density, from the most apparently solid to the most ephemeral and subtle. Ultimately, there is no way to say *what* this indivisible wholeness *is*. No label, concept or formulation—whether scientific or metaphysical—can capture the living actuality.

No one knows for sure what happens after death, and I may be surprised; but I assume that dying will be just like going to sleep or going under anesthesia. Conscious experiencing—my movie of waking life and the experience of being present—will vanish as it does every night in deep sleep or under anesthesia. And, as in deep sleep, I won't be there to miss myself or my movie of waking life. The fear of dying only exists during waking life, and only as a fearful idea. In deep sleep, the problem—and the one who seems to have it—no longer exist.

The more closely we explore this whole compelling appearance that I call the movie of waking life, the more we find that it has no more substance or enduring reality than a passing dream. We might think of it as a play of the universe, a dance of consciousness, a marvelous and deep entertainment, with no meaning or purpose except to play, to dance, to enjoy and explore and express itself, and then, to dissolve— back into that unfathomable mystery prior to consciousness, subtler than space, in which nothing perceivable or conceivable remains.

In my view, what happens after death is a flat earth question. Worrying about what happens to us when we die is like worrying about what happens to us if we fall off the edge of the earth. People used to worry about that, but their fear was based on a misunderstanding. Just as there is no edge to the earth, there is no actual boundary, no edge where life begins or ends. The things we are worrying about are all conceptual abstractions, artificially pulled out of the whole. Like the lines on a map dividing up the whole earth, birth and death are artificial dividing lines on an indivisible reality.

Just as no wave is ever really fixed in any permanent form or separate from the ocean, no person is ever actually a fixed or solid "thing" separate from the totality. This unbroken wholeness or unicity is ever-present as the still-point of Here-Now, and ever-changing as the thorough-going flux and impermanence of experience. This wholeness cannot be found or lost because it is all there is, and there is nothing and nowhere that is not it. Nothing stands apart from it to "get it" or "lose it," and it never departs from itself. Stillness and movement, immutability and impermanence, mind and matter, are simply different ways of seeing and describing this indivisible actuality.

Of course, there's no denying the everyday reality of death. Every living being is a unique and precious expression of the universe, a unique point of view, a unique and unrepeatable pattern of energy. When someone we love dies, they are gone, never to return, and one day, this life we are experiencing right now will end. In so many ways, death is the greatest wake-up call there is.

Someone sent me a wonderful cartoon for my sixty-fifth birthday. It pictured a long line of cute penguin-like creatures waddling in single-file across a vast plain that extended as far back as the eye could see, and at the front of the line, the creatures have arrived at the edge of a cliff, a very steep precipice—and the captions reads, "Man, I guess it really was about the journey and not the destination."

When the future disappears, we are brought home to the immediacy that we may have avoided all our lives—the vibrant aliveness Here-Now, the only place where we ever actually *are*. Whether it is the personal death that awaits each of us, or the inevitable planetary death in which the earth itself will be no more, or even the end of the entire known universe, death is the single reality that most clearly informs us that the future is a fantasy and that the person and the world and everything that we have been so concerned about are all fleeting bubbles in a stream.

When we believe that a single, fragile, vulnerable, impermanent bubble is all we are, we live in fear of death. And yet, paradoxically, at the same time, we long to pop the bubble of apparent encapsulation and limitation and dissolve into the vast, unlimited wholeness that we seem to have lost, the no-thing-ness where all our problems and concerns vanish into thin air.

We all know, intuitively, that this bubble is not all we are, nor are we some kind of lost soul trapped inside it. The wholeness we long for is actually all there is. The bubble has never been a solid, separate, independent, unchanging thing. By embracing the actuality of life just as it is, something shifts. And surprisingly, the more closely we tune into the bare actuality, the less substantial it seems, and the more mysterious, unresolvable and extraordinary it reveals itself to be. Pain, whether physical or emotional, becomes more interesting and less frightening, and even if fear arises, that too becomes interesting rather than fearful. *Everything* reveals the jewel in ever-new ways.

We often have the idea that dignity means being in control, not being overwhelmed by emotion, not screaming or crying in pain, not losing control of our bowels, not vomiting on ourselves or peeing in our pants, not losing our minds, and so on. Most of us are conditioned to feel that bodily functions and emotions are a bit dirty or unspiritual and best hidden away. At the very least, they must be controlled.

As we age, and for some people much sooner in the wake of an illness or a disability, all this begins to crumble away. We may start having falls or losing our cognitive skills. We may not be able to function independently anymore. We may need help, sometimes with very intimate tasks. We may lose bowel control, perhaps in a crowded restaurant while eating Sunday brunch with a large group of friends—that happened to my mother in her last year of life. If you've been with people who are dying, you know that there are usually body fluids involved and all sorts of messy things that don't fit our limited and unreal picture of dignity. We may end up in bed, in a nursing home, in restraints, in terror, screaming—this happened to a friend's father. I have an ostomy bag now, following an anal cancer, and I've had some pretty messy moments while managing the bag one-handed—I lost my right hand before birth. Are all these events undignified? Are they humiliating? Or are they simply part of life?

This book is not about getting control and staying young forever, nor is it about avoiding or denying any of the messiness and painful loss that aging and dying and living inevitably involve. This is not a self-help book that tells you how to stay active and feel perpetually young, nor does it promise any kind of afterlife "for you" through heaven or reincarnation. Rather, this book is about fully embracing death, and therefore life, wholeheartedly and relaxing into the total disintegration and loss of control that growing old and falling apart— and living and loving and being awake—actually entails.

Our usual approach is to tiptoe around the word death, replacing it with euphemisms, as if speaking the word itself would be too raw, too disturbing. Growing old is a natural and unavoidable fact of life that we are constantly trying to deny, hide, or cover up with wishful thinking, hair dye, Botox, erectile dysfunction drugs, cosmetic surgery, euphemisms, and inspirational stories about age-defying, ninety-year-old super-heroes who are still sky-diving and having hot sex. All of this promotes the popular notion that we can always be young and healthy and at the top of our game. I'm all for staying fit, challenging ourselves, enjoying life to the fullest, and having a positive attitude toward old age; but in the final analysis, growing old is one long surrender, letting go into a process of subtraction and unraveling, a demolition project in which things fall apart and every form we know and love is lost. It usually involves some degree of physical pain, and it isn't always pretty or easy.

Old age is an adventure in uselessness, loss of control, being nobody and giving up everything. That sounds quite dreadful when we have been conditioned to believe that we must be *somebody*, that we must strive to get better and better, that our lives must have purpose and meaning, that above all, we must be useful and productive and always *doing* something and *getting somewhere*. This book is here to suggest that the loss of all that is actually not bad news. It may even be immensely liberating!

This book explores growing old and dying—and more importantly, being alive—both through the lens of my personal story and from the larger, impersonal perspective of what might be called nondual spirituality. And when I use the word spiritual, I don't ever mean spirit as opposed to matter, or spiritual as opposed to secular. Spirituality as I mean it is a perspective that sees *all* of life as sacred, and by sacred, I mean worthy of devotion, full of wonder, inconceivable and ungraspable. The kind of spirituality that has attracted me is about direct experience, not belief or dogma, and it is focused on Here-Now, not on some imaginary future. This is the perspective you'll find in this book, and it includes everything from vaginal dryness to politics.

Many so-called "nondual" or "spiritual" books sound so abstract. The author seems to have crossed some finish-line and risen above the human mess once and for all, and the reader wonders why he or she can't seem to do the same. For years, I labored under the delusion that "I," this person called Joan, was somehow lacking, not quite all the way "there" yet. Of course, as a person, we are never perfect in any ideal way, and any "there" that we imagine one day arriving at is a fantasy, for *nowhere* actually exists outside of Here-Now. Having known many spiritual teachers up close, I know for a fact that I'm not unique in having human imperfections.

In the end, we're all frauds and liars, magicians and tricksters, pulling the wool over our own eyes and playing peek-a-boo with ourselves; and we're all Zen Masters in thin disguise as well. After all, the one behind all the masks is the One and Only, the ever-changing, dancing emptiness that is no-thing and everything.

My life as the Joan character is essentially no different from any other life because, when you boil all our seemingly very different lives down to the basics, the central themes turn out to be quite universal. At the same time, every snowflake, fingerprint, cloud formation, person and moment is utterly unique and unrepeatable. I am showing up intermittently as a particular human being and simultaneously as the vast presence being and beholding it all. I am both the ocean and the wave, and in this, I am no different from anyone else. I speak in this book as both the ocean and the wave, and my perspective moves freely between relative and absolute, which, in nonduality, are understood to be "not two."

All our stories are ultimately dreamlike fictions, however relatively true they might be, and all the characters in this story, including the main character, "Joan Tollifson," are mirage-like phantasms. At the same time, every character is as real and miraculous as every snowflake, and our stories are every bit as much a manifestation of this unfolding as ocean waves and cloud formations, all of it the cosmic play. Imagination is a powerful and creative force, every bit as real as so-called "material reality," which may itself be nothing more than a dreamlike imagination of consciousness.

There is something that draws me to stories, and I find that all stories are my story, for in this holographic universe, each of us contains the whole. I love movies, plays, TV shows, novels, gossip. The best stories open the mind and the heart. They entertain and delight. They shake us loose from our moorings. They reveal new depths, insights and possibilities. Of course, some stories—the conditioned ones that repeat over and over in our heads—create the illusion of bondage and separation ("I'm a loser, I've ruined my life, I'll never get," or "You're a loser, You shouldn't have done that, You've ruined my life."). So, stories can function as both an avoidance of life and a deep and intimate engagement with life. I love the stories that take us to places we've never been, the stories that wake us up, the stories that invite us to see something new, or to see more deeply. I also love waking up from stories. I love silence and stillness. I love the absence of stories. Like a child, I love blowing bubbles and popping them, building sandcastles and smooshing them, going into the movie theater, getting totally absorbed in a story, coming back out again into the larger movie of waking life, and then sitting down in meditation and dissolving into wordless presence. It's *all* beautiful. And that kind of play is exactly what this book *is*.

It weaves personal narrative and meditative explorations together, telling a story and then erasing it, dispensing the dharma and then revealing the messiness of the drama behind the scenes that is usually hidden from view in most spiritual or nondual books. I write in this way simply because I do. I find it interesting to go back and forth between the abstract and the particular, the personal and the impersonal, the relative and the absolute. Something in that tension, that juxtaposition of construction and deconstruction, creation and erasure, intrigues me. The ultimate discovery is that there is no actual separation between form and emptiness, purity and impurity, sacred and profane, spiritual and material, perfection and imperfection, nirvana and samsara, undivided boundlessness and its expression as a unique person or an unrepeatable snowflake.

My mother once told an ER nurse that my books are about being who you are. This can be heard on many levels. It can mean being the limitless Here-Now. Or it can mean fully playing our part as the character we are pretending to be in the movie of waking life, playing that part wholeheartedly, without restraint or apology, without holding back, without trying to be someone else instead, being exactly who we are in this moment with utter abandon, "following your bliss," as my mother would say. I think my mother intended "being who you are" in both of these ways when she said it, the undivided wholeness and the fully-lived character. Maybe they are actually one and the same. Maybe that is part of the great discovery that is called awakening, liberation or enlightenment. And maybe the other part of that great discovery is that the fully-lived character and the undivided wholeness aren't ever what we *think* they are. Maybe the fully-lived character is *exactly* what we *actually are* in this moment, not how we *imagine* we *should* or *could* be, *if only*. Likewise, maybe Ultimate Reality or nirvana or supreme enlightenment is not a distant memory or a future hope, but rather *this* present moment, *this* aliveness that is endlessly appearing and disappearing, inhaling and exhaling, dying and being born—right here, right now, just as it is.

This book is definitely not a seven-step guidebook to perpetual bliss or to never growing old. It is rather an invitation to let everything fall apart, as it does anyway, and as it must for anything new to emerge. This falling apart is a waking up from the obsessive concern with self-improvement and self-preservation, and a release from the fear of disintegration, imperfection and death. Perhaps in this exploration we will discover together that our worst fears are not really as terrible as we had imagined, and that what appears to be an obstacle or a hindrance is actually the gateless gate and a jewel beyond all price.

Part I: Chicago

2003 – 2008

CHAPTER ONE: Stepping Through the Mirror

Popping the Bubble

The day my ninety-five-year-old mother Dorothy died, we blew bubbles over her bed, her Lift-Off Bubbles, we called them. It was an extraordinary day, full of love and joy, laughter and tears. It was her last party, and she died just as the sun was setting. She lifted off, nothing to nothing, dust to dust, ashes to ashes, a snowflake evaporating in a fire. I sat with her cooling body, holding her bony hand, touching her face, her forehead, the curve of her ear, all these familiar landscapes I knew so intimately over so many years. Although we called them her Lift-Off bubbles, it was utterly clear that there is no one to lift-off and nowhere else to go. The Dorothy Show is finished and yet never finished, for it is inseparable from the whole universe. The bubble of apparent encapsulation bursts, and now Dorothy is everywhere and everything, sparkling in this new November sunshine, dancing in the leaves. Each life is like a bubble, and when the bubble pops, there is no more imaginary separation. The space inside the bubble is the same as the space outside the bubble, as it always was. The bubble itself was nothing but space bubbling. Each bubble is brief and fragile, but immensely beautiful. Floating, shimmering, wobbling, billowing, bedazzling, and then popping. Oh, how I adored my mother's smile, her voice, her face, her nose, her hands, her sense of humor, her light, all the wonders in her eyes—the Dorothy Show, ephemeral and precious. Pop! Gone now, and always right here.

What Happens Next?

The temple bell stops—
but the sound keeps coming
out of the flowers.

—Basho

3

Our loved one who has died was never a separate, fixed, persisting thing. They were a waving of the ocean, and they are both gone forever and totally present right here—in our hearts, in our cells and genetic material in some cases, in our minds and memories, and in the whole universe.

I don't believe that Mom and Dad and everyone else who has died are up there in some fairytale place called heaven, or down in some fiery hell, or that they have all been reincarnated intact in new bodies somewhere else. I think those are ancient myths that come in part from a desire to assuage the fear of death, and in part from an intuitive knowing that there is actually no-thing to die. But such myths all make and perpetuate what I see as a false assumption, namely that there is a persisting self or soul that exists as a separate, discrete, independent, continuous "thing."

The individual waves in the ocean are never the same from one instant to the next, and they aren't ever really separate from the other waves or from the whole ocean. Even in the midst of waving, the water that was briefly part of one wave moves on to be part of other waves. The boundaries are imaginary. The waves have never actually been anything other than a movement of the ocean. Nothing is ever really lost.

The "me" who fears that "I" might disappear has never had any real substance or continuity. It is a thought-form, a mental image, an idea that disappears many times in any ordinary day when we're not thinking about ourselves or looking in the mirror. And even the first impersonal *sense* of being present and aware vanishes completely in deep sleep, and no one is leftover to miss it. When the bubble pops (or the snowflake melts), it doesn't reincarnate as a new bubble or go to bubble heaven. It vanishes back into the bigger whole from which it came. The movie is over, but the ripples of it continue infinitely.

The bodymind is nothing but thoroughgoing impermanence. It never really holds still in any fixed form. It only *seems* to do that if we don't look too closely. And it is never actually separate from the environment in which it exists. It wouldn't be here without sunshine, air, water, food, all of its ancestors and everything that nourished and sustained them. In short, without the whole universe being as it is, this bodymind could not be here. This bodymind is a continuous process of smaller forms dying and being born. It is not the same bodymind from one second to the next. It is in perpetual exchange with its so-called environment. The boundaries are as imaginary as those between one wave and another. Like waves or whirlpools, all the apparent forms we see are ever-changing patterns that take shape briefly and then dissolve.

In death, this pattern of activity that we call "Joan" dissolves back into the larger field, the wholeness from which it has never actually been separate. We fall easily into attempts to pin down that ineffable wholeness as being this or that—primarily "consciousness" or primarily "matter." Ultimately, *whatever-this-is* defies all attempts to grasp it and nail it down, for it is not an "it" in any way whatsoever. It is *this,* right here, right now. What is this? No word-label-concept, no explanation, no metaphysical theory or philosophy will ever contain the living actuality of this moment. The actuality itself is at once totally obvious and utterly mysterious. It is utterly beyond all attempts to control, understand or make sense of it. Nothing we say about reality is ever the truth. The words can only be a map, a pointer, a description, an approximation. Don't get stuck on the words.

Identified as the separate "me," we inevitably feel insecure and incomplete. We don't like uncertainty and feeling out of control, so we keep trying to grasp what we believe will save us. We try desperately to make sense of everything, to nail things down, to get a grip, to get control. And yet, the faster we run on the mental treadmill of thought, chasing the proverbial carrot of Ultimate Understanding, Total Happiness and Complete Mastery, the more confused, desperate and miserable we seem to become.

What truly satisfies the longing of the heart is right here, never absent, but often overlooked because we are so busy looking for something else or trying to make sense of it all conceptually. The so-called awakening journey, the spiritual path, the pathless path from Here to Here, is about waking up *now* to what is obvious, immediate, simple and never hidden in any way. It is about discovering what brings forth happiness and what brings forth suffering. It is not about belief or philosophy. It is actually about letting go of all the answers and beliefs, and waking up to the inconceivable immediacy and simplicity of this very moment—*being just this moment,* the only actuality there is, and perhaps discovering the jewel at the very core of our being, the aware presence in which the whole universe is contained.

And far from being a long and complicated undertaking, this is always already fully accomplished whether that is recognized or not. But we may apparently have to go on what *seems* to be a long and complicated journey before we really understand what that means and how simple this is, and before the willingness shows up to simply relax and let go into this utter simplicity.

What Revealed Itself When Mom Died

Dorothy was dead, and this alive presence filled the whole room and the whole universe. All imaginary dividing lines were erased. Like a wave in the ocean, she had no beginning and no end. My mother was an ever-changing process inseparable from everything else in the universe, a process that continues, not only in all the beings whose lives she touched, but as the movement of the whole universe, for there is nothing that is not touched and brought forth by everything else. The spark of life that we see, recognize and love in the beloved is the light that is seeing only itself everywhere.

As I sat with my mother's cooling body, I saw that when conditions changed—when organs wore out and stopped working, when the stars and the galaxies and the subatomic particles and everything else in the universe shifted—suddenly the Dorothy Show no longer manifested. Inside Dorothy, her unique Movie of Waking Life came to an end, and outside of Dorothy, the happening each of us knew as Dorothy ended forever. Inside and outside, it was like the end of a favorite TV series, like the last episode of *The Sopranos.* And yet, the ripples continue infinitely. In a very real sense, nothing had died because no separate, independent *thing* had ever formed in the first place. Death is at once the ultimate boundary from which there is no return, and at the same time, no boundary at all.

There is no end and no beginning. There is simply one seamless, boundless movement that is always Here-Now. Dorothy is gone forever, and yet, Dorothy is right here.

What do we even mean by "Dorothy"? Any *idea* or *image* we have of a particular person is a mental abstraction, a conceptual reification of ceaseless flux, inseparable from the consciousness in which it appears. "Dorothy," as any kind of persisting entity, was a creation of smoke and mirrors rather like the illusion of continuity and narrative created by the pages of a flip book, or the frames in a movie appearing in rapid succession. In reality, each moment is absolutely new. No-thing persists over time. Time itself is a mode of perception, a construct of consciousness. Consciousness divides up what is actually a dimensionless whole into apparent parts existing in what appears to be space and time. The brain is a pattern-maker, and in this movie of waking or dreaming life, there are apparent patterns, such as a whirlpool, a waterfall, a symphony or a person, but these "things" are never anything but continuous change that never departs from Here-Now. Dorothy was an activity of the universe in the same way that a wave is an activity of the ocean.

Our true immortality is not in fighting off death and keeping the body alive forever, nor is it in some individual "soul" or separate unit of consciousness called "me" that leaves the body and either goes to heaven or reincarnates in a new body. Our true immortality is the seamlessness that is without beginning or end for it is always Here-Now. Just as the eye cannot see itself, the hand cannot grasp itself, the fire cannot burn itself, and the sword cannot cut itself, so we can never find unicity or totality as any kind of object because it has no other, no opposite. There is no way to stand outside of it and perceive it. It is all there is. It cannot depart from itself. As Rumi so beautifully expressed the miracle of awakening: "I've been knocking on a door. It opens. I've been knocking from the inside."

To discover this, to see through the mirage of separation, is to pass through the gateless gate. The gate is said to be gateless because when the illusion of separation and duality is seen through, when the bubble of apparent encapsulation pops, when you see that both time and space are a kind of illusory construct, you realize that you were never not Here, that *this* has never been absent. It is clear that there was never anyone apart from this who passed through any gate. Nothing was ever lacking, and nothing new was found. The gate was imaginary. But at the same time, there is an undeniable difference between knowingly *realizing* this and being confused and entranced by the *story* of separation and lack, which is why there is said to be a gateless gate rather than no gate at all. As the Advaita sage Nisargadatta put it, "Your begging bowl may be of pure gold, but as long as you do not know it, you are a pauper."

Thought is inherently dualistic. It divides, labels, categorizes, and explains reality. This is a useful function in many ways, not to be discarded. But it can also lead to immense confusion and unnecessary suffering simply because we tend to mistake our thoughts and the stories they spin for reality. By shifting the focus of our attention from thinking to presence itself—sensing, feeling, awaring, being—and by spending time in silence and stillness, we may come upon a felt-sense of spacious openness at the very core of our being, a space in which this whole universe is held. And when we enter deeply into any apparent form with open attention, that form reveals this same spacious presence, this same ever-changing formlessness and absolute immovability. I'm not talking about some exotic, mystical, psychedelic experience. I'm pointing to a recognition that is actually very ordinary and always already here, although commonly overlooked in favor of the solidity of our conceptual maps. Awakening, as I mean it, is simply a shift of attention (now) from what we *think* is happening to actual present experiencing.

To awaken to this unbroken wholeness is not about picking up an idea or a belief system. It is a felt-reality, an absence of unnecessary self-centered thinking and a present-ness to the actuality of this moment, a letting go. Our faith or trust in this living reality grows as we open to it. I don't mean faith in some belief or idea, or trust that a certain outcome will happen. I mean a deep peace with life as it is, a deep knowing that all is well, that everything belongs, that the deepest truth is unconditional love and the absolute freedom of groundlessness. This recognition is rarely a permanent, one-time event. *What is recognized is ever-present and never actually comes and goes, but the recognition of it, the opening to it, the dissolving into it seems to happen again and again, always Now.* What I'm talking about is a kind of transcendence, but not a detached, dissociated or dualistic kind of transcendence that ignores the world, turns away from suffering or denies our humanness. It is rather a way of entering evermore deeply into the living actuality of what is.

Unbroken wholeness is the ever-present actuality. What comes and goes is the mirage of apparent separation, the feeling of being a person in a story, the ever-changing weather of experiences positive and negative—all of that comes and goes. Here-Now (boundless awareness, the Ultimate Subject) is omnipresent. And nothing actually exists *outside* of this, or *other* than this. To awaken is to recognize the sacred everywhere, to live in devotion to this luminous presence, to wake up again and again from the dream of what we *think* is happening.

From this awake presence, it is clear that death is nothing to fear, not because "I" as the person will live forever, but because that apparently limited "I" is only an intermittent and momentary dreamlike happening in a much larger happening—the true "I" to which we all refer prior to name and form. That true "I," the Original Face, the Ultimate Subject, the One behind all the masks, is closer than close, most intimate, all-inclusive, being and beholding it all.

And contrary to our usual way of thinking, the realization of this need not—and usually doesn't—arrive with thunderclaps and lightning bolts. It is, in fact, very simple, very ordinary. It doesn't even really arrive, for what is recognized is never not here. There is no "me" who *has* this realization, for in it, there is no separation, no division, no boundary, no subject and object, no inside or outside. Waking up is the falling away of the persistent belief that "this isn't it," that "I am nothing but a separate little person in a huge alien universe outside of me," that "I'm not quite fully all the way there yet." Awakening is the recognition that the one who seems to be at the center of "my story" is nothing more than a mental image, a bundle of sensations and memories, a character in a dream, a mirage that appears and disappears intermittently in a field of conscious experiencing, which is itself like a bubble or a whirlpool in a shoreless ocean of unnamable vastness. This radiant presence Here-Now has layers of density, from the most apparently solid to the most subtle and ineffable, and they are *all* included in what is.

In deep sleep, everything perceivable and conceivable vanishes, as does the one who cares about all of this. Every night in deep sleep, the caretaker, the controller, the author, the observer, the scorekeeper, the seeker, the judge, the critic, the decider, the phantom helmsman is gone. The no-thing-ness that remains is the groundlessness, the emptiness, the infinite potential from which the entire universe is born and to which it returns, moment by moment.

Waking up is like dying. Dying to the past. Dying to the known. Dying to all your thoughts, ideas and beliefs. Dying to who and what you think you are. Dying to all hope of something better. Dying to everything. Dying even to any *idea* or *experience* of no-thing-ness or liberation. Letting go of every attempt to hold on, to control, to survive as anything in particular. Losing everything that can be lost and discovering what remains.

What Remains

Where is Dorothy? Gone! *What* was Dorothy? Nothing of substance can be grasped. She was an ever-changing dance of emptiness. And the very heart of her being, what I loved most deeply in her, is right here, for it is the very heart of all being—this vast presence, this alive nothingness, this silent stillness. The expression of this vast emptiness in apparent form, as Dorothy and Joan and the whole world, cannot be denied. It is a celebration, a magic show. Form and emptiness, relative and absolute, appearance and disappearance, ocean and wave—one seamless whole.

I cry and feel grief, but it is a pure grief, like a clean fire or a cleansing rain, almost an ecstasy at times. I feel a great peace and love and groundedness, a new strength. Bits of my mother's life are migrating into my apartment now—a few red pillows, a purple sweater, her fuchsia colored shawl—and already this place is changed. And I am changed. Nothing seems real now except the absolute simplicity of *what is* minus *all* ideas about it. Her death re-turns me to what is real and authentic, to ground and groundlessness.

Leaving my last class at the college where I teach before Thanksgiving, I see out the huge picture window in the hallway that winter has arrived with wild ferocity. Wind is raging and it is dark and bleak looking out there. Snow is blowing furiously by the window, the first snow. Outside, as I walk to my car, it is cold and dark and bare branches are tossing in the wind. And now, on Thanksgiving morning, the sun is out and the world is white and glistening.

My mother, who was so utterly real only a few months ago, and for as long as I can remember before that, is absolutely gone. And in my living room is a small cardboard box with a label that says: "This package contains the cremated remains of Dorothy Tollifson."

It's more like gravel than ash, and it's inside the box in a plastic bag not much bigger than an eggplant. A small parcel really, it weighs about ten pounds maybe—all that remains of an entire woman.

She's absolutely gone, and yet, she's right here. Not as a bag of ash or a disembodied spirit waiting to reincarnate, but as this whole universe. And she's here in my heart, always.

Of course, the Dorothy Tollifson who played with me as a baby has been gone for decades. I barely remember her. Without photos, I probably wouldn't be able to picture that young woman at all. The Dorothy who saw me off to college back in 1966 has also totally disappeared—a dim memory and a few photos are all that remains of her. The same is true of the seventy-year-old Dorothy who lived so openly and gracefully through the death of my father, the man she loved with all her heart. In fact, death is happening every moment. Continuity is an illusion. Some pattern apparently persists, something that allows us to recognize someone on the street whom we haven't seen in decades. But every cell in their body has been completely replaced in the course of those decades. There is literally no-thing left of the person we knew before. And yet, we *think* it is the same person, this shimmering flame now extinguished. And yet something *is* the same in every passing appearance, and that something is Here-Now, everywhere and nowhere.

Dorothy waving from atop an elephant in India. Dorothy in a huge-brimmed red hat in the Gay Freedom Day parade in San Francisco. Dorothy marching for peace in Washington, D.C. Dorothy moving mysteriously from youth to old age. Dorothy smiling at me from the photo on my wall. Dorothy in a small box. Dorothy embedded forever in the fabric of my life.

I sort through her possessions. Her clothing. Her jewelry. The art she collected. Her books. Her wine glasses, cereal bowls, teacups, napkins, towels. Her sheets and blankets. Her bags full of old birthday cards and letters from her daughter. Her prayer wheel. Her hearing aids. Her table cloths. The remains of a life.

Her middle-aged daughter going forward. Walking on into her own crumbling away.

The Fire of Impermanence

A monk asked Daizui, "It's clear that the fire at the end of the kalpa will completely destroy the universe. I'm still not clear whether there's something that won't be destroyed."

Daizui said, "It will be destroyed."

"IT will be destroyed along with everything else?" the monk asked.

"Gone with the other," Daizui said.

—Daizui's Fire at the End of the Kalpa (*Book of Equanimity* Case 30, *Blue Cliff Record* Case 29)

I've been told that Cocteau, the famous French writer and artist, was once asked what he would save if his house were burning down, and he replied, "the fire."

There's an old Zen story in which the teacher and student have been talking late into the night, and finally the teacher tells the student it's time for the student to leave and go back to his sleeping quarters. The student opens the door and says, "It's very dark outside." The teacher offers the student a lighted candle to find his way home. Just as the student receives the light, the teacher blows it out.

All of these stories point to the possibility of holding onto nothing at all, dying to the past, moment by moment. What remains is not some dreadful, dead nihilistic void. It is *this* right here, right now—exactly as it is, before we try to understand it, grasp it, control it, or figure it out.

Right now, in this moment, "the end of the kalpa" (or "the end of the world") is a thought. Wanting something to continue, or fearing that nothing will, is also a movement of thought. "Nothing" is another thought. The "IT" that the student hopes will survive the end of the kalpa, *whatever* we take that "IT" to be, whether we imagine that it is the personal self, the soul, boundless awareness, consciousness, the One Self, or whatever—"IT" is, *in that moment of asking the question,* only a thought, an idea, a mental object. Past and future are thoughts. We scare and confuse ourselves by thinking about "things" that do not actually exist! This is what the student here is doing. But in the immediacy of Here-Now, no such questions arise. When we let go of *all* our concepts and ideas, no problem remains.

Whenever we relax into simply being this moment, without judging it or trying to improve it, our imaginary dilemmas vanish into thin air. But then, as soon as we *think* about this and try to hold onto some sense of freedom or spaciousness as a particular experience, we mentally separate ourselves from it. We shrink—in our imagination—back down into that little capsule-self, and we turn the vastness of unbound presence into an object, a remembered *experience*, which we then try to repeat. Instantly, we're seemingly back in the world of confusion and lack, trying to regain what seems to have been lost. But no experience is permanent. What we are sensing in those moments of stillness and presence is never actually lost. It is right here, right at the very heart of the confusion itself, beholding it all.

Death is another word for impermanence, and impermanence

sounds scary until we realize how *complete* impermanence is. If we still think there are solid, separate, persisting, semi-permanent *things*, like you and me and tables and chairs, and that all of these *things* are impermanent, we suffer. But when it is recognized that impermanence is *so complete* that no solid, separate, persisting *things* ever form in the first place to even *be* impermanent, then impermanence is actually another word for seamless unicity, the undivided wholeness of life from which nothing stands apart. Impermanence is freedom. It is Cocteau's fire, the fire at the end of the kalpa, the fire of every moment. In Vedanta, they call it the Self. In Buddhism, they call it no-self, emptiness, non-clinging or groundlessness.

This emptiness isn't a bleak, nihilistic void; it is the red fire engine streaking past, the aroma of morning coffee, the exquisite song of the hermit thrush at dusk, the listening silence that remains when the sound is finished. And that silence, like the emptiness of deep sleep, is not a dead void but a vibrant aliveness.

Death is the fire that strips everything away. The whole story of our life, all of our apparent achievements and failures, and for that matter, all of human history and the entire history of the universe, is like mist evaporating in the sunlight, smoke curling into the air, waves rolling on the ocean, cloud formations changing shape in the sky, or last night's dream dissolving in the morning light. In other words, nothing that appears, including the person we appear to be, has any persisting form or any graspable substance.

When we are fully awake to the vibrant aliveness Here-Now, we recognize that life is more like a dance or a song than a grueling, goal-oriented task. The beauty of life lies precisely in its playfulness, its purposelessness, its groundlessness. It doesn't "mean" anything other than the indefinable *suchness* of each moment, exactly as it is. Death is that which makes life so surprising and impossible to grasp. Death is the freedom that offers a new beginning in every moment. Death is the great liberator thinly disguised as our worst fear.

What About Near-Death Experiences, Reincarnation, Memories of Past Lives?

I am not quite sure whether I am dreaming or remembering, whether I have lived my life or dreamed it. Just as dreams do, memory makes me profoundly aware of the unreality, the evanescence of the world, a fleeting image in the moving water.

—Eugene Ionesco

What we call NDEs and memories of past lives are real *experiences*, and they're as real as any dream, but that doesn't prove what people often assume it does. In one sense, as consciousness or unicity, there is nowhere we are not, just as the whole ocean is there in every wave. But "the wave" is never a solid, fixed *thing* that reincarnates whole-cloth, so to speak, as a new wave. That's the false assumption. Thought, and to some extent conditioned perception, separates, divides, freezes and reifies what is actually an indivisible whole.

I personally suspect that NDEs occur as waking consciousness is either slipping away or returning, as a kind of dream, not during a state of actual brain death. But as far as I can tell, there is no way to scientifically know for sure. Past-life memories can be explained in many ways. None of these things *prove* that "my" individual conscious experiencing survives death or that there is some kind of cohesive soul-like entity that travels through different lifetimes. My movie of waking life, and even the bare, impersonal knowingness of being present and aware, vanishes every night in deep sleep. What remains is devoid of all content, all experience, all *sense* of presence. Nothing perceivable or conceivable remains. That doesn't mean there is *nothing*, but there is nothing *experienceable*.

We could say that consciousness or presence is reincarnating from moment to moment as the apparent character it is playing in the movie of waking life, and that the world as it appears in our movie is reborn from moment to moment as the coherent and continuous whole it seems to be. Certain patterns and stories are reborn moment

15

to moment, giving rise to an apparently consistent personality. And it seems obvious that our "personal" or "individual" consciousness is not walled off from other "personal" or "individual" streams of consciousness, or from the larger "universal" whole. *Remember, these are all words, dividing up the indivisible.* Just as no wave in the ocean is walled off from the other waves or from the whole ocean, and just as water moves from one wave to another as the waving movement rolls along, it seems apparent that "my mind" and "your mind" are not really separate. Thus, we have those seemingly inexplicable but very common events where you think of an old friend, and a second later the phone rings, and it's them. Or the way someone suddenly "knows," as one of my aunts correctly did, that her husband's plane had just crashed. Or the way I knew on several occasions before I got the word that a person close to me who was dying had just died. Or like out-of-body experiences—I had one of those in a car crash once—where consciousness seems to have left the body and is watching it from a place beyond.

Our True Body is the whole universe. This is there in the Buddhist teaching of emptiness and interdependence, in modern science, in the Advaita notion of One Self, and in our own direct experience if we look closely. We are the holographic jewels in Indra's Net, each only a reflection of all the others. Reality seems to have infinite layers, dimensions or perspectives from which it can be seen, and who knows how it all works? No formulation can capture reality. Thought only imagines that it is describing reality. When we let go of the *need* to describe and understand, we can melt into simply *being* what we are—presence itself, Here-Now, utterly inexplicable and yet obvious and unavoidable.

While the notion of an individual soul as a discrete and persisting entity that travels through time makes no sense to me, I *can* relate to "soul" as a word pointing to a certain aspect of the mysterious event we call "a person" or "life." Zen teacher John Tarrant sees soul as "the part of us which touches and is touched by the world," the vital counterpart of spirit, the part that transcends the world and goes toward the light. Some people see "soul" as a kind of amorphous cloud of information not bound by space or time. Perhaps the word soul might even describe the felt-presence of a loved one who has died, not as an actual entity or a ghost, but as some energetic pattern that is alive in us and in the whole universe—the infinite ripples of a life, rippling on. Words like heart and soul, when I use them, do not refer to some objective or material *thing*, but to a quality that is unlocatable, boundless and ungraspable.

When the snowflake hits the ground, when the flame is extinguished, when the wave subsides, when the bubble pops, they are finished. That's the beauty of it. That's what makes life so alive, so fresh. And yet, the indivisible immediacy of *just this* is never born and never departs from itself. It just keeps changing its appearance. What we are concerned about—the survival of "me"—is so small. What we truly are is so vast.

Of course, it's possible that I will be very surprised at the moment of death. Maybe I will find myself hurling down a long dark tunnel, passing through the bardos one-by-one, sailing into the white light, slipping into a new body, arriving in some heavenly realm where my parents and all my dead friends and beloved pets will be awaiting my arrival, or plunging down into some fiery hell where it turns out all lesbians go after all. But if any of that *does* happen, it will only be another passing dream in the Great Dreaming, empty of substance. And it won't be happening to Joan Tollifson—that corpse will be burned up and dropped into the Pacific Ocean.

And none of this actually seems very important to me. For me, THIS life, right now, is what matters, not hypothetical past lives or imagined future lives. Heaven and hell are right here. And it's the *presence* itself that really matters, not the ever-shifting content, whether that content is a shopping mall in Chicago, a dream of flying through the air, an experience of kundalini rushing up the spine, or a magnificent near-death experience. All experiences are gone in an instant, and they are all dreamlike.

When we look closely at the past in *this* lifetime, we find nothing substantial—a bunch of notoriously unreliable and partial images and narratives that are endlessly revised and reconstructed, occurring

Now. How much less real or reliable the "memory" of previous life-times? How real or substantial is *any* of it? Does *any* of it actually refer to something objectively and inherently existing?

Although I don't believe in reincarnation or the soul, I *do* feel the presence of my mother and father in my heart, and I even joke frequently with my mother—in my mind. My parents show up in my dreams sometimes, as do others I've known who have died. I don't interpret this in the literal way that some people do, but I do feel we have within us the imprint of all the people who have touched our lives. No one is ever really gone, in one sense. And in another sense, no one was ever here in the first place as any-*thing* graspable or separate from the whole.

The Mysterious Head

As I was looking through the photos from my mother's memorial celebration, I came to one that showed the back of someone's head looking up at the pulpit as one of the ministers was speaking. This mystery head had white hair, and it looked like the back of Mom's head! Something about the shape, the way it's tipped, the hair... it definitely looked like the back of Mom's head! As if Mom were there watching her own memorial. And I thought to myself, "Who *is* that?" Then I noticed that this mystery person was wearing the same scarf I was wearing that day, and sitting where I was sitting. Yes, indeed, it was me!

This reminds me of something that happened perhaps a decade earlier when Mom had broken her hip and I had come to Chicago from Springwater, New York, where I lived at the time, to be with her during her recovery process. She was around eighty, and it was a time in her life and in my own view of her when she was just crossing the borderline from a very prolonged "late middle-age" into being truly old. We were at a physical therapy session in the hospital, waiting for the physical therapist, and I looked across the room and saw a middle-aged woman sitting next to her elderly mother, who was in a wheelchair. It was a very poignant sight at that moment because I thought to myself, all too soon, that will be my situation: I will be middle-aged and my mother will be an old woman like that. And then I realized I was looking into a mirror. The opposite wall was a mirror. I was looking at myself sitting next to Mom.

Stepping Through the Mirror

I was still relatively young when I experienced that collapsing of time in the hospital mirror. My hair hadn't turned white and menopause hadn't yet swept through my body. In my mind, a vast and promising future still stretched out ahead of me. I still hadn't decided what to be when I grew up or where to settle down and live. But one day I would figure it out. Things might not be quite right yet, but given time, they could and certainly would improve. My real life would begin any day now. This was all a kind of warm-up act like the preface to a book. That's what I thought. Old age and death seemed so remote as to be nonexistent. Of course, I knew intellectually they would happen to me, but in some less rational and more primal way, it seemed as if these were things that would never *really* happen, not to me, or at least, not for a very, very long time. When I worked in a law office years ago, we'd joke about how people would come in to draw up a will "just in case" they died. Yes, my mother had turned into an old woman right before my eyes that day in the mirror, but she had bounced back and once again seemed invincible and full of energy, someone indestructible and immortal who would certainly always be there because she always had been there.

But by the time I found myself back in Chicago fifteen years later, living there and accompanying my mother on her journey to death, my mother was in her nineties and I was in my fifties and it suddenly hit me with a new and visceral intensity that there was no future. It had all been a fantasy. There had only ever been this placeless immediacy from which I have never moved and this eternal Now in which, and *as* which, everything appears and disappears.

CHAPTER TWO: The Immediacy of Presence

Here-Now

Whatever time of day or night it is, whatever season, however old you are, it is always Now. Whatever location shows up, it always shows up Here, in the immediacy of presence, this unlocatable placeless-place where we always already are. However far we travel, every step of the journey happens Here, and when we reach our destination, we are still right Here. Time and space are a kind of mental construct, a mode of perception. We think of time as a linear progression, but the only actual reality we ever experience is Now, which is timeless and eternal. Likewise, the only actual place we ever are is Here in this immediacy or present-ness, which is unlocatable and infinite. We can never step out of Here-Now. Memories of the past, fantasies of the future, thoughts about elsewhere can only appear Here-Now. When the past was happening, it was happening Now. When the future arrives, it will be happening Now. If we take a trip from San Francisco to New York, the airport shows up Here, the plane flight shows up Here, and when we reach New York, we are still Here. Now is the only eternity, and Here is the only infinity that actually *is*.

What is the same in every different experience? Here-Now (immediacy-presence-consciousness) is the common factor in every experience, isn't it? This immediacy, this present-ness, this boundless awaring presence is the water in every wave, the screen that is equally present in every scene of the movie. To paraphrase an ancient statement, Here-Now is like a sphere, the center of which is everywhere and the circumference of which is nowhere. Here-Now is the Ultimate Subject to which the word "I" most deeply refers if we trace it back deeper than name and form.

The screen (the still-point of Here-Now) is the ground without which the movie could not appear. As an analogy for consciousness or Here-Now, this is a three-dimensional screen with no borders or edges—it is omnipresent; there is no place where it is not. In the movie, there seems to be a great deal happening: progress and regress, evolutionary development, heroes and villains, plot twists and turns, purpose and meaning, cause and effect, good and evil, free will and choice. The movie is full of drama and action, but the screen is empty of all that. The screen has no preferences. It never takes sides—it reveals everything equally and clings to none of it. The movie involves time and space, but the screen never moves away from Here-Now. In the movie, we have close-ups and long-shots—we may seemingly be squeezed into a narrow constricted tunnel or stand overlooking a vast spacious panorama, but the screen itself never actually contracts or expands. And the fire in the movie never burns the screen. When the movie ends, the screen remains, untouched by all the drama that has taken place within it.

But unlike the movie screen, the mirror, the ocean, or any of the other common analogies that are used for the ever-present, eternal, infinite aspect of this dancing emptiness, Here-Now (consciousness-awareness-presence) is not an object or substance that can be set apart, seen, grasped or measured. It is not a "thing" apart from the flow of experiencing. It is our most undeniable and fundamental certainty, the reality in every dream, the common factor in every experience, and yet, we cannot get hold of "it" as an object. What is liberating is to *recognize* this dimension for yourself, here and now. *Believing* in it as some kind of *idea* is just more mental baggage—another object in the movie, as is identifying it as any *particular* experience (this but not that). Once we name this omnipresent ground of being, there is always the danger of reifying it and creating a false duality in the mind between awareness and content, emptiness and form, subject and object, screen and movie. But as they say in Buddhism, form *is* emptiness, and emptiness *is* form. Not two. The division is purely conceptual, a helpful map to use for a moment on the pathless path, but then equally important to discard. Subject and object are one seamless whole.

Spiritual awakening typically begins with the recognition that there is something Here-Now that isn't caught up in the story, something that *sees* the thoughts *as* thoughts, something that has the capacity to stand back and observe, something that is beholding "me" and "my story" and "my body" and "the world" and the whole movie of waking life—a bigger context that is always present no matter what the content—a light that illuminates everything. This is an essential discovery. Awareness is the key ingredient in psychotherapy and in all forms of addiction recovery and social justice work. It is also what allows us to recognize that we are not limited to this bodymind, that this bodymind and the whole universe are appearing in us, not the other way around. As awareness, as presence, we are being and beholding it all.

Awareness is subtler than any form. It is invisible, shapeless, boundless, weightless. It has no size, no limits, no place where it is not. It cannot be measured or grasped. It's not an object. It is the Ultimate Subject. Awareness is another name for Here-Now. It can also be called unconditional love, for it accepts everything just as it is.

Some people get caught up in trying to *identify* as awareness and not as a person. But we are *already* boundless awareness. The one who wants to *identify* as that is a mental image, a thought-form. That whole project is rooted in a misunderstanding ("I'm not there yet"), and it requires a subtle effort, all of which reinforces the very thing it is trying to point beyond.

Awareness is already present, beholding it all. Awareness is here before that appearance, during that appearance, and after that appearance. *Everything* that shows up—our thoughts, our emotions, our moods, our most expanded spiritual experiences, our most mundane or contracted experiences, our whole spiritual search—*all* of it is passing through, like weather. *None* of it is personal. It comes and goes.

Here-Now doesn't move. Our *being*, and our actual direct experience, has *never* for one instant *ever* been anything *other* than Here-Now, aware-presence—*just this*. Even when consciousness is totally bamboozled by the story of "me," and even when a huge storm of emotion-thought is passing through the bodymind, it is all happening Here-Now in the utter stillness of presence. And instantly, whatever appears disappears. Thus, it can be said, nothing ever happened.

But we don't need to *deny* the person or the relative reality of history either. While I don't feel *limited* to this body, I don't feel that I'm *not* the body either. To *deny* the body seems absurd. On one level, *of course* I'm Joan Tollifson! If you poke this body with a sharp object, I feel pain. But the more closely I explore the body, the less solid it seems, and the more it dissolves into indeterminate formlessness, inseparable from everything that is supposedly not the body. And *all* of that happens in this vast field of awareness. I find no boundary between awareness and what appears within it. Without the words and the concepts, it is one, seamless, undivided, unbroken whole. I'm not *limited* to the body or encapsulated *inside* it, and the "body" is not the solid, persisting, independent "thing" we *think* it is.

It can, however, be very helpful to *notice* when we are identifying as a person. Sometimes in daily life that's functional, but often it isn't. When we think, "I'm not awake yet," or "I don't get it," or "I've ruined my life," as what are we speaking? In that moment, consciousness is identifying with and speaking as the apparently separate self. And we might ask, is this self, the apparent subject of these thoughts, real? Or is it a thought-form, an idea, a mental image? If the thought arises that, "I need to stop identifying as me," to whom does this thought refer? We can also discover that *all* these thoughts are happening by themselves; the thinker is just a mental image, another thought-form. Thoughts are ephemeral bursts of energy, a happening of the whole universe, an activity of consciousness—gone as soon as they arrive. Sometimes, particular thoughts or patterns of thinking tend to re-play over and over. They seem to refer to *something*, but that something never actually exists in the way we think it does.

The present moment is a fleeting instant between past and future, gone before we can even perceive it, but Now is timeless and eternal. There is no end to Now. Nothing comes after or before Now. We may *think* the past is really back there, but actually, when it happened, it happened Now, and Now, it has vanished completely.

If we're not awake to the wonder and aliveness of it, the present moment has a very unspectacular quality—it consists of seemingly ordinary things like door knobs and pieces of paper and toothpaste and office cubicles and bodily sensations and stray thoughts and television commercials and barking dogs and cans of soup and farts and traffic jams. It never holds still. It is thoroughgoing impermanence, vanishing as soon as it appears.

Without thought, this moment is without plot or narrative. It has no meaning or purpose. There is no main character, no "me," at the center of it. There is simply present experiencing—a snowflake landing in a fire. It may all seem quite solid if we don't look too closely, but if we pay attention, we find reality is actually fluid, ephemeral, effervescent, impossible to grasp or pin down. It keeps changing shape without ever moving away from right here, right now. It is completely obvious, never hidden, and yet strangely elusive if we try to take hold of it. It is at once immovable and constantly in motion, unchanging and yet totally in flux. It is an unbroken whole of infinite diversity. It defies all words and categories.

Now is holographic—it contains the past and the future. Everything happens Now, and yet, a symphony wouldn't make any sense, it wouldn't be music, without the *context*, without a memory of the notes that have come before and an anticipation of what might come next, without the sense of progression and *relationship* between what came before and what is arising now, and without the expectation of what may come next. The same is true of a novel, a play or a movie. This is precisely what makes it meaningful to us. But at the same time, we can see that each note happens Now, that the future resolution will happen Now, and that the context for the whole unfolding symphony (or story) is Now. Past and future are Now, memory happens Now. "Relationship" is simply a description of this seamless happening that *all* happens Now. That Now-ness doesn't *deny* past and future. It *includes* them. No concept can ever capture reality, so beware of fixating on one side of any imaginary conceptual divide. Life itself cannot be pinned down or captured by formulations.

When we're fully alive to the naked reality of the present moment, it turns out to be an astonishing and extraordinary miracle, this luminous awaring presence bursting forth as flowers, leaves, mountains, oceans, chairs, tables, planets, rabbits, giraffes, zebras, people, birds, tornados, planets, stars, random acts of kindness, horrifying acts of cruelty—one seamless and shimmering display, appearing and disappearing in the vastness of Here-Now.

But when attention is caught up in thoughts and what Zen teacher Joko Beck called the "self-centered dream," we don't notice what shines and sparkles right here, right now. We don't notice the beauty of the simplest and most ordinary things—white clouds moving through a puddle of rainwater on the sidewalk, late afternoon light on a dilapidated building, a colorful piece of trash blowing down the street, the exquisite mountains and valleys in a crumpled Kleenex on the table, the sounds of rain on the roof.

We imagine that everything of value and importance is "out there" somewhere, somewhere else, in the future, *after* we finish graduate school or get a promotion or get married or do another retreat or attend another satsang or find another teacher or have some transcendent experience or get enlightened or stop smoking cigarettes or go on a diet. *Then* we will find happiness, or so we imagine. *Someday* we will become the person we are supposed to be—that is the story. Until one day we look in the mirror and see death looking back at us, and it hits us that *this* is our life, right now, just *exactly* as it is. And as someone said, whenever you die, it will always be today.

Waking Up to Here-Now

It was in Chicago when I came back to be with my mother in her final years that this realization hit me full force. My own body was showing the first really undeniable signs of aging and falling apart, and I had only to look at my mother's body to see what was ahead. Several friends who were my age died, and to my amazement, I noticed that some of my closest friends were turning seventy and even eighty—how did *that* happen? Friends of mine, my peers (!), were having strokes and heart attacks and hip replacements and were even going into nursing care facilities and retirement communities!

It seemed like only yesterday that we had all been going through the wild and reckless adventures of our youth. We were the generation that came of age in the 1960s and broke all the rules, the generation of sex, drugs and rock-'n'-roll, of civil rights and social change. We were the Weather Underground, the Black Liberation Movement, the lesbian-feminist revolution, the radical fairies, the dykes on bikes, the acid-trippers of Woodstock, the Stonewall rebellion, the explorers in Eastern religion. We were the rebels, the men with long hair and beards, the women who threw off our bras and high heels, put on pants and work boots and got jobs no women had ever done before, the free love generation that vowed never to grow up and become normal. How could *we* be turning into old people? It was astonishing and unexpected. I never in my wildest dreams expected to ever *really* be eighty years old. I'm not quite there yet, and I may or may not make it all the way to eighty or beyond, but it has become abundantly clear to me that old age is real and that I am not immune from it.

I saw with sudden, undeniable clarity that there was no future. I wasn't going to medical school or law school or divinity school after all. Chances were, I wasn't going to write a series of Pulitzer Prize-winning novels, make a million dollars or find the love of my life. These were all just dreams.

This was not an entirely new insight. I had written books and given talks about this for years. I had seemingly realized this many times before. But I've noticed we seem to realize the same basic lessons again and again, and that, as the old saying goes, we teach what we need to learn. A friend of mine once said to me regarding one of my books, "Joan, have you *read* this book?" It seems I am often the last one to get my own message. And something felt very different this time—this sense of no future was visceral in a new and different way. At thirty, we know intellectually that we will get old and die someday, but we don't actually believe it. But there comes a point when we know it in our bones. It is *happening*. Getting old is no longer abstract—you cannot deny it. And as someone famously said, old age is not for sissies. It is one long descent into progressively more and more loss of control, loss of independence, loss of mobility, loss of self-image, loss of loved ones, and ultimately, loss of *everything*.

I used to think enlightenment meant crossing some magical

finish-line and living forever after in a state of perfection and perpetual happiness. But enlightenment isn't about becoming perfect, I discovered, or finally getting control of my life and fixing it all up at last. The whole search for perfection and future happiness turns out to be a kind of distraction that obscures the realization that this moment already *is* the Holy Reality.

When we first hear that "this is it" or that we already are what we seek, this can seem pretty hard to fathom. "My life" as a person often looks like one big mess—struggles with addiction and compulsion, bouts of depression, waves of anxiety and doubt, outbursts of anger and rage, failures and mistakes of all kinds, stories of unworthiness and failure. And yet, this is the grit that creates the pearl, the mud in which the lotus blooms, the suffering that calls us home.

Death itself doesn't frighten me. What frightens me, *when I think about it,* is the stuff that happens *before* you die—the pain and suffering, the loss of control. Having dementia or being in some dreadful nursing home wearing a diaper, racked with pain and unable to move, totally at the mercy of overworked and underpaid nursing aids who may be insensitive, negligent or even abusive, while a senile roommate talks incessantly in the next bed and watches Fox News on TV all day long at full volume. What a nightmare!

But when *thinking* about all of this drops away, there is no problem. Instantly, colors brighten and everything feels spacious and open and full of wonder. There is no "me" anymore, and no problem, only the simplicity and wonder of Here-Now!

As a particular experience, this brightness and wonder can't be held onto. It doesn't stay put. In the inner weather, just as in the outer weather, some days are brighter, other days more overcast. Consciousness, by its very nature, seems to enjoy tricking itself, playing hide and seek, jumping back on the hamster-wheel from time to time and chasing after its own tail just for the fun of it. Again and again, day after day, the movie of waking life starts rolling. I fall helplessly into my part as Joan—my personal drama and the world drama appear unbidden—attention is attracted by various headlines and sucked into myriad captivating plotlines. Emotions bubble up.

Consciousness becomes absorbed in its own creations, and in the blink of an eye, it has become identified as this Joan character who is passionately fighting with ghosts and chasing after mirages.

Perhaps from the perspective of consciousness or the universe, this is all a form of deep fun and endless discovery. The universe plays Hide and Seek with itself. The rope looks like a snake. Consciousness, pretending to be Joan, is momentarily fooled and runs away from itself in terror. What a hoot!

Certain forms of entrancement have seemingly fallen away for the Joan character over time, and others seemingly happen less often and with less severity and duration, but the divine hypnosis, as one teacher aptly called it, still happens. And actually, there is no one at the center of these experiences and behaviors or the thoughts about them. *All* of this is simply a happening of life, like the weather—one moment cloudy, another moment clear, sometimes a thunderstorm or an earthquake or a tsunami, sometimes calm and placid. The Buddha's enlightenment is not separate from me, nor is Hitler's delusion. We are one whole happening.

I've learned that even people who have a polished and successful exterior can be suffering or unraveling in all sorts of ways behind the scenes. I've encountered many people like the fashionably-dressed, physically beautiful, happily married, successful psychotherapist who told me that she spent the evenings compulsively cutting up the bottoms of her feet with a razor blade, or the brilliant and gorgeous writer who told me that she and her seemingly perfect husband hadn't slept in the same bed in seventeen years. And of course, we have a long history of gurus and spiritual teachers molesting their students, getting drunk, embezzling funds, committing suicide, having angry outbursts, or in countless other ways demonstrating that old conditioning runs deep. No one is entirely unstained, even those who appear spotless. The koan of embodied life seems to have nothing to do with reaching some state of imaginary transcendent perfection for the character, but rather being at peace with exactly how it is, even the not-being-at-peace that sometimes arises.

I was very close to my mother, loved her dearly with all my heart, and yet, I can honestly say that her death and everything leading up to it was one of the most profoundly liberating and beautiful experiences of my life. And in a funny way, even though I am terrified at times of what may lie ahead, I am also excited about this new adventure of growing old and vanishing completely.

CHAPTER THREE: Dying

Dying

Someday the sun will explode. Could happen in the next six seconds. Could happen in the next six billion years. But it will *happen.*

—Wallace Tollifson, my father

If I go up in a puff of smoke, don't feel bad. That's what I'm praying for. Just call the Cremation Society. The card is on the refrigerator.

—Dorothy Tollifson, my mother

I was born without the hand that signifies purposeful doing. My life was about unraveling rather than producing, subtracting rather than accumulating. When I was very small and first heard about death, I dreamed recurrently about a person whose arm fell off, then the other arm, then each leg, until nothing was left. I was already on my way toward this mysterious disappearance.

—Joan Tollifson, *Bare-Bones Meditation: Waking Up from the Story of My Life*

Death is a long process—at least, for those who die as my mother died, it is a long process. You lose one thing after another. I watched my mother slowly lose her hearing. She loved the theater, and she would go to plays, but she could no longer hear them. She would attend lectures, but she could no longer hear the speaker. The hearing aids didn't really help. She couldn't tell if the batteries in her hearing aids were dead or alive, and with her failing eyesight and trembling hands, she had endless trouble trying to see and execute the minute operations required to replace these tiny batteries in their tiny little resting places

31

with the tiny little doors on the tiny, tiny hinges. These fragile little doors often snapped off in the process of trying to change the battery, and then her one-handed daughter—that would be me—would work miracles and reattach the tiny little doors to their tiny little hinges. Mom went to dinner with friends, but increasingly, the conversation was inaudible to her. She would answer her telephone and be unable to tell who was calling her or what they were saying. She faked her way through conversations, parties, and discussions. Sometimes this worked well and sometimes it didn't. Occasionally, someone would tell her they had terminal cancer and Mom would tell them how wonderful that was. Once she reported to me that someone important to us had died, but that she wasn't sure who it was.

Although she was basically fully with it to the end, she lost some of her finer cognitive abilities and some of her short-term memory. If she tried to read a novel or watch a movie or even the simplest TV drama, she couldn't track the story anymore or remember who the characters were. She would pretend, and she fooled many of her friends, but I could tell she was increasingly clueless. Even in the simplest TV programs, everything moved too fast and was too complex. Not being able to hear it very well didn't help either. And she had a few episodes of strangely atypical behaviors that felt like dementia, where she became paranoid that a friend had turned on her, a thought-form that was totally unlike my mother.

Her lungs began to give out. And her legs. And her spine. She had pain. She rarely spoke of it, but I knew. There was a lot of pain, excruciating pain. She got shots in her spine to try to alleviate some of it. But they didn't totally work. She lost more and more of her mobility and independence.

My indomitable mother, who once charged through life at full speed with an amazing stride, was on a cane, then a walker, and finally in a wheelchair. Young people hurrying down the streets, talking on their phones, frequently ignored her smiles, and occasionally even laughed at the sight of this ancient old woman with her white hair pushing her clumsy walker ahead of her. It took hours to get dressed, to put on coats and shoes, to walk half a block. She lost control of her bowels. She had humiliating accidents in public places, in restaurants and stores, in front of friends and strangers. The skin on her legs became as thin as tissue paper, and as her legs filled with fluid from congestive heart disease, sometimes the skin would simply burst for no apparent reason. Blood and fluids would pour out. Because she had lost much of her nerve sensitivity, she often wouldn't notice. She would be trailing blood and fluids across the carpet, oblivious to it all. I watched as some of her friends came by less and less often, invited her out to fewer and fewer activities. When they did include her, she sat alone in the crowd unable to hear. My mother, the most extroverted person I ever met, spent more and more time by herself, alone in the crowd or alone in her apartment, cut off from fully enjoying even those entertainments generally available to us when we are home alone—books, TV, phone. Death is a long, slow process.

Everything unravels. My mother, a proud and independent woman who dressed with colorful pizzazz and cared greatly about "running her own ship," was having to accept more and more help and take more and more orders from "Baby Boss," as she called me. In her final years, I handled her money, paid her bills, hired her nursing help in the final month, and in the final days, decided how much morphine to give and when. Had she lived one more day, I would have had to decide whether or not to let them insert the Foley catheter.

People would say to her, "You're going to live to be a hundred!" And she'd reply, "Oh, I hope not!" She had a tremendous love for life, but she was ready to go. She knew it was time, and she wasn't one to overstay her welcome at a party or hesitate about leaping into the unknown.

Compared to many people's final years, my mother's were very blessed. Up until her last week, she still had some mobility and, despite some minor cognitive loss, she was mostly quite with it. She died at home, surrounded by people who loved her. Not everyone is as lucky. A friend tells me how his father's life ended. His father had dementia and, in the end, had to be in a nursing home because the family could no longer manage him. He was often terrified, although no one knew what it was that so terrified him. He would jump out of bed, trying to flee from his imaginary terrors, but he was no longer strong enough to walk, so he would fall and injure himself. Finally, to keep him safe, he had to be strapped to a gurney. He no longer recognized or was comforted by the presence of family. He was in utter terror, crying and screaming, straining to get free. This is not the ending most of us are hoping for.

My uncle, whose leg was amputated in his last year of life, would also get up in the middle of the night, forgetting that his leg was gone, and fall. My mother's oldest friend had dementia and managed to get on the elevator one day in the nursing facility and ride down to the basement where she got off. It was dark down there, and she didn't know where she was. They found her, hours later, huddled in a corner in terror. Dying can be a long and difficult process—at times even terrifying.

Where does death begin? Perhaps at the moment of birth? Or before? Certainly, by the time you are middle-aged and watching your mother's body and mind disintegrate in front of you as your own body wrinkles and sags, certainly by then it is dawning on you with a very visceral certainty that you too are going to disintegrate. And this disintegration may well be a long, painful, frightening, lonely and at times humiliating process.

And you wonder, who will be with you as you undergo this process? You realize that you have no children, no partner, no siblings, and that most of your friends are ten or twenty years older than you. If you reach your mother's age, they will all be dead and gone. Suddenly you realize how alone you might become. You realize your mother is the oldest and probably the closest and most intimate relationship you've ever had. You see her in person almost every day and speak to her many times by phone every day in her last years. And suddenly it hits you that after she is gone, you could be lying unconscious or paralyzed by a stroke on the floor of your apartment for weeks before anyone would even miss you. You'll be one of those old people they find years later mummified in front of their television set. The only person who was woven into the daily fabric of your life is dying, the only person who has known you forever. But then you notice that this is all thought and imagination, that right now, you are fine. You relax back into the present moment.

Yes, death takes a long time to wear us down, and it isn't always pretty. But through all of this long decline, my mother became ever more beautiful and transparent, shining with love, lighter and lighter. She surrendered to this disintegration and loss with a grace that was awesome to behold. Resistance of any kind fell away and in its place there was ever-deeper acceptance and an abundance of pure joy. Mom would look out the window and say, "I'm so blessed." Where someone else might see only dreary city blocks down below and the ugly side of a high-rise, my mother saw sheer beauty. She relished every last moment of life. She accepted the mounting losses and humiliations with graceful equanimity.

She said many times in her last year, "It's so freeing to realize that nothing really matters." My mother was an exuberant woman who loved life, loved people, loved animals, loved plants, and cared deeply about the world. She didn't say "nothing really matters" in a way that sounded nihilistic, despairing or cynical, but rather, in a way that sounded truly free. Joyous. The burden of accomplishing something— becoming somebody, fixing the world, doing the right thing—was dropping away. The need for a solution was dissolving. My mother became more and more translucent and filled with light. She was alive with simple presence, profoundly awake to the beauty and the holiness of every ordinary moment. Oh, she had her occasional moments of irritation and crankiness, all part of the show, but overall, she radiated love and joy. And being with her, I also noticed that there was beauty everywhere, even in death and disintegration, maybe even *especially* there. I would look at things like body fluids and excrement and soiled clothing and old, deteriorating flesh, things that might once have seemed downright ugly, scary or repulsive, and I would see only beauty.

The Beloved Is Everywhere

I'm at work at the city college in Chicago where I teach English to the most remedial of students—many are immigrants, others are survivors of a childhood in the housing projects, some are ex-gang members, some are just back from the wars in Iraq or Afghanistan, others are on their way to these wars, many are single mothers working two jobs and going to school and never sleeping at all, others have severe learning disabilities and attention deficit disorders of various kinds, most all of them are people of color although there are a smattering of Polish immigrants and other white folks. All of my students are people who failed the basic English entrance exam for a two-year city college. Although they are all high school graduates, they write at about a third or fourth grade level, and I do not exaggerate.

It's midterm week. Big week. Busy. After my morning classes finish, I'm in my office grading papers, and I pause to call my ninety-four-year-old mother as I do every morning. She's had a fall, tells me she is sitting on the floor surrounded by broken glass. "I'm fine," she says. "Don't worry." My mother believes in positive thinking. She does not dwell on her misfortunes, or even see them as misfortunes. If asked by a friend or a new doctor whether she has any medical conditions, my mother always says no, even though in fact she has emphysema, spinal stenosis, arthritis, and congestive heart disease. My mother lives on the sunny side of life.

I hang up and call a friend in Mom's building who promises to go immediately to Mom's apartment, and then I rush to my department head and tell her I need to leave, and together we rustle up a substitute for my remaining classes. I call my friend Valjean (a woman my age who will be dead from lung cancer by the time I write this several years later) and she reminds me to keep breathing, and then I gather up my half-graded papers and take off for Mom's.

There is blood all over the place. The friend I called in the building has already cleaned up the glass. I bundle Mom up and take her to the ER. We spend the next eleven hours there. She has three broken ribs and a deep cut in her hand, but is otherwise fine. It is a long time before we know this, however.

The ER is having a very busy day. Car wrecks, gunshot wounds, heart attacks—these folks come by ambulance and are brought in through another door. Those of us deemed less urgent by the triage nurse are seated in a waiting room. We wait. Hours go by. A crazy man wearing an oxygen mask screams over and over that he doesn't want to go back to Vietnam. A woman with a newly broken leg gives me a quarter for the vending machine. A toothless eighty-seven-year-old woman stands right in front of me, inches away, and then lifts up her shirt and pulls down her pants to show me the shingles outbreak all over her body. Moving even closer, she sits in the chair next to me and leans into me, talking and talking and talking, story after story, breathing on me, her breath sour-smelling. My body recoils; I am not Mother Teresa. But I love this old woman, too.

Finally, they call my mother's name. We enter the sanctuary. We have a cubicle. A nurse gets us settled. She is a radiant, rock-steady woman who exudes genuine heartfelt love and calm. I feel we have been ushered into God's Kingdom. A handsome young medical student comes to check my mother over. He flirts with her, asks her out on a date. They play together. The woman doc who heads the ER comes over eventually. A big woman, solid, no bullshit—pure Chicago—she uses her fingernail to peel apart the wound on my mother's hand, checking for shards of glass.

Later when the shift changes and the young medical student is going home, he comes to say goodbye and wish us well, and a male nurse takes over. Another radiant being, he immediately begins talking with Mom about how "All is One." He asks me what I do. I say I teach college English. My mother pipes up and says I write spiritual books. He asks me what kind. I say, "They're about the simplicity of what is. Nothing traditional or systematic, just this. This moment, here now." I go on, "This right here is my idea of spiritual." The male nurse lights up. Yes, he sees it that way too. Later, he comes over with the blood pressure equipment, wraps the cuff around Mom's arm. "We have to pretend I'm here for some reason," he says.

The Beloved was everywhere. *Is* Everywhere. Is *Everything*. The overflowing emptiness (or no-*thing*-ness) dancing its Crazy Cosmic Dance. Galaxies exploding in the night sky. Sheer beauty. Amazing grace.

CHAPTER FOUR: The Long Road Home

Que será, será

The first musical recording my mother bought for me when I was a child was a single of Doris Day singing *"Que será, será,* whatever will be, will be." Mom brought it home from the stationary store one afternoon in the 1950s and played it for me on our Victrola. I listened carefully.

My father, who read books about Einstein and the fourth dimension, was a determinist who told me early on that the universe was an interconnected and interdependent whole in which everything was the cause and the effect of everything else. He told me that waving his arm at just that moment was the result of infinite causes and conditions and could not be other than exactly that wave at that moment. He told me this applied to every thought, every impulse, every apparent "choice" we seemingly made and every action we seemingly initiated and carried out, big or small. He also told me the sun would eventually explode, that there was no essential difference between a table and a person, that it was all a subatomic dance of energy. All of this made perfect sense to me. He was an atheist as well, and for a brief time in my childhood, I offered classes in a tent in our backyard to the Catholic children next door on how God did not exist, until my mother told me I had to stop.

My mother, who was deeply spiritual but who had no interest in organized religion back then, considered God another word for love. Later in life, after I had left home and my father had died, she sold our home in the suburbs and moved into downtown Chicago. She was in her seventies then, and she wanted community. There was a church right across the street from the apartment building where she first lived after her move into the city. She liked their social service programs in the housing projects, and so she joined. She didn't believe all the dogma—she believed in love, and in the kind of inclusiveness and generosity of spirit that Jesus embodied. My mother couldn't see the hymnal as she was nearly blind, but she would belt out the hymns with great enthusiasm, except that she'd be singing nonsense syllables like *blabityblablabla,* and she would grin at me mischievously out of the corner of her eye as she sang.

As a child, I was inexplicably drawn to religion. I invented religions and religious rituals in my bedroom during quiet time every day. As a pre-teen, I devoured books on world religions. I felt most drawn to Buddhism, but I didn't know any Buddhists. As a teenager, I briefly found Jesus and spent every evening trying to convert my amazingly patient and tolerant father. In college, I read Alan Watts, took a class on Zen and Vedanta, met several Zen teachers, learned to sit zazen (Zen meditation), and dropped acid, which greatly expanded my view of reality.

In my youth, under the influence of my Republican father and the overwhelmingly conservative town where I grew up, I was a Young Republican who loved Ayn Rand, shook hands with Dick Nixon, supported Barry Goldwater and thought we should nuke Vietnam. But by the time I reached high school, I had changed from a conservative to a progressive. I was reading James Baldwin, opposing the war in Vietnam, and my new heroes were Martin Luther King Jr., John F. Kennedy, Malcolm X and Ho Chi Minh. And in my twenties and thirties, after I sobered up from a serious plunge into alcohol and drug abuse, I was involved in a variety of social change movements and finally the radical anti-imperialist left.

I wanted to change the corporate-dominated, for-profit, capitalist and imperialist system into a cooperative, socialist, for-the-people system where we would all share the resources and work together for the common good. We would care for Mother Earth and for one another. Imperialism, colonialism and global exploitation by greedy, power-hungry corporations and empires would be finished. The disparity between rich and poor would be eliminated or at least greatly lessened. Racism, sexism, classism, heterosexism, ageism and all other forms of discrimination, prejudice, injustice and inequality would be no more. We would have peace instead of war, love instead of hate, justice instead of injustice, inclusion instead of exclusion, compassion instead of bigotry, and universal healthcare for all.

Today, in my worldview and in my opinions on current events, I still lean to the left politically. I still pay attention to what is going on in "the world." I still feel sorrow when I see suffering, injustice and cruelty. I can still imagine a world that would be organized cooperatively rather than competitively, where humans would live in harmony with the ecosystem, where things like racism, sexism, imperialist exploitation, genocide and fundamentalism would be largely gone. But I recognize now that even if all of this came to pass, some new problem would crop up to replace those that had finally been vanquished. I have come to see that there is no end to problems.

I've also come to recognize that life is inherently unfair. Some baby birds are eaten in the nest by predators, some fall from the nest and die, some take flight and survive into adulthood. Eventually, they all die and become food for some other life form. There is a great deal of violence and inequity in nature: predators stalk and rip apart their prey, parasites live off their hosts, some ants work like crazy while others are lazy and do very little. Apparently different ant colonies have even been known to invade each other, take captives and turn them into slaves. In many species, a female in heat seems to have little choice about being stalked, raped and impregnated, and life can be tough on the males too, as when the female praying mantis routinely bites off the male's head after sex. Species survive for a while and then go extinct. Nature unleashes hurricanes, volcanoes, tidal waves, ice ages, earthquakes, thunderstorms and tornados as a matter of course. Stars explode, meteorites and asteroids crash into planets, galaxies are born and die.

In our human world, some people are born into grinding poverty or live their whole lives in war-zones, while others are born into unbelievable affluence and live their entire lives in peaceful, idyllic settings. Some children are abused in horrific ways, while others are treated with love and respect. Some people come into this world with healthy, strong, gorgeous bodies, while others are born with hideous deformities, disabilities, and painful, debilitating illnesses. Some people work from childhood to old age doing grueling, back-breaking, monotonous work without ever being paid a living wage, while others are independently wealthy and live in the lap of luxury without ever lifting a finger. Some people are raped, mugged, tortured, imprisoned or murdered, while others glide through life seemingly unscathed.

Some of the injustices in life appear to be caused by nature at large, while others seem to be caused specifically by human nature. Those that are apparently caused by human nature seem to be potentially within our power to correct. And so, healing and corrective activities spring up, things such as medicine, therapy, religion, social service programs, civil rights organizations, political revolutions, addiction recovery programs, aid organizations, meditation, yoga, awareness work, pharmaceuticals, and so on, all designed in some way to bring about a more equitable community and a happier world. Many of these bring forth positive results, but then new problems appear. And no two humans seem to completely agree about exactly what a fair, just, happy world would look like. Religious images of Jesus nailed to a cross dripping blood or the Hindu goddess Kali wearing her necklace of skulls and eating her offspring don't come out of nowhere, and our attempts to sanitize and purify life or to create some future utopia are inevitably disappointing.

It dawned on me gradually that this phenomenal manifestation can only appear in polarities and contrasts. You cannot have up without down. If you're going to have beautiful sunsets, delicious meals, passionate love affairs, cute puppies and moments of deep peace, then you're also going to have rape and murder, thunderstorms and volcanoes, mass extinctions and genocides, suns flaming out, excruciating pain, fatigue and exhaustion, mistakes and false starts, and all the ways of seemingly being broken and lost. And, although we often think otherwise, all of our uniquely human weather is in some sense every bit as natural as hurricanes, cloudy days, thunderstorms, lightning strikes, erupting volcanoes, catastrophic earthquakes, swirling tornados, fire storms, tsunamis and animals ripping apart their prey or eating their young. *All* of it is the Divine Dance, the Great Play, the Cosmic Self-Revelation. All of it is a waving movement of the great shoreless ocean, and *none* of it is what we *think* it is.

The whole appearance is empty of inherent, objective, observer-independent reality. The world is not actually "out there" in the way we think, and there is no separate me "in here" looking out at it. That is all a conceptual picture we've learned, not what we actually *see* or experience directly. All apparent objects only exist conceptually, as ideas, and to some degree as conditioned perceptions. Babies don't see tables and chairs—they must *learn* how to draw boundary lines around the various shapes and colors they see, how to put things into abstract categories, and thus, how to "see" such things as tables and chairs and not just ever-changing blobs of color and shape. "My body" is an idea. The actuality is ever-changing sensations and movement, inseparable from everything I think is *not* my body. The universe is one seamless happening.

In this movie of waking life, there seem to be ever-changing, interdependent cycles of creation and destruction, evolution and disintegration; but it all happens Here-Now in this eternal present. Whatever appears to be happening in "the world" has a relative reality, and we can't deny that relative reality. Here it is, showing up plain as day, as real as it gets on one level—but it's never what we think it is. All of it is ultimately an insubstantial, fleeting appearance, gone before it arrives. A whole lifetime vanishes like last night's dream.

Each person's movie of waking life is totally unique, although they share certain apparently common features. The person is a character *in* the movie, and the movies are all movements of consciousness. The movie is at once real and unreal. It is real in the sense that the *experiencing* of it, the *presence* of it, is undeniable. It is unreal in the sense that none of it is happening in the way we *think* it is, as some sort of coherent, substantial, persisting, observer-independent, objectively-existing actuality. That doesn't mean that the pain doesn't hurt, but it doesn't have the solidity we think it does.

I discovered that what we consider good and what we consider evil are so relative to our point of view and so thoroughly intertwined with one another that it is finally impossible to completely pull them apart or to say where one begins and the other ends. Furthermore, what looks like conflict and disorder at our human level of reality may be in perfect harmony and order at another level of reality when seen in a larger context. The extinction of the dinosaurs, which from their perspective might have seemed quite terrible, made way for new life forms, and in the same way, our demise may open the way for something entirely new to appear. Locusts, viruses, cockroaches, parasites, cancer cells, serial killers and child molesters all have their part to play in the dance of existence, even if we don't like it. One day, as my father told me years ago, the sun will explode and this solar system will be no more. The show will be over. Whether this happens billions of years from now, in the next moment, or at the moment of death, everything perceivable and conceivable will be erased, as it is every night in deep sleep. In reality, all of it is a momentary appearance, fleeting and dreamlike.

I also discovered along the way that the political left can be as oppressive as the political right, and that people often become the thing they are fighting against or, maybe more accurately, what we are fighting against is often, if not always, our own shadow, our own mirror image. There is no left without the right and vice versa. They exist relative to each other, creating and defining each other. They go together like yin and yang. That doesn't mean there can't be what *seems*, from our point of view, like improvement, progress, or evolutionary development, but any improvement will inevitably give rise to new problems and, sooner or later, whatever goes up will eventually come down. Up contains down, and down contains up. And no two people agree completely about what constitutes improvement.

Several centuries ago, oppressed and persecuted people from Europe came to North America, where they wiped out most of the Native Americans, enslaved the Africans, shot the buffalo for sport, took over half of Mexico, and eventually created the world's most powerful global empire whose inhabitants sucked up much of the world's resources in no time at all. In a similar circuitous twist, Jewish people who had survived the horrors of the Holocaust and anti-Semitism went over to Palestine, where their ancestors had lived centuries earlier, and drove the people who were living there now, the

Palestinians, off their land into refugee camps, ghettos and occupied territories. Likewise, idealistic socialists trying to create an egalitarian people's government have ended up exterminating hundreds of thousands of these same people in order to preserve and defend "the people." Followers of Jesus, the Jewish teacher who famously said, "Love your enemies as yourself," and "Let he who is without sin cast the first stone," have incomprehensibly ended up persecuting Jews, burning women as witches, mounting crusades, owning slaves, shooting abortion doctors in the head in church, waging endless wars, calling for vengeance and retribution, and amassing vast personal fortunes on the backs of others who toil for minimum wage. Who is the oppressor and who is the oppressed? Who is the real terrorist?

Disillusioned with politics, I turned to spirituality. But the koan of how these two seemingly different perspectives go together—political and spiritual, relative and absolute, immanent and transcendent—is a koan that seems to stay with me, taking different shapes over the years but always seeming to reappear, never entirely resolved.

At first, I was drawn to something like Christian liberation theology or engaged Buddhism—a socially-conscious, politically active, progressive spirituality that took a stand for the underdogs and the oppressed and sought to bring forth a better world. But as I continued to explore meditation, I came to see issues such as poverty, war, racism and sexism as symptomatic manifestations of a far deeper problem—the belief that we are each a separate self in a fractured world. I saw how we habitually mistake the map-world of conceptual thought for the actual territory of life itself without noticing that we are doing this. I saw how the thought-sense of being an encapsulated separate self gives birth to psychological fear and desire, which is different from the instinctual animal fear and desire that is a functional part of our biology. I saw how this psychological fear and desire spirals into addictions and compulsions, competing belief systems, long-held resentments and demands for retribution, and finally into all the insanity we see in the human world. We identify with various groups and individuals and fight to defend them, while regarding other groups and individuals as enemies and seeking to destroy them. I saw how

45

humans are hypnotized by our abstract thinking and overwhelmed by our powerful emotions, and how this swirl of emotion-thought gives rise to that basic sense of discontent, restlessness and unease that motivates much if not most of our human activity. We humans seem to be slowly destroying the very Earth upon which we depend for our survival, and no one seems able to stop the juggernaut.

I saw that by being aware and paying attention to the present moment, we can wake up from this hypnosis that is causing so much of our human suffering. I thought that perhaps we might even be able to stop the juggernaut before it was too late. This is a popular vision these days, that we are on the verge of a New Age, a new consciousness, a New Earth, in which humanity will perhaps no longer be caught up in ceaseless conflict and division. Imagining that we are on a wonderful evolutionary path toward a "New Earth" can be very energizing and uplifting, and it may even be true, but I've grown more aware of the dangers of purification fantasies and idealistic quests for some imagined utopia. Sooner or later, the sun will explode. And that's not bad news. Ultimately, the whole movie of waking life, including the entire history of the universe, is a passing dream.

But it *seems* very real, and in that context, where daily life is lived, I still feel that intelligent meditation and awareness work can be tremendously beneficial to both individuals and the world at large. And I certainly *do* see a life-changing shift, one that can happen in any moment, from entanglement in me-centered thought to the freedom of open aware presence. I'm still an enthusiast for meditation, meditative inquiry and awareness work of all kinds—and for progressive politics as well.

But no sunny day is ever a permanent state of affairs. We in the West have often tended to think of polarities as separate forces in conflict with one another, and we want and expect one side to ultimately defeat the other. But in reality, as they realized long ago in the East, polarities are inseparable and only exist relative to each other. Without them, the manifestation could not appear at all. Polarities are interdependent aspects of one whole event. Up is meaningful only in contrast to down, and no such place as "up" or "down" actually exists.

The ceiling is "up" in relation to the floor, but "down" in relation to the sky. It's all relative. In the boundlessness of outer space, without any reference points or gravity, there is no up or down. Astronauts aboard the International Space Station apparently sleep "standing up" in small vertical sleeping closets, but of course, in zero gravity, there is no difference between standing up and lying down, so they are literally sleeping on air. At the subatomic level, there is no actual separation between one polarity and its opposite. You can't find any actual place on a coin where heads become tails. The dividing line is conceptual. And the very notion of heads and tails only makes sense *within* the discrete, bounded conceptual abstraction that we call "the coin." Take away that conceptual boundary that defines the coin, and there are no heads and tails anymore. And of course, at a subatomic level, "the coin" is nothing but continuous change and mostly empty space, inseparable from everything that we think is not the coin. When you look closely with awareness, you can't actually find a border in your actual experience where what you think of as "inside of you" turns into what you think of as "outside of you." You can't actually *find* any *real* boundary line between subject and object or between awareness and content. You can't find any separate or persisting *things*. It is all one seamless and ever-changing event in which there is variety and diversity but not separation. There is no such thing as up triumphing over down, or light permanently vanquishing darkness.

Of course, there is a natural urge to relieve suffering, to wake up, to clarify, to explore and heal. But it's a very slippery slope between that natural, healthy aspiration and something much darker like the imperialist adventure, the Holocaust, the Stalinist purges, ISIS, Islamophobia, the war on terror or the war on drugs. Humanity has been slipping and sliding around on that slope since time immemorial. And in some sense, the entire manifestation, including all the slipping and sliding, is a fleeting dreamlike appearance that has no intrinsic, enduring reality. Whether the movie playing in the Theater of Mind is a horror story about the fiery end of the world in a catastrophic nuclear holocaust or a romantic fairytale about the New Earth and the New Humanity living in blissful vegan harmony in some organic Garden of Eden, it is always a fleeting appearance in consciousness, a dance of energy. Once consciousness divides up and mentally solidifies what is actually an incomprehensible and unbroken flow into *something* that seems permanent, substantial and coherent, *that* is always in some sense a delusion, empty of actual substance.

Spiritual paths and practices spring up in response to our confusion and suffering in much the same way that various chemicals, hormones, endorphins and antibodies spring up in the body in response to infection, pain or injury. It's all part of the natural movement of life, happening effortlessly by itself. Life creates *both* the antibodies *and* the viruses, the white blood cells *and* the bacteria, the medicine *and* the illness. Like the two sides of a coin, disease and medicine—delusion and enlightenment, samsara and nirvana—go together inseparably, and *both* are equally an expression of this undivided living reality.

The dark side of my life, the things that would be called suffering and misfortune—having only one hand, getting cancer, nearly dying from alcohol abuse, having a finger-biting compulsion that still flares up—these things have also brought insight, wisdom, compassion and humor into my life, and whatever shows up, the other side of the gestalt is always there as well, the light in the darkness and the darkness in the light. We can never have a life of only positive emotions and happy events. No one gets through this life unscathed. And as has so often been noted, the defect is where the light gets in, the suffering is what motivates us to seek liberation, and delusion is what opens the door for enlightenment. As Thich Nhat Hanh once said, "No mud, no lotus." Clearly, in *all* of this, there is an energy at work, an intelligence, a movement far beyond our limited human ability to understand or control. We do what life moves us to do, and we don't *really* know what's best for the universe or how it all works.

I've come to feel that liberation is never about resolving everything in some neat and tidy way, finding The Answer, knowing with certainty how the universe works, crossing the Finish Line once and for all, and never again being troubled by any pesky human emotions; but rather, it is about *seeing through* the imaginary problem, not once and for all, but *Now*. Every apparent answer or solution that can be formulated and grasped, quickly becomes part of the imaginary problem once we cling to it or mistake it for the Truth.

Over time, I found that my attention was moving away from trying to fix the outer world and more toward exploring the inner world. I was glad *somebody* was still working to save the environment and correct all the massive social and economic injustices, but I was no longer drawn to that endeavor. Zen became the focus of my life. I lived briefly at a Zen Center in Berkeley. From there, I got involved with Toni Packer, a former Zen teacher who had left the tradition behind to work in a more open way, without hierarchy, dogma, rituals or religious trappings. I was on staff at the retreat center she founded in rural northwestern New York for five years. We did eight or ten silent retreats every year and, during those years at Springwater, I spent lots of time in nature, wandering in the woods and fields.

It became crystal clear to me during those years that everything is one whole undivided happening and that this awaring presence Here-Now is boundless and limitless. And one day—I remember it vividly—it suddenly became clear that *everything* belonged, that *everything* was part of this wholeness, even our industrial civilization, air pollution, human cruelty, factory farms—the whole catastrophe. It was *all* a part of nature, an activity of this indivisible *no-thing-ness,* whatever we call it. There is nothing *other* than this seamless unicity doing what it does. When we ask, "Who am I?" or "What is this?", and we look deeper than any superficial answer, any word or concept we've learned, we find nothing we can grasp.

The actuality Here-Now is our most obvious, immediate, undeniable, ever-present reality; and yet it is unfathomable. We tend to overlook it in favor of the abstract map-world that thought has painted. But all the while, the actuality is effortlessly and spontaneously functioning in perfect harmony. It is ever-changing, and yet always Here-Now. It never departs from itself. It is by nature open, aware, intelligent, radiant, allowing everything, clinging to nothing. And somehow, it all belongs.

I wrote my first book at Springwater during my years on staff. And that's where I discovered Nisargadatta Maharaj and Jean Klein.

Eventually, I left Springwater for the Advaita satsang world. I spent time with many satsang teachers including Jean Klein, Gangaji, Francis Lucille, Isaac Shapiro and Adyashanti. I did The Work with Byron Katie. Eventually, I encountered radical nondualists like Tony Parsons, Leo Hartong, Sailor Bob, Nathan Gill, Chuck Hillig, Karl Renz and Darryl Bailey.

From radical nonduality, *you get nothing*. Or put differently, you get *everything*, just as it is. Radical nonduality is not about improvement or progress. It offers a *description* of reality, never a *prescription* for how to fix it. It suggests no path, no methodology, nowhere to go, nothing to do other than what is already happening effortlessly by itself. It isn't *against* doing things like meditation and yoga, but it isn't suggesting any of this either. It points to the fact that *whatever* happens in any given moment is the Only Possible and that *all* of it is nothing but a kind of impersonal, evaporating, dreamlike appearance—clouds changing shape, smoke curling into the air, waves rolling on the ocean—nothing graspable, nothing fixed, nothing that can be resolved or finalized or pinned down.

This radical perspective points relentlessly to the choiceless nature of reality and the absence of anyone running the show. Everything is a spontaneous and automatic happening that can never be captured or grasped by words, concepts or formulations. Our brain sees patterns where none actually exist. It turns chaos into order. But the order is imaginary. We are always clueless. Life is an unresolvable, incomprehensible, indeterminate mystery. And that's not a horrible or depressing thought, but rather, a liberating and beautiful realization.

In discovering our complete and absolute powerlessness, our utter lack of control, there is immediately great peace, true freedom and unconditional love. It is the freedom for everything to be just as it is. It is not the peace that is the opposite of war or upset, but rather, it is the peace that *includes* war and upset, the peace that is at peace with war and even with our resistance to war. It is the unconditional love that accepts everything. In this discovery of choiceless unicity, there is immediately compassion for oneself and all beings, knowing that in every moment, we are all doing the only thing possible. No wave can ever go off in a direction other than the one in which the whole ocean is moving.

From this radical perspective, enlightenment doesn't mean a utopian society of people who are gentle, kind, happy and vegan, nor does it mean hiding out in some kind of pure and transcendent awareness that stands safely apart from this messy world. It means exactly *what is, right here, right now.* The sound of machinery, the exhaust fumes from the city bus, clouds blowing across the sky, the song of a bird, breath coming in and going out, sensations in the body, a fart, a twinge in the tooth, the ache of grief, the fire of jealousy, the darkness of despair, the fragrance of roses, the smell of garbage, the warm patch of sunlight on the carpet, the mental movies that play in the imagination and then suddenly pop like bubbles, these words pouring out uncontrollably, the awaring presence, the unfathomable intelligence-energy being and beholding it all—not the conceptual "things" that these words inevitably suggest, but the bare, undivided, indeterminate, unresolvable actuality itself, the present-ness of it, the immediacy, the no-thing-ness showing up as everything. The nondual absolute includes *everything* and sticks to nothing.

This doesn't mean being a doormat, or not fixing a flat tire, going to the doctor, practicing yoga or meditation, or marching for civil rights if we are so moved. Nonduality *includes* our impulse to fix what is broken as well as our ideas, opinions, angry outbursts, waves of fear—the whole dance. It simply points out that the apparent individual is not the author, the source, the controller, or the doer of our impulses, choices and actions—and that nothing is what we think it is. There is no one here who can choose one response over another. Our personality, including all our neurotic quirks, couldn't be any different in this moment from how it is, and likewise, the child molester, the genocidal dictator, the school shooter, the factory farmer, the terrorist, and the serial killer are all expressed as they are because of infinite causes and conditions. There is no choice in the matter—we don't "decide" to be Ramana Maharshi or Adolf Hitler—and it is the same seamless energy dancing as both.

This can be easily misunderstood. Ramana Maharshi once said,

"Whatever is destined not to happen will not happen, try as you may. Whatever is destined to happen will happen, do what you may to prevent it." And that is absolutely true. But if your child is running out into the traffic, do you stand silently by and think to yourself that "whatever is destined to happen will happen," or do you yell, "Stop!" and run out to get them? *Your response is also destiny.* You can't leave your own urges, impulses, thoughts and actions out of the picture—they too are the play of totality. If your child gets hit by a car anyway, it is indeed very helpful to *realize* that this was the Only Possible at that moment, and that realization may lessen your suffering and free you from guilt or self-blame. But that realization doesn't block you from acting, it doesn't prevent you from grieving the loss, and it certainly doesn't make any of those human responses "wrong" or "unenlightened." No child ever actually existed in the way we think—as a separate, persisting, independent entity—and yet, we can't deny the tangible reality, preciousness and uniqueness of every child either. We can't land in either the relative or the absolute, or cling to emptiness or form, personal or impersonal. It is *all* included!

Life includes rose gardens and concentration camps, song birds and cluster bombs, Ramana Maharshi and Martin Luther King Jr., Buddha and Hitler, relative and absolute—the whole show. Like it or not, there is space Here-Now for absolutely *everything* to be just as it is, and *all* of it is empty of any solid, inherent, observer-independent existence.

If I don't see this, if I feel that I am a separate fragment, then when I am confronted with someone on the opposite side of the political spectrum, or someone who is treating me, or some group with which I am identified, unjustly or with great cruelty, it is easy to strap on the suicide belt, literally or metaphorically, and blow us both up in a fit of rage. This of course only pours gasoline on the fire. America's "war on terror" is a classic example of this on the global scale.

When, on the other hand, I can really *see* that the original insult or act of cruelty comes from ignorance and pain, when I don't "take delivery" of it, as Nisargadatta used to say, then I can meet the original insult or act of cruelty with love, compassion, generosity and understanding. When I see only God everywhere, I will quite naturally meet hatred with love. That doesn't mean I won't try to put the serial killer and the child rapist behind bars or that I might not try to kill someone like Hitler to save many others. But I'll do all of that in a very different spirit than if I am filled with hatred and blame and fear, seeking vengeance.

But even when this whirlpool called "Joan" *does* "take delivery" and get angry or upset or hurt, that too is nothing but unicity doing what it does, and it is the Only Possible *at that moment*. If "Joan" then "decides" (or more accurately, feels compelled) to meditate, and eventually wakes up from her anger, that too is the Only Possible, and there is no "Joan" who is doing *any* of that. The anger, the meditating, the heart opening is *all* a happening of the whole universe.

In the end, I woke up from radical nonduality as well, at least as any kind of system that could be formulated and pinned down. I found that radical nonduality could also become something to grasp—a new ideology, a comforting answer, a way of closing down rather than opening up—like putting on a new set of blinders or getting stuck in a new kind of fundamentalist dogma. I found that *anywhere* we try to land and *anything* we try to grasp or cling to is false. Truth is the openness that sticks to no conceptual formulation or explanation of life but rather remains with the freshness and groundlessness of not knowing and non-clinging. When we wake up from *all* the answers, truth is what remains.

Truth cannot be put into words. It is alive, ever-fresh. To be awake is to live in devotion to Here-Now, without the handrails of any ideology, belief system or authority. Sometimes devotion means that I sit on a cushion and engage in something that looks like formal meditation. Sometimes it means I sit in my armchair watching the clouds blow past the mountains or feeling into the fear and anxiety that is sweeping through my gut or my chest. Sometimes it means I pick or bite my fingers and notice that I am compelled to do this and unable to stop myself, and that this, too, is an inconceivable movement of life itself. Sometimes it means discovering anew that there is space here for everything to be as it is, and that in that spacious and unconditioned awareness, empty of all judgments and goals, everything changes, and the truly new emerges.

In the years that followed, I returned many times to Springwater for retreats with Toni and others who are teaching there now. I attended Buddhist retreats with Steve Hagen, Anam Thubten and John Tarrant. In the last two decades, I've enjoyed and been touched by expressions as wondrously diverse and as seemingly irreconcilable at times as Eckhart Tolle, Karl Renz, Norman Fischer, Ramana Maharshi, Dogen, Rupert Spira, Barry Magid, Jon Bernie, Peter Brown, Pema Chödrön, Dorothy Hunt, Gilbert Schultz, John Butler, Pamela Wilson, Mooji, Dan Harris and Jeff Warren—to name just a few. Some are friends, some I've heard in person, some I've read or heard online, some I've met with or been on retreat with.

Every teacher (or non-teacher) I've heard, read or been with has pointed out or illuminated a different facet of *what is,* and/or been just what I needed at that moment to pull whatever rug I was currently standing on out from under me. I've heard things from one that I couldn't hear from another. Sometimes expressions that are wildly different in style and form have brought me to exactly the same realization. Teachers will affect everyone who hears them differently. All expressions are fluid. You can't really pin them down. There is a resonance between speaker and listener, an aliveness, which is where the juice really is. All of the diverse perspectives I've explored are reflected in some way or other in my own work.

In the mid-1990s, after my first book, *Bare-Bones Meditation,* was published, I began holding public and private meetings, giving talks, and occasionally traveling and offering workshops and retreats elsewhere when I was invited. I've always been rather allergic to the word teacher, preferring to think of myself as a friend on the pathless path. And I've always remained rather low key, turning down most of the invitations I've received to travel. I began writing this book after my second book, *Awake in the Heartland,* was published. While I was writing this book on aging and dying, two others emerged— *Painting the Sidewalk with Water* and *Nothing to Grasp.* Finally, this book on death and the end of self-improvement, after its seemingly unending gestation, appears to be nearing birth. Or is it death? They are strangely alike, those two.

What Do We Really Want?

What really matters? What do I most deeply want? These are wonderful questions to live with and explore. Many decades ago, probably in 1989, I attended a seven-day Zen sesshin, or meditation retreat, with the late Maurine Stuart, who was dying at the time from cancer. She gave me that question, what do you really want, as a koan—a question to work with on the retreat.

I spent many days obsessively thinking about the question, twisting and turning in mental anguish, trying to figure out what it was I really wanted. Did I want to stay with Zen or go back to the nontraditional approach I had been pursuing? Did I want to stay in California or move back to New York? Did I want to live in a big city or in the country? Round and round the mind went. What finally became crystal clear, in one of those magical moments of total clarity when the mind stops and the clouds part and you're simply completely awake to the obvious, what finally became crystal clear is that what really matters, what I most deeply want, is to be fully present and awake right here in this moment, right now, just as it is.

And today, decades later, if I had to give one single key to awakening, it would be that it's all about Now—not yesterday or tomorrow or forever after—but right here, right now. It's not about some better or different experience, but rather, it's here in the immediacy of *this* experience. And *this* experience is ever-changing, impossible to capture in any concept, label or storyline. It doesn't hold still. We never step into the same river twice, and we're never the same person from one instant to the next. Presence is alive and moving, yet always Here-Now.

When the attention isn't lost in thought-stories, it doesn't matter if I'm in the city or the country, if I'm working in an office or living at a Zen Center, if my bank account is big or small, if I'm partnered up or single, rich or poor, writing a book or taking out the garbage. The joy, the love, the freedom is in the presence, the aliveness, not in the particular circumstances or momentary forms that life is taking. *All* forms are beautiful! All forms are equally an expression of this aliveness, this seamless energy. And all of them are gone in an instant.

We humans spend so much precious time and energy trying to escape the Now. We *think* we want better weather, a nicer living situation, a different partner, more money, less fatigue, more sex, fewer wrinkles, a different job, more cooperative or successful children, whatever it is we think will make us happy. But every job, partner, location, living situation, and spiritual path has its upside and its downside. The weather is always changing and nothing stays the same. Trying to find happiness in a passing form is inevitably disappointing. That doesn't mean we can't enjoy the passing forms or that we shouldn't try a different job. But if we think that any of this is what will truly, deeply satisfy the longing of the heart, we are always in for a disillusionment.

CHAPTER FIVE: Beyond Self-Improvement: Embracing What Is

The Tyranny of Self-Improvement

All the great spiritual teachings ultimately point to a freedom that has nothing to do with self-improvement or control.

—Darryl Bailey

Self-hate is pervasive in our culture, the feeling that we're never good enough, that we always need to be improved, corrected or fixed in some way, the sense of shame and deficiency. Our society is obsessed with self-improvement, eternal youth, the *pursuit* of happiness. People feel tremendous pressure to eat the right food, go to the gym, excel in school, become somebody, be a winner, and never get old. We are deluged with stories about exceptional people and over-achievers. We read about ninety-year-old skydivers, quadruple amputees climbing Mt. Everest, people born into poverty who have become billionaires—and these become the standard against which we all feel measured. To be average or ordinary, to fail and be imperfect, is our worst nightmare.

Of course, it's great to hear inspiring stories, to challenge ourselves, and to have a more positive picture of what's possible in life if you have a disability or when you're old. And I'm all for eating well and taking good care of ourselves. There's nothing wrong with having goals and aspirations. That's all part of the natural movement of life doing what it does. But it can easily become oppressive.

Many parents have huge expectations for what their children should do in life. Children feel the pressure. Many parents give their adult children the supposedly encouraging message that they will *someday* do something great, which of course carries with it the *subtext* that right now, whatever they're doing is *not* that great.

When I mentioned the title of the book I was working on, *Death:*

The End of Self-Improvement, to one of my oncology nurses, she was ecstatic. *Yes!* she said with a huge smile. She started talking about what she called "the tyranny of exceptionalism," something that she'd been reading about that clearly resonated deeply with her. She told me that, in order to get her health insurance at work, she has to wear one of those wrist monitors that counts how many steps you take every day. If she doesn't wear it or if she doesn't take enough steps, no health insurance. I was stunned.

If we get sick, we're often given the message that we must have done something wrong. Maybe we were having too many negative thoughts, not meditating enough, not having the right relationship to our money. Make we drank too much coffee, ate too much chocolate or not enough kale. Cancer is blamed on everything imaginable. And as we move into old age, we often get the message that we must battle death and fight to live as long as possible. To die is to fail.

The spiritual journey becomes a quest for the biggest awakening experience. We compare ourselves to our favorite spiritual superheroes and feel inferior, never quite all the way "there" where we imagine they are or were. People announce themselves as "Awakened Ones" and then have to prove it and live up to it, which can result in enormous layers of self-deception, dishonesty and bullshit.

What a relief to finally let all this go!

The Curious Paradox

You are perfect just as you are, and there's room for improvement.

—Shunryu Suzuki

The curious paradox is that when I accept myself just as I am, then I can change.

—Carl Rogers

So, am I suggesting we should all sink into sloth and torpor, conclude that liberation is a pipe dream best abandoned, gorge on junk food for the rest of our lives, and allow such things as disabling depression, destructive addictions, racism, sexism, environmental devastation or animal cruelty to continue unchallenged? Is that the message of this book?

Clearly not. After all, how genuine transformation happens has been one of the main interests of my life. I've experienced and seen undeniable positive changes in myself and others through meditation, psychotherapy, somatic awareness work, spirituality and nonduality. I've seen positive changes in society as a result of political movements, some of which I've participated in. The women's movement, the gay liberation movement and the disability rights movement have all made my life much easier and less painful. The changes I've experienced from inner work include sobering up from near-fatal alcohol and drug use, and leaving behind bouts of depression and such debilitating patterns of emotion-thought as self-doubt, self-hatred and shame. As someone who has spent much of the last four decades writing books and articles, putting on retreats, giving talks, answering emails, and meeting with people about waking up from false beliefs and exploring the possibility of being liberated on the spot, it would certainly seem that the alchemy of transformation has been central to my life. Of course, all of what I've just described only exists in a story constructed by memory. But relatively speaking, I'm all for positive changes.

Paradoxically, though, every time I've gone through therapy or delved deeper into some spiritual path or non-path, what has always emerged front and center at the root of it all is the willingness to be as I am; to be, on the human level, in some sense imperfect, incomplete and unresolved; and to see that this very person, warts and all, is already whole and complete, that this bodymind and everything it thinks and wants and does is a movement of the whole universe. Rather than trying to reach some ultimate perfection of "me," or some imagined supreme enlightenment, it turns out that true happiness is a matter of simply being Here-Now, which is actually unavoidable; but what can fall away or no longer be believed are the thoughts and stories *about* this present happening, the interpretations, judgments, and ideals.

Even when people take up meditation to reduce stress and improve well-being, as many people do nowadays, even then, they soon learn that the usual result-oriented, end-gaining approach of trying really hard to get somewhere else—seeking, resisting, evaluating, judging, and so on—doesn't work. Meditation, even as a wellness practice, begins with allowing everything to be as it is. In a way, even to say "allowing" or "accepting" is saying too much. Everything already *is* allowed to be as it is—obviously!—because it *is* as it is. So it's more like simply *acknowledging* how it is, *being* present experiencing, which we already are. It's not a *doing*, in other words. It's more like *not* doing anything extra. Relaxing. Being what you cannot *not* be. And as the pathless path unfolds, *everything* is discovered to be an expression of this radiant presence that we are. Nothing needs to be pushed away or kept out. *Everything* is spiritual.

An interest in how change happens and the total acceptance of *what is* may seem like two diametrically opposed movements, but in fact, I have come to see that true healing, transformation and liberation begin with the simple acceptance of this moment and this world, just as it is. As counterintuitive as it may seem, embracing imperfection, allowing everything to be as it is, loving what is—*this* is the gateless gate to a fresh start and the utterly new. Oddly enough, *this* is the secret of freedom.

My first Zen teacher, Mel Weitsman, said that "our suffering is believing there's a way out." The Tibetan Buddhist teacher Chögyam Trungpa famously said that enlightenment is not final victory, but rather, final defeat. Another one of my Zen teachers, Joko Beck, spoke of Zen as "having no hope." She also used to say, "What makes it unbearable is your mistaken belief that it can be cured." None of these teachers were pointing to a state of despair, resignation or hopelessness, which is the flip side of hope, equally rooted in an imaginary future. Instead, they were pointing to how we can waste our lives in hopeful fantasies and "the pursuit of happiness" while missing the living reality that is Here-Now. We dream of the perfect location, the perfect house, the perfect career, the perfect partner, the perfect child, the perfect enlightenment experience, the perfect self, the perfect society, the perfect world, the perfect present moment—and all the while we are missing out on the actuality and perfection of life as it is.

That doesn't mean we should all vegetate passively on the couch or be a doormat for abuse. In fact, we cannot suppress or deny our natural desire for exertion and movement, our urge to take action, to respond to life, to seek pleasure and avoid pain, to dance the particular dance that each of us is moved to dance. There is a natural impulse to pursue what attracts us, to heal what is broken, to clarify what is obscure, to explore new territory, to discover and develop and extend our capacities and capabilities, to envision different possibilities, to help others, to bring forth what is within us. Astronomy, quantum physics, going to the gym, learning a foreign language, practicing meditation, playing music, taking up yoga, exploring various forms of awareness work, working for social justice, writing books, making art, raising children, starting a business, planning a trip to Mars, performing brain surgery, climbing mountains, rescuing abandoned cats and dogs, developing new software programs—*all* of this is the natural movement of life, something the universe is doing, just as the seed flowering into a tree, or the ecosystem evolving in ever new ways are all the natural and spontaneous play of life. *Everything* is included.

I went into therapy to sober up from near-fatal drinking back in 1973 and several more times over the years, and it's quite natural to want to find a solution to certain painful situations such as depression, anxiety, self-hatred, or addictive and compulsive behaviors that are hurting ourselves and others around us. And if we have glimpsed the possibility of living without self-doubt, shame, worry and self-concern, we naturally long to return to that place of freedom and happiness that we have tasted. People go into therapy, take up meditation, go to satsangs, and listen to radical nondualists out of just such a longing.

But paradoxically, it is in some sense the very *search* for happiness that makes us miserable. That search is predicated on the belief in deficiency and lack, the belief that "this isn't it." It is all about a "me" that doesn't actually exist and a future that never arrives. The end of self-improvement is the realization of what is always already whole and complete, the wholeness that includes the apparent brokenness.

The character we take ourselves to be, which is a mental construction made up of ever-shifting images, memories, thoughts, stories and sensations, has no independent will or volition in the way we imagine it does. That image we see in the mirror is just an image. It has no power to do anything. If we watch closely, we can *see* that all our urges, interests, abilities, feelings, and thoughts—*including this watching and the interest and ability to carry it out*—all arise from an unfindable source. The "we" who seemingly does all this is merely a grammatical convention.

That doesn't mean we don't have what *feels* like volition and choice. Obviously, we do. One neuroscientist calls the sense of being a self with agency a neurological sensation. But if we watch closely as choices and decisions unfold, we can *see* that it is all happening by itself. There is no little helmsman, no self, no "me" inside our head sitting at some giant control panel pulling levers or authoring our thoughts. Our desire to get drunk or sober up, go into therapy, take an aspirin or march for civil rights is *all* an expression of the totality, as are the outcomes of all such actions. Our emotional reactions and ruminations, our thinking, our apparent successes and failures—this is *all* happening by itself. The little "me" who seems to be authoring my thoughts and making my choices is not actually doing any of that because that "me" is nothing but a mental image, an idea, a thought-form.

That "me-thought" arises spontaneously either before an action or after an action, taking credit or blame. "I should do that," or "I did that." In any moment when that thought-sense of being a separate and vulnerable "me" is absent, nothing is taken personally. We are no longer concerned about outcomes in the same way. We are no longer plagued by guilt, shame, blaming others, or the anxiety of thinking we might "get it wrong" and "ruin our life." We are simply doing what life moves us to do, as is everyone else, which has actually always been the case. We naturally have compassion for ourselves and others being just as we are in each moment. And the "we" in all these sentences is only a grammatical convention. The sense of separation is absent, and even when it shows up, it is only an appearance. No wave can ever go off in a direction other than the one in which the whole ocean is moving. We are *all* a movement of the whole, not isolated agents capable of going the wrong way.

But this gets very subtle. It doesn't mean becoming passive, or picking up the *belief* that "I" have no free will, that "I" am a helpless robot being pushed around by the universe. That belief is still centered around the idea of a separate entity, a self, now believed to be powerless. That is delusion. Our urges, interests, actions—*and our sense of choice*—are all part of how life functions and moves. And we are not separate from, or *other* than, life itself.

The capacity to make better choices can obviously be developed through education, athletic training, psychotherapy, meditation, yoga, and in all kinds of ways—*all* of which happen choicelessly, even as it *appears* that "I" am choosing them.

There is a palpable shift that occurs when attention drops out of the thinking mind into stillness and presence. When that happens, in the light of awareness, there is an increase in responsibility (response-ability), the ability to respond rather than react, to move in a more wholesome—holistic, whole, intelligent—way. This is the beauty of meditation, psychotherapy, various forms of inquiry, and somatic practices such as Feldenkrais, Continuum or yoga. They bring awareness to where we are stuck and show us what else is possible. We become less ensnared in old conditioning, and a new range of possibilities opens up. The habitual me-system is no longer always running the show. We are no longer totally a slave to conditioned neurology. We (as awareness) have more choices, more possibilities, at least sometimes.

Of course, this shift out of thinking and into aware presence happens choicelessly, in that there is no "me" who can bring it about by an act of independent will. But this shift may indeed require an *apparently* intentional move that we call a choice, a movement that itself arises choicelessly. The possibility of taking a time-out when we're angry, of not lighting up a cigarette when the urge arises, of choosing to meditate when we feel upset, is only there when it is. *Whatever* happens is *always* a movement of the whole. But our functional *sense* of agency is part of that larger movement, part of how the universe, or consciousness, functions. In a sense, we have no choice but to act *as if* we have choice.

We can't land on either free will or no free will because both are conceptual abstractions of a living reality that cannot be captured in *any* conceptual formulation. The map is not the territory; the word is not the thing. Therefore, it's so important not to get fixated on one side of a conceptual divide between two abstract ideas, such as choice or choicelessness, self or no self, practice or no practice, effort or effortlessness, because neither side is totally true. It's very easy to turn what begins as a genuine insight into a limiting or oppressive belief, a new fundamentalist dogma that we then cling to and defend.

Liberation is never about getting the right ideas or the right beliefs. It's always about direct insight. Believing that there is "no self" is useless, and as a concept, this is a very easy one to totally misunderstand. But if we simply pay attention, we can begin to notice that there are many moments in any ordinary day where we're not thinking about ourselves and feeling like a separate person. We're just driving the car, making love, dancing, washing the dishes, changing a diaper, calculating a bunch of numbers, folding the laundry. There's no "me" in the picture until a thought arises, such as, "Why do *I* always have to be the one who changes the baby's diapers?" or "I'm a bad dancer," or "I wonder if she likes me." Instantly, with that thought, the mirage of "me" appears on the scene. And we can notice that this mirage is just another passing experience, another weather event in this vast open space of awareness. The awaring presence being and beholding it all is unbound. Present experiencing is without a center or a periphery. It has no inside or outside.

Of course, for most, if not all of us, the me-system does not permanently disappear never to show up again. In moments of inattention and stress, old conditioning tends to return, and for a moment, whether that moment is a few seconds, a few hours or a few weeks, we again feel angry, hurt, defensive, entitled, guilty, or whatever we feel. But more and more, this can be seen. Sometimes we don't see it. And sometimes we only see it hours or years or decades later. But through practices such as meditation and psychotherapy, we can begin to catch it more quickly, to see it as it is happening, and sometimes even as it is just *about* to happen, that first tiny seed. We begin to notice how our lip quivers, how our throat constricts, how blood rushes to the head, how our gut tightens, how we are holding our breath or barely breathing—these first tiny signals of upset. In the absolute sense, everything is already perfect, while in the relative sense, there's always room for improvement—*and that's part of the perfection!*

Life is a kind of balancing act in a way, between the recognition that everything is perfect just as it is, and the impulse or aspiration, which is part of this perfection, to grow and transform. If we pay attention, we can begin to *feel* the difference between misery-inducing self-improvement and what we might call healthy aspiration, genuine transformation or true happiness. There are no rules for precisely where one ends and the other begins. And in the absolute sense, *everything* is equally an expression of unicity, *including* misery-inducing self-improvement and the illusion of personal will. But on a functional and relative level, just as we can distinguish apples from oranges, we can distinguish what we might call healthy aspiration or genuine transformation from the kind of misery-inducing self-improvement that is itself a manifestation of the very problem it is trying to solve.

Self-improvement is always focused on the future, while true happiness is only ever found Here-Now. Self-improvement begins with the *rejection* of this-Here-Now, while healthy aspiration begins with the *embrace* of what is. Self-improvement is endless postponement. The finish line is never reached. Genuine transformation is the recognition that waking up only happens Here-Now. Self-improvement is rooted in a sense of lack and deficiency, whereas true happiness understands that the defect is an essential component of perfection. Self-improvement wants one polarity to triumph over its opposite, which is never going to happen, while genuine transformation recognizes the inseparability and collaborative necessity of both apparently opposing forces.

Self-improvement is oppositional and violent. It thinks in terms of *fighting* cancer, waging a *war* on drugs or a *war* on terror, *killing* the ego, *vanquishing* thought. Genuine transformation comes from unconditional love. It has no enemies. It recognizes everything as the Beloved. It sees only God everywhere. It embraces everything, recognizing everything as itself. What we resist tends to persist because by resisting it, we are validating its reality and giving it power. The more we oppose and vilify something, the stronger, more defensive and aggressive it seems to become. Not resisting doesn't mean staying in an abusive relationship, being a doormat or not taking action to correct an injustice. It is pointing to something much more immediate, a way of being in this very moment that allows intelligent action to emerge. You can treat cancer without *fighting* it, and it is only the ego that wants to kill the ego.

Self-improvement is rooted in the illusion of an imaginary self with free will and choice trying to control and fix a separate and enduring "thing" that doesn't actually exist, whether that imaginary "thing" is "me" or "you" or "the world." Genuine transformation moves from wholeness and recognizes that whatever is appearing Here-Now is the Only Possible in this moment.

Happiness arises from a fundamental trust or faith in the Way It Is (the Tao), while self-improvement moves from fear and insecurity. When I speak of trust, I don't mean trusting that things will go my way, but trusting that whatever happens, all is well in the deepest sense. This isn't a belief—it's a faith that emerges from presence.

Self-improvement inevitably ends in disappointment, because it is the nature of form to break down and fall apart. Genuine transformation begins from the recognition of what is beyond any particular form and yet completely present as every form. It points to a freedom and joy that isn't dependent on outcomes.

Self-improvement is rigid and perfectionistic, driven by beliefs, expectations and old answers, while genuine transformation is flexible, open to new discoveries and rooted in not-knowing. Genuine transformation listens for what life itself wants, while self-improvement imagines that "I" know how everything "should" be. Self-improvement is judgmental, self-righteous and narrow-minded, while happiness and real change are the release of all that.

Self-improvement is primarily thought-based, while genuine transformation emerges from aware presence. Thought divides; awareness joins. Thought is dualistic; awareness is nondual. Of course, there is a place for intelligent thinking—reason, intellect and analysis are marvelous tools. I'm not in any way disparaging thinking. I have great appreciation for the scientific method and for human reason. But awareness is upstream from thought. And in many situations, thought is the wrong instrument.

There is a place for healthy aspiration and intention, for creative imagination and visualization. Social change work of any kind obviously relies to some degree on our ability to identify what causes suffering and to imagine a different possibility. There is no exact or fixed line where that healthy and functional use of memory, imagination and thinking crosses over into a painful obsession. But we can become more and more sensitive to where we are coming from when we envision or work toward a change in ourselves or in the world. We can begin to *feel* the difference between perfectionistic self-improvement and genuine transformation, between self-righteousness and love. And we can recognize that the best place to begin any kind of change is always with simply being aware of how it *is* right now.

Otherwise, it's easy to wind up recreating and reinforcing the very problems we are trying to solve. When we fail to go all the way to the root of our problems, we often end up reproducing the original problem in a new form. We've seen this in many political revolutions, in various technological developments that have had unintended consequences, and in spiritual practices that end up reinforcing the root illusions. We easily end up digging ourselves into deeper and deeper holes. Humanity is now on the verge of wiping itself off the face of the earth, all because we have made one well-intended "improvement" after another.

How would it be to not know how we or the universe or this moment "should" be?

Patterns of thought are deeply conditioned and, as we grow up, we begin to think that we actually *are* the voice in our heads, the thought-stream, and we come to believe that whatever this voice says is reliable and true, and that we are somehow authoring our thoughts as well. We even begin to think that there is nothing outside of thought, that thinking is the primary reality. "I think, therefore I am." We are easily hypnotized and entranced by our thoughts. One of the reasons I feel insight meditation is helpful, or a process such as The Work of Byron Katie, or many intelligent forms of psychotherapy, is that recognizing thoughts *as* thoughts is not always as easy as it sounds, and realizing that there is so much here other than thought—as obvious as that seems once it's obvious—can be surprisingly elusive. It is, as they say, the open secret, hidden in plain sight, the elusive obvious.

We can argue over whether thought is *causative* of emotions and behaviors or whether it is simply an *aftereffect* of what originates below the level of conscious awareness. I suspect both perspectives are true, each perhaps more so in some instances than others. Clearly, waking up isn't *only* a matter of questioning our thoughts and beliefs but, in my experience, that's an important element.

Bringing awareness to the body, feeling sensations, tuning into aware presence in a way that is non-conceptual and not thought-based is the other part of the equation—opening up to the non-conceptual immediacy of the sensory-energetic actuality Here-Now and recognizing the boundless awaring presence that we are and that everything is. And that can happen in many different ways.

We don't ever reach any ideal perfection that we can imagine, or if we do, it doesn't last. So any true aspiration must be balanced by the realization that life is in charge, not me. We must discover the willingness to allow life to unfold at its own pace, in its own way, the willingness to fail again and again, without taking that personally and turning it into a story of personal lack or a reason for self-hatred. Shunryu Suzuki said, "The life of a Zen Master is one continuous mistake." Or Zen teacher Elihu Genmyo Smith: "Mistake after mistake is the perfect way." Our failures, disappointments, mistakes, and even humanity's most horrific actions, are all part of this whole fabric in some essential way. We know from our own experience that our most difficult and challenging experiences are often the ones that open us up and teach us the most.

It's not uncommon for people who take up some form of nonduality to get stuck in the absolute for a while—and in some cases, forever. They get the mistaken idea that they aren't supposed to have goals or preferences of any kind, that they shouldn't want anything to change. They keep asserting over and over that there is no self, no choice, nothing to do—that everything is perfect as it is, that nothing is even happening. But it's quite natural to want to change what hurts. And it's quite useful to be able to *see* when we are making a mistake or missing the mark. Of course, we are never out of integrity in the absolute sense, and in that larger sense, every mistake is perfectly placed, but in the relative world of everyday life, the ability to identify mistakes and correct them is vital to our survival as individuals and as a species. It's part of how life is functioning and evolving. Perfection isn't a matter of not making any mistakes. It's about the ability to learn from them, to get up and keep going, to not take mistakes personally or get lost in shame, guilt and self-hatred, to start fresh Here-Now.

Sometimes when we have an idea that "everything is perfect as it is," we forget that working to improve things is part of what is. We leave ourselves and our own abilities, inclinations and actions out of the picture in some way. So, nonduality doesn't mean we shouldn't meditate or pray or take vows or see a therapist. It doesn't mean we shouldn't go to the gym and exercise, or that we leave a flat tire flat forever because we are "allowing everything to be as it is," or because "we are powerless and have no choice." That is a misunderstanding. And waking up from our entrancement in thought, from our habitual tendency to mistake the map for the territory, doesn't in any way mean that we can't, or shouldn't, think or conceptualize or use maps. It simply points to how all these activities come from life itself, not from the phantom self. All our *ideas* of success and failure are just that, ideas.

The peace and freedom we long for is found in one place only: Here-Now. Of course, we can't *make* ourselves stop seeking and resisting on command, and any attempt to do so is only another form of seeking and resisting. All that can happen is to *see* this habitual pattern of seeking and resisting whenever it arises. We can't even *make* that happen—but it *does* happen, when it does.

It's fine to have practical goals, such as getting a college degree. But we don't need to get hooked on the fantasy that we will be happy only if and when we get that degree, or that we *need* that degree to be happy. Our attention can be on the present moment even as we move toward the goal.

Awakening is not about denying relative reality. What happens in the world both matters and doesn't matter. As a human being in the play of life, it breaks my heart to see someone torturing an animal or abusing a child. It breaks my heart to remember some of the insensitive, abusive or hurtful things I have done in my life. Having the bigger view, the absolute perspective, helps me to see all of this in a bigger context, to hold it more lightly, more compassionately, more gently, to be more flexible, open-minded and open-hearted—to see beyond the story that the world is going to hell and I have to fix it, or that I am a terrible person who should crawl into a hole and die. To recognize how ephemeral and insubstantial, how subjective and dreamlike it all is, is very liberating. But it doesn't mean I don't care, that my heart doesn't break sometimes, or that I may not be moved to act.

In Zen, there are a bunch of precepts, and they say that from the absolute perspective, it is impossible to break them, and from the relative perspective, it is impossible *not* to break them. Just by being alive, we break them. Not killing, the first precept, is broken every time we eat, every time we take a step, every time we wipe our forehead, every time we inhale. Life feeds on life. But in the absolute sense, no-thing is born and no-thing dies; so we can never *actually* kill anything. From the absolute view, there are no mistakes. From the relative view, there are many mistakes, and it's important to recognize them, correct them, learn from them, apologize for them, or whatever is appropriate in the situation. We cannot land on either side of the equation—both perspectives are important.

Seeing this, we begin to love the imperfections in life, the mistakes, the defects, the things that don't go our way, the upsets. We begin to see the Beloved everywhere, even in our disappointments and disturbances, maybe even especially there, where we would least expect to find it.

I've heard that when Katagiri Roshi was dying, he said, "Enlightenment is not dying a good death. Enlightenment is not *needing* to die a good death." Even if you are screaming in pain, or yelling in anger, or having the thought, "How am I doing? Is this a good death? Am I impressing my students?"—even *that* is simply *what is*. It's not personal. When it is seen as impersonal weather, a whole new moment opens up. There is no trace from the past, and there is no one here to take delivery. The universe begins anew.

CHAPTER SIX: The Pathless Path

A Deep Soak in Reality

Meditation works by itself. You don't have to "do" anything.

—John Butler

As we age and become more incapacitated and limited in terms of our physical and cognitive abilities, the enjoyment and exploration of the present moment remains always available. We could call this meditation, although that word conjures up so many different things that I always hesitate to use it. As I mean it, meditation is not about trying to get somewhere or control anything. It focuses only on the immediacy of Here-Now, on what actually *is*. We're simply being present—alert, open, relaxed—allowing everything to be as it is and exploring the nature of this awaring presence, this present experiencing.

Zen teachers like to emphasize that Zen is useless. It's not about getting anywhere. It's about waking up to the naked actuality of *this* moment, before we think about it or try to understand or explain it, or get something out of it, or figure out what we think it means. It's about discovering the absolute right here in the naked actuality of *whack!* (if the Zen Master hits you, as in the old stories), or *caw-caw-caw* (if a bunch of crows happen to be flying over), or *whoosh-whoosh-whoosh* (if you're listening to traffic). No gap. No "me" hearing a "sound" or feeling a blow. Just *whack!* Immediate. Not two. No question of "What does it mean?" No explanation possible. *Just this!*

In my first book, *Bare-Bones Meditation: Waking Up from the Story of My Life,* I described how my first Zen teacher, Mel Weitsman, told me that the whole point of a Zen sesshin, a long silent meditation retreat, is to have no way out. When I told him I could see the benefits of that kind of practice, he cut me off. "Benefits, benefits," he repeated with irritation. "No! Just do it! This isn't about benefits. It isn't about getting something or becoming somebody. It's *just this*. Nothing else!"

73

It took me decades to really hear that.

Just this! No separation! If you're analyzing it, trying to make sense of it, trying to *do* it, or trying to get something out of it, you're missing the utter simplicity of *this*.

Mel once described a Zen sesshin as "a deep soak in reality." On a sesshin, you sit in silence, often for a whole week, hour after hour, day after day, night after night. If you are able to do so, you sit cross-legged on a cushion, otherwise you sit upright in a chair. Either way, you don't move at all during the timed sittings, which are interspersed with short periods of very slow, silent walking meditation. Meals are eaten in silence, in a ritualized way, typically while still sitting on your cushion. All your usual distractions and occupations are removed, so it is an intimate encounter with the bare actuality of this endlessly changing present moment.

You encounter many different states of mind: boredom, restlessness, fear, anger, grief, frustration, love, joy, wonder, gratitude for the simplest things. There is upset and tranquility, peace and turmoil, the sounds of rain, the screech of tires, the barking dog next door. Sitting cross-legged for hours on end, or even sitting for hours in a chair, you encounter physical pain, at times excruciating. You discover the relativity of time—how a second can be an eternity and an hour can pass in an instant. You encounter resistance and the desire to escape, and you discover the possibility of letting go and dissolving into the very heart of pain and suffering, which, to your great surprise, opens into the unbound vastness that you come to find is present in every breath, every sip of tea, every bird song, and every moment of life, however dark and unbearable it may seem. You find freedom and spaciousness in the midst of limitation, and you discover the transcendent in being just this moment, exactly as it is. You discover the space in which everything is happening, the openness of presence, the ungraspable fluidity of everything. Your usual obsessions and concerns are gradually washed away and dissolved. Everything becomes simpler and simpler.

Whether you are sitting for seven days or ten minutes, in this form of meditation, instead of *avoiding* the actuality of life and endlessly racing toward a future that never arrives, you are fully experiencing life as it is, waking up to the naked actuality of *just this*. And the more deeply you enter into *just this,* the more you find that it isn't what you thought it was, or what it seems to be. And you begin to notice the endless ways we mentally separate ourselves from this naked actuality by labeling it, thinking *about* it, judging it, dividing it into categories, turning it into stories with a plotline and a main character ("me"), and adding things to it that don't exist, such as victims and perpetrators, and *what if's* and *if only's*. In silent stillness, listening openly with the whole bodymind, you find there is no division anywhere, no center, no solidity, no body in any sense—only this vast, infinitely spacious, listening presence that you are.

Of course, you don't need to sit motionlessly through excruciating pain for days on end in order to discover all this. Nor do you need to sit in any special posture or wear special robes or anything like that. I left formal Zen behind. I prefer an approach that is open, explorative, playful and enjoyable rather than one that is rigid, grueling and pain-ful. Meditation as I mean it is simply about exploring and enjoying the actuality Here-Now, and that can happen while sitting quietly in an armchair, riding to work on the bus, sitting in a waiting room before a medical appointment, even during a medical or dental procedure or during a storm of upsetting emotion-thought, in a prison cell, or on your deathbed. In short, anywhere and anytime. Silent retreats and daily meditation can be helpful, I recommend both if you're drawn to them, but true meditation is nothing more nor less than simply being awake here and now.

I take time every day to sit quietly, doing nothing. I don't do it to get somewhere or attain anything; I just do it. Sometimes I do it deliberately—sitting down on my meditation cushion every morning and often again at night before bed—and sometimes it simply invites me at various times throughout the day as I'm sitting in my armchair, on a park bench, in a waiting room before an appointment, or wher-ever it might be. When I hold meetings, I usually begin with being together in silence. We set aside all our usual doing and we rest in simply being this present happening. We're not seeking any particular outcome, trying to get into any special state, or trying to get rid of anything that shows up. We're not trying to suppress thinking, but we're not deliberately engaging in it either. When thinking arises, we simply notice it. We begin to see how it spins stories, creates virtual realities and stirs up emotions, and how easily these imaginary scenarios can capture the attention and hypnotize us into all kinds of dramas and apparent conundrums. Whenever thinking is noticed, we simply return attention to the bare happening of the moment—the sounds of traffic, sensations in the body, breathing, whatever is showing up. The content is secondary—that, too, is a kind of virtual reality, a creation of the brain and consciousness. The aliveness is in the awaring presence itself, the awake space in which everything is happening, which is found to be the very nature of everything. The more deeply we enter into this presence, the more it unfolds into ever-more subtle dimensions.

If we look for the self who is supposedly at the center of all this, we find *nothing* at all. We find no place where "I" begin or end, no boundary between what we call "inside" and what we call "outside." The "seer" and the "thing seen" are realized to be ideas; the actuality is undivided *seeing*. The seeing itself can never be seen. It has no shape, no size, no beginning or ending. It is most intimate, closer than close, and it contains the whole universe, all of space and time. This listening presence cannot really be contained by any name or label, for it is not a "thing;" but it can be recognized, felt, dissolved into. The words are never quite right, for there is nothing separate from it that awakens to it or dissolves into it.

In this kind of meditation, we're not looking for any particular experience. Everything is allowed to be just as it is, without judgment. And if judging or trying arises, we simply notice that and allow that to be as it is. Nothing is rejected.

Go deeply into any form—visual, tactile, somatic, kinesthetic, auditory, olfactory, gustatory—or into the silence, the stillness, the listening presence—and you find nothing solid, nothing that can be separated out from the whole, nothing you can grasp. Presence gets ever more nuanced the more deeply you explore it. And you're not exploring from the outside. There is no explorer and something else being explored; there is only exploring. It is doing itself. Everything is a movement of the whole. *Everything*—hearing, breathing, moving, sensing, being. Even thinking, imagining, conceptualizing and emoting are *just this*. Nothing is left out. Nothing is *other* than this.

Although deliberate or formal meditation may happen at certain times, there's no real boundary between meditation and the rest of our life. More and more, we begin to enjoy the simplicity of presence throughout the day—hearing sounds, seeing shapes and colors, feeling all the sensations in the body, feeling the spaciousness in which it all happens, the spaciousness that beholds and permeates everything. We begin to notice and appreciate the beauty that is everywhere, even in things we usually think are "ordinary," "undesirable" or "ugly." Nothing is seen as a distraction or an obstruction anymore. *Everything* is included. The bathroom and the office are just as sacred as a temple, and being stuck in traffic is just as spiritual as attending a satsang. You can be in satsang right there in the traffic jam. Samsara *is* nirvana. Nirvana is not some different place or some better experience; it's just a different way of seeing or beholding what we *thought* was samsara.

That shift from resistance to devotion, from the sense of separation and encapsulation to the recognition of boundlessness, can be challenging when we are caught in an upsetting situation or emotion. Something inside us doesn't want to let go of our suffering, our resistance, our protective armoring, our self-defense, our self-image, our self. This is one of the many things that we discover through meditation—our attachment to our self and our self-image, to being right, to our views, to our sense of separation, our ego, our identity, even to our suffering and pain. We begin to notice how we do our suffering. And we also begin to notice how *all* of it is happening by itself—*no one* is actually *doing* any of it—all of it is an impersonal happening, like weather.

When something arises that you don't like—an unpleasant sound, a pain in the body, a critical remark, fear or anxiety, whatever it might be—what happens if you open up to it completely? What *is* this fear or pain or sound or feeling of being criticized if you don't label it or try to explain it? Can it be explored with interest, curiosity and wonder, in the same way you might explore the body of your beloved or a beautiful work of art? When I say explore, I don't mean to *think* about or *analyze* it, but simply to *feel* it. Go right into the very core of it with open attention. Allow the sensory-energetic actuality of it to unfold and reveal itself completely. Resist nothing. *Be* the happening of this moment, just as it is.

Gradually, we discover that it is possible, at least sometimes, to be with something we would normally resist without resisting it, to feel an itch without scratching it—whether it is a literal itch or that seemingly irresistible feeling of urgency, restlessness and unease that drives so much of our human behavior. Gradually, we discover that if we do nothing to resist or change it, if we are simply open to the bare actuality of the sensations, letting it all be as it is, what seemed unbearable is actually bearable and survivable, often even interesting, and never what we thought it was.

In fact, counterintuitively, if we don't move away, if we lean into what bothers us and open to it completely, it often dissolves completely. It may return again, but in that moment, it often disappears. In this way, we learn a new way of being with pain, whether it is physical or emotional, and a new way of being with desire and fear. We are less and less pushed around and bamboozled by the powerful tides of emotion-thought, and more and more able to see freshly and clearly. And when we *do* get bamboozled, *as we all do,* then meditation simply means being bamboozled—exploring what goes into bamboozlement, how it works, what keeps it going, how it feels in the body. If confusion, despair, tensing up, or trying to make something happen are showing up, then simply *be* confused, *feel* the despair in the body, *be* tense, *feel* what it feels like to try. Be curious about *all* of it.

We cannot *make* ourselves not think, so meditation is not about control, suppression or resistance, but rather a way of shedding light on the compulsive patterns and habits of thinking, *seeing* them clearly—discovering through open attention how that whole sticky, messy realm of emotion-thought operates—feeling put down, ignored or misunderstood, defending ourselves and our opinions, looking for approval, judging ourselves and others, trying to control things, feeling entitled, seeking better experiences, beating ourselves up—all the things that are going on in our mental world, and simultaneously in our whole bodies. And the more all this is seen clearly, the less power it has to hypnotize us and run our lives. Instead of being totally swept away by all this, meditation is a way of noticing and waking up from this whole entrancement.

Waking up only ever happens now. Perhaps, for a few rare individuals, there may be a sudden, dramatic, more or less permanent shift of some kind, but for most of us, this is a lifelong, moment-to-moment (Now) awakening. Old habits die hard, usually slowly, and sometimes never completely. Comparing ourselves to others or to ideas we have about perfection only creates suffering. We're not looking for perfection. And we're not looking for fireworks.

No experience is permanent, so trying to have a permanent *experience* of expansion or unity or boundlessness or bliss is inevitably disappointing. All experiences come and go. Liberation is not about having special experiences or dramatic breakthroughs. In fact, all of that can actually be a huge distraction, a golden chain as they say in Buddhism.

It may seem at first that we are alternately "getting it" and then "losing it," but actually, as we eventually realize, presence-awareness (Here-Now) is never actually absent. We're never *really* in the rut we *think* we're in. Aware presence is the very *nature* of Here-Now. And we never actually leave Here-Now. Awareness (Here-Now) is what we *are*. In any moment, if we stop and check, presence-awareness is here. It is all there is. Thoughts, feelings, sensations, experiences, emotions, moods—these *all* come and go. But Here-Now, boundless awareness, is the ever-present still-point in which it all appears and out of which it is made.

There are two popular directions in spiritual practice. I call them zooming in and zooming out. They've also been called the path of wisdom (non-attachment or exclusion) and the path of love (inclusion, non-separation, devotion or non-duality). Zooming out has a kind of purity—it recognizes and embodies pure light, clarity, emptiness—while zooming in is more earthy, soulful, messy, and full of everything.

Zooming out is the *neti neti* approach—"not this, not that"—recognizing that I am not anything in particular—not the body, not the mind, not my thoughts, not my emotions, not the personality, not my life story. *Anything* perceivable or conceivable, *even the first bare sense of impersonal presence*, what is often called the I AM, is negated. *Not this, not that*. What I truly am is beyond all imagining, prior to all experiencing, prior to consciousness, subtler than space, subtler even than the first bare sense of presence. It is the Ultimate Subject that can never be seen, the eye (the True I) that cannot see itself.

Zooming in takes the opposite approach. It *includes* everything—"this, too." There is *nothing* that is not the Self. Everything belongs. Nothing is a distraction or an obstacle. Nothing is *other* than this boundless unicity. Thoughts, emotions, unpleasant noises, air pollution—*nothing* is excluded. *Everything* is what is. And the more closely we enter into any form that appears—whether it is a chair, a dog, a thought, a feeling, a mental image, or even consciousness itself—the more it shows itself to be infinite, unresolvable, ever-changing and inseparable from everything else. This absolute intimacy, this complete inclusion, is unconditional love. It is the very nature of awareness to accept everything and to cling to nothing.

Many teachings use both zooming in and zooming out. I have found both approaches useful. They are different medicines, useful in seeing beyond different misunderstandings, but don't cling to either of them. Whatever medicine is needed in your life will appear, and if it is no longer needed, it will disappear. That's been my experience again and again. For myself, this ever-fresh exploration, discovery, awakening and deepening Here-Now is my greatest joy in life. Sometimes zooming out; sometimes zooming in—but which is which? Without a reference point, you can't say which way is in and which way is out, and both are movements of an indivisible unicity that never moves away from itself.

If any of this feels like a task that "you" are *trying* to *do*, the thinking mind is adding something extra—the image of the meditator, the "me" who supposedly needs to get somewhere other than Here-Now, and the idea of a "there" that this phantom is trying to reach. Whenever we seem to be tangled up in confusion and despair, that can be an invitation to stop, look, and listen—and perhaps to sit quietly, not doing anything, letting everything be just as it is. However disturbing it may be, it's simply weather passing through. It has no owner, no doer. It's not personal. It will unwind and untangle itself at its own pace, in its own time. Presence-awareness is here before this cloud, during this cloud, as this cloud, and after this cloud has passed.

One of the things we can begin to notice is how often we are trying to control life. As you go about your daily life, you can begin to notice how often you have a strong opinion, how often you want to convince someone else of your viewpoint or change how something is being done, how much you are trying to control your own body and mind in various ways. In sitting quietly, we may notice this on ever-more subtle levels as a tension or contraction in the body that is almost always there. When we die, we let all this go. The body relaxes completely, and the mind does too. When we die, we must at last give up all our efforts to control ourselves, our children, our partners, our friends, our parents, our work situation, our living situation, our country, our planet, our species. All our opinions and ideas, all our plans, all our fears and dreams. We let it all go.

And as a kind of meditation, it's possible to imagine dying right now, feeling into the experience of letting go completely, giving up all control. Leaving behind your life story, the past, your future hopes and expectations, your ideas about how the world should be, your concern over climate change or the upcoming election or what kind of future your grandchildren will face. Letting go of the need to continue. Actually, we do this every night when we relax into sleep or when we go under anesthesia. But we can explore what it's like to let it happen while we are fully awake.

As a Zen teacher once said to an eager new Zen student who was telling her the story of his life and his whole spiritual journey, "Why are you still carrying that dead corpse? Drop it!"

Whatever appears Here-Now—however real it may seem—is an

appearance in the movie of waking life, a painting painted by consciousness. What's really going on here is ungraspable and inconceivable. Conditioned perception divides this seamless play of energy into recognizable forms and patterns. Thinking and conceptualizing further divides, solidifies, freezes, reifies, abstracts, and then creates narratives about what is seen, turning inconceivable formless fluidity into "me" and "you" and "my life story" and "chairs," "tables," "abortion," "gay marriage," "police brutality," "the Middle East," "Donald Trump," "Brexit," "enlightenment," "consciousness," "awareness," and so on. Suddenly, these all seem like solid, actual *things*, and many of them evoke powerful emotional responses. It's not that this whole process is wrong. It is all part of the dance, part of how the universe is functioning, part of what consciousness does. We can't avoid conceptualizing, abstracting, story-telling, thinking and emoting, but when we don't *see* all of it for what it is, we become easily bamboozled by mirages: "I really am a loser," or "You ruined my life," or whatever the story asserts.

The thinking mind gets easily fixated on trying to work all this out mentally. Thinking has its place, but the models that thought creates are not the reality they are modeling. We can use maps—they're helpful—but eventually we need to let them go and just *be* the territory itself. The living actuality Here-Now is where the juice is. Maps can only take us so far. Meditation is about the living actuality Here-Now. We can never get hold conceptually of exactly what that is because it keeps shapeshifting. At the same time, it's obvious, immediate and utterly unavoidable—*Whack!* Just this!

Of course, the pathless path may take many different forms and involve different things at different times. It may utilize techniques, methods and intentions at times—inquiries of various kinds, koans, mantras, breath-counting, thought-labeling, attempts to zoom out or in, to transcend or include. Or it may throw all techniques, methods and intentions away. It may involve a strict formal practice at one moment and the abandonment of all that in another. Each of us has a unique path—no two are identical. No one else knows what you need. Your life, just as it is, *is* your path. It cannot be otherwise. Teachers and books like this one may be helpful—they certainly have been for me and often still are—but ultimately, there is no outside authority who can tell us what to do. Life is doing all of it.

Meditation as I see it is an open exploration and enjoyment of being alive. And this exploring and enjoying is an activity of *this* that is being explored and enjoyed. The universe is exploring and enjoying itself. Consciousness is exploring and enjoying itself. Life is exploring and enjoying itself. It's one whole undivided happening, and there's actually no way to get it wrong. It is always doing you, not the other way around.

Meditation is an open mind and an open heart—not landing anywhere, not clinging to anything, welcoming everything.

How Can I Get Rid of the Self and Stabilize as Pure Awareness?

Who is asking this question?

Isn't it consciousness, identifying as the phantom "me," trying to gain the ultimate advantage *within* the story by pulling itself up by its own bootstraps and getting rid of itself in order to be a better, more awakened self? Can you see the joke?

Life in samsara revolves around "me," the main character in our favorite movie, *The Story of My Life*. The story is all about *my* problems, *my* search, where *I* am on the path of awakening, what *I* still lack, how *I* compare to various others, *my* successes and failures, *my* desire to be fully awake, where *I* still fall short, and so on. It might include such storylines as, "I'm a failure, I'll never get it, I'm almost there, I had it once but I lost it, I understand it deeply but I haven't fully embodied it, I'm all alone, nobody loves me," and so on.

It's all fiction. And it's all about me. And that "me" is a mirage.

Then there are meta-stories, stories *about* the stories. Spiritual people are often hypnotized by meta-stories, and the whole spiritual journey is itself a giant meta-story as soon as we begin *thinking* about it. The main story might be, "I'm a failure," and the meta-story is, "How can I wake up from that story?" So there's "me" who is a failure, and another "me" who recognizes that this is only a story and wants to wake up from that story. Another popular meta-story might be, "I've seen through the me-illusion, I know I'm boundless awareness, but I keep forgetting. I keep getting sucked into that thought-sense of being me. How can I stabilize as pure awareness?" It's another layer of the same basic story. It's all about *me*—me on a progressive (or regressive, or not yet complete) journey through time, trying to get from some imaginary "here" to some imaginary "there." The "me" gets split into two parts, the "me" who can't stop feeling like a separate self, and the "me" who is trying to fix that problem. It's all stories within stories, and imaginary selves within imaginary selves—turtles all the way down, and *all* of it is empty of substance. *All* of it is unicity doing its dance.

Waking up is simply *seeing* this—*seeing* (again and again, *now*, as it happens) how consciousness has shrunk down to this capsule-size and identified itself as a character in a movie of its own creation and then as the observer-fixer of that character. Waking up is seeing through the imaginary problem, the imaginary self who seems to have it, and the imaginary observer-fixer self who wants to fix all this. Waking up is *recognizing* the space, the boundless awareness, the indivisible radiant presence in which it all appears and out of which it is all made, and recognizing that nothing actually stands apart from that, ever.

Notice how thought may pop up right now and say, "Yes, but..." *This is a very common and seductive hook.* To awaken is to catch that "Yes, but..." as it arises, to *see* that *it's only a thought* and not follow it down the rabbit hole. Because *so quickly,* from that one little thought, the whole story of me and my problem can reassert itself. It's fascinating to see how the mind will defend and argue for the reality of our suffering and our story. It is, after all, a very convincing illusion. And it's all about me! And me loves to think and talk and worry about itself.

Awakening is simply *seeing* any attempt to move away from this very instant, from Here-Now, from the simplicity of this moment, back into the story and identity as a person—*and* any attempts *not* to do that, because the latter are the same game in meta-form.

All of this, the whole dance, the apparently getting lost and the apparently getting found, appears Here-Now. The True Self, the Ultimate Subject, is beholding and being it all. This limitless presence is open, free, unconditioned, lacking nothing. The one who wants to grasp all this, have some permanent experience of unicity, stabilize in pure awareness, or never again experience the sense of being a separate me—that one is the phantom again. It's a thought, a sensation, an energetic contraction, a mirage, an event in a dream. It has no substance, no reality. This aware presence is completely stable, never absent, ever-present, always Here-Now. You have never for one instant ever been apart from it. It is all there is, and you are That.

The often heard instruction to "be here now," to bring attention to the present moment, is a beautiful and valuable pointer on the pathless path. But it can easily become an oppressive new task for the phantom "me" to do or to fail at. So it's equally important to see that being Here-Now is unavoidable—it is what we are and all there is. This unbroken wholeness never deviates from itself. We're never really in the trap we think we're in. Both the trap and the one being trapped are illusory.

The notion of "no self" has been greatly misunderstood. The illusion being pointed to is the image we have of this entity with free will and choice that is supposedly authoring my thoughts, making my decisions and having my experiences—the main character in all these stories, including the observer-fixer, the spiritual superego who is correcting the ego. That entity in all its guises is a mirage composed of ever-changing thoughts, sensations, memories, and mental images. It is a grammatical convention—the subject or the object of a verb. It doesn't exist as an actual entity. It's more like an activity. There is no actual "self" inside our head. But of course there *is* a pattern of energy here that we call the body and patterns of behavior that we call the personality, and there *is* a functional sense of location and identity with the body—we answer to our name and can distinguish between our fingers and the carrot we are slicing up for lunch. We remember where we live, who our partner is, what bills we need to pay. We still have preferences and opinions. None of that disappears unless we suffer a brain injury or some kind of cognitive impairment. And none of that is a problem. *Attachment* to our preferences, or *believing* in our stories can be a source of suffering, but *all* of that, even the experiences we call "suffering and confusion," are simply passing appearances in the dreamlike movie of waking life, all of it a play of unicity, a dance of emptiness.

CHAPTER SEVEN: Doom and Gloom

My Mother's Last Winter

The first snowfall. In the early morning, only the silent sound of single leaves descending one by one. The pond in the park half-frozen. The tree outside my window bare now.

Winter fills me with dark shapes. Ecstasy mingles with unimaginable pain and grief. The night vanishes in a pool of daylight. Snow descends in slow motion, falling upward into the sky.

A magical ride home from work, leaves whirling in wind gusts, not just a few leaves, but thousands of leaves all swirling and dancing, flying madly through the air, careening this way and that, changing direction. The Nutcracker Suite playing on the car radio. All of it so wonderfully ridiculous, this whirling wind and spray of birds tossed briefly across the sky, turning this way and that, blowing a clear night of sparkling stars into the emptied sky. The next morning, the world glistens with clear light, shining everywhere, cold and fresh, gleaming. What wild madness!

Mother Earth Is Dying: Is There a Cure or Is It Time for Hospice?

It was the best of times, it was the worst of times, it was the age of wisdom, it was the age of foolishness, it was the epoch of belief, it was the epoch of incredulity, it was the season of Light, it was the season of Darkness, it was the spring of hope, it was the winter of despair, we had everything before us, we had nothing before us, we were all going direct to Heaven, we were all going direct the other way—in short, the period was so far like the present period, that some of its noisiest authorities insisted on its being received, for good or for evil, in the superlative degree of comparison only.

—Charles Dickens, *A Tale of Two Cities*, 1859

I was born a few short years after the atomic bombs were dropped on Japan. I am part of the first human generation to grow up under the threat of worldwide nuclear annihilation. During my childhood, people were building bomb shelters in their backyards, and in school we practiced how to "duck and cover" in the event of a nuclear war. Obviously, we all had our heads in the sand, and most of us knew it.

I also grew up in kind of protective bubble. As a middle-class white American born in the middle of the twentieth century, I lived in a world of rising incomes, central heating, air conditioning, electric lights, an unlimited water supply coming out of the taps, grocery stores stocked with every food one could want, extraordinary advances in modern medicine and palliative care—in short, a world of abundant comfort and prosperity that seemed safe from predators and the ravages of wild nature. It was a world that believed technology could accomplish anything, that America was invincible, that everything was getting better and better. Aside from the looming threat of a nuclear war, it seemed we were safer and more comfortable than human beings had ever been.

But before long, scientists were discovering that human activity was causing climate change and the mass extinction of many species. As I move into old age and approach the death of this bodymind, there is compelling scientific evidence that humanity as a whole may well be moving toward our collective death as a species. To many, this is looking not only increasingly likely but quite possibly inevitable and irreversible, given the damage already done and the apparent lack of political will to make the radical changes needed to slow this down. Some think that, even if everyone woke up tomorrow and started doing everything possible to prevent further warming, it is too late. Others are more optimistic about the prognosis and the possibilities. Of course, nobody knows with absolute certainty what's coming or what's possible because we've never been here before.

Perhaps people throughout the ages have felt that the end was near. Certainly, many people throughout history have lived through wars, famines and plagues in which everyone they knew perished. And, of course, death is an ever-present possibility for any form. Even without destructive human activity, the planet, the ecosystem and the human species would still be vulnerable and ultimately passing forms that will eventually be wiped out, whether slowly or explosively. This has always been true whether people knew it or not. Even the sun will eventually explode. But most of us in the developed world live with the illusion of security.

But now the polar icecaps are melting faster than expected. The weather is becoming ever more Biblical: mile-wide tornados, gigantic hurricanes, powerful tsunamis, unprecedented wildfires, heat waves, droughts, catastrophic floods, epic blizzards. Evidence suggests that global water supplies are diminishing. Cities in India have already run out. Sooner or later, residents in some American city will wake up one morning, turn on their taps, and no water will come out. Small island nations are already going underwater as sea levels rise or as devastating hurricanes sweep through. Climate refugees are already on the move in many parts of the world, not to mention those fleeing New Orleans after Hurricane Katrina. Food riots have erupted in some parts of the world. Nuclear reactors have been built on earthquake faults, in the path of tidal waves and tsunamis, and in Fukushima we saw the results.

Scientists tell us the earth has gone through many periods of extreme warming and cooling, so climate change itself is nothing new, nor are geological periods when conditions on Earth could not sustain human life. Those conditions have apparently come and gone many times over the geological ages. Scientists also tell us that there have been mass extinctions in the past when most of the species living on the planet have disappeared, so extinctions are also nothing new. But the sixth mass extinction and the catastrophic climate change now underway are caused mainly by human activity. We are now living in what has been termed the Anthropocene, an epoch in the geological history of the planet characterized by the advent of the human species as a geological force.

Of course, human beings are as much an expression of wild nature as rain forests. Our highways and highrises, our pesticides, technological developments, oil drilling and mountaintop-removal, as well as our attempts to combat climate change are *all* every bit as much a movement of nature as ant hills, beaver dams, lightning storms and asteroids. But we tend to think of ourselves as being apart from nature, and we tend to imagine that we can control nature, which to some extent, in very limited ways, we can. But ultimately, nature is way bigger than we are, and natural events don't always end in survival, even of the fittest.

It has seemed to many of us for a long time that our whole industrial civilization is like a cancer that will eventually destroy the host, an unsustainable system predicated on continuous growth on a planet with finite resources. The predictions for what this collapse might entail are not pretty. The social order as we know it will break down.

There is a certain collective dis-ease in the air alongside a collective denial vaguely reminiscent of the orgy-filled days prior to the fall of the Roman Empire. As ice caps melt and sea levels rise and the human population multiplies like cancer cells and locusts, reality TV shows feature such entertaining events as women undergoing "extreme makeovers" and having plastic surgery in front of the cameras, multiple potential trophy wives competing to win a marriage proposal from a single eligible bachelor who rejects one after another in front of a national TV audience, wife-swapping families, celebrities eating worms, and all manner of truly unbelievable insanity.

We had eight years of George W. Bush, the 9/11 attacks, the wars in Iraq and Afghanistan, and the ill-conceived, oxymoronic and suicidal "war on terrorism." We had the erosion of civil liberties, a frightening new emphasis on jingoistic patriotism and nationalistic fervor, people wearing flag pins on their lapels and flying American flags everywhere, the widespread open use of torture and rendition and imprisonment without trial, a growing right-wing populist and militia movement armed to the teeth and steeped in xenophobia and narrow-minded Christian fundamentalism or white supremacy, more and more crazy people armed with assault rifles shooting other people at random. We had school shootings, freeway shootings, drive-by shootings, gang wars on the rise, weapons of mass destruction falling into more and more hands, desperate and dispossessed people willing to engage in suicide attacks, talk of inevitable biological and nuclear attacks on US cities—with Chicago always mentioned as a likely target. We had the ever-growing corporate takeover of everything, the rapid growth of artificial intelligence and social media, and a world increasingly dominated by greed, speed, over-consumption and the manipulation of fear, desire and information.

The feminist revolution I had helped to carry out was being slowly undone. Women's reproductive rights were being dismantled piece by piece, abortion doctors wantonly killed off.

Many of my students at the college were single mothers working two jobs and going to school at the same time, trying to give their kids a better life. One young woman would fall asleep on her desk every morning during my early grammar class after working the night shift at the post office. The children of these single mothers were not just in day care, they were in night care as well. I wondered, how was this absence of maternal care going to affect a whole generation of children?

People were texting and talking on cell phones while driving, walking and eating dinner, everyone was frantically multi-tasking and drowning in email, Twitter and information overload, no one was paying complete or careful attention to anything at all anymore it seemed. The entire population seemed to be increasingly distracted, scattered, sped up, sleep-deprived, in debt up to their eyeballs, and overwhelmed.

On factory farms, animals were treated in ways so monstrously cruel that it was beyond belief that anyone could think it was okay, but many people seem to view animals as "produce"—sort of like lettuce or bananas—rather than as sentient beings. On top of that, frogs, honeybees and rain forests were disappearing at an alarming rate.

In short, it seemed that I was facing not only the death of my mother and my own impending demise, but also the decline of the American empire, the rapidly progressing death of the natural world and wild nature, the likely death of humanity, and perhaps the end of all life on Earth. Humanity appeared to be on a rapidly accelerating lemming-like run toward the edge, and no one seemed able to apply the brakes. In fact, an alarmingly large number of people seemed fully convinced that all we needed to do was to step on the gas and accelerate even more and everything would be just fine. And what did I know? Maybe they were right. After all, a hundred years ago, who could have imagined nuclear energy or people actually landing on the moon or planning a trip to Mars? Maybe some unimaginable new scientific discovery or a global shift in consciousness *would* save the day.

There *are* credible people who feel that all of this doomsday dystopian thinking is greatly exaggerated. They argue that much of our fear is a form of catastrophizing, reflecting the way our brains are hardwired with a negativity bias. We are apparently programmed by our biology, for survival reasons, to focus more on bad news and on what can go wrong than on good news and on what can go right. The news media tends to emphasize disasters because that's what sells, and with twenty-four-hour cable news and social media, we are literally deluged with bad news. Every day we hear about mass shootings and terrorist attacks, and we watch those planes crashing into the Twin Towers over and over and over again, putting us into a collective state of unrelenting trauma.

But even if some of our doomsday thinking is exaggerated, from what I understand, the current science overwhelmingly supports the view that we are in a grave crisis and that, even if we take corrective action, the kind of extreme weather events we are already seeing will continue to worsen, impacting the social fabric in many ways. How many refugees from foreign lands will each of us welcome into our own communities? How much of our comfortable lifestyle will those of us in the developed world be willing to give up if need be? How will each of us respond if the taps go dry or the government collapses? Will we pull together and cooperate or lock our doors and grab our guns? Probably, most of us will do some mix of both. I can find both tendencies in myself, and I can see both tendencies manifesting around me and throughout human history. And the person who saves our life may not be the person we expect. It might be the very person we have demonized.

Admittedly, I tend toward the apocalyptic view, and maybe that's partly a bias of my personality. But even if we do survive climate change and manage to avoid a nuclear catastrophe, eventually, all forms die. Nothing is forever. Death is a natural part of life, not something to fear.

From the absolute perspective, the end of life on Earth would be just another changing shape in the ceaseless flux of unicity, another flash of lightning in the sky, another momentary wave on the ocean cresting and dissolving, another dreamlike appearance passing away. Nothing real is ever created or destroyed. But I lose sight of this absolute perspective on occasion and become caught up in the movie of an impending doomsday. "Doom and Gloom" my mother would call me at such times. "Here comes Doom and Gloom," she would joke.

My mother was more like Pollyanna, the eternal optimist, or perhaps the great Olympic track and field star Carl Lewis, who said, "If you don't have confidence, you'll always find a way not to win." He also said something beautiful once about the faster you want to go, the more relaxed you have to be.

Apparently, the survival of the species depends on having both the glass-half-full types like Pollyanna, and the glass-half-empty folks like Doom and Gloom. Both the optimists and the pessimists, the cautious and the hopeful, the obsessive worriers and the carefree dare-devils, have their roles to play. Without the worriers checking and double-checking for possible dangers, the species would probably have been swallowed up by predators long ago. But without the carefree risk-takers, we would never have crawled up out of the ocean onto the land. Still, sometimes I got tired of the obsessive-compulsive, checking and double-checking part of me that always seemed to be scanning for errors and focusing on what could go wrong. I have often envied people like my mother and Carl Lewis who seem to believe anything is possible, those relaxed and carefree long-distance runners sailing through life with full confidence.

It wasn't all doom and gloom from my perspective, of course. On the brighter side of relative reality, we had all kinds of progressive things happening as well: society was becoming more diverse and open to differences, science and reason were replacing superstition and magical thinking more and more, worldwide social change organizations and green networks were springing up everywhere, people were more and more environmentally conscious, Eckhart Tolle reached millions around the world through a series hosted by Oprah Winfrey, more and more people were taking up meditation or going to satsangs and waking up to the bigger reality. In so many ways, the world had changed for the better in my lifetime, but many new problems had arisen, and many old ones remained.

CHAPTER EIGHT: Challenges on the Pathless Path

Encountering the Dislike of Old People

It is hereby prohibited for any person who is diseased, maimed, mutilated, or deformed in any way so as to be an unsightly or disgusting object to expose himself to public view.

—City of Chicago Ordinance, 1911

Maybe in some way, all of us are biologically programmed for survival reasons to find youth and bodily perfection attractive and to find disability, deformity, and old age repulsive—better for the survival of the species to mate with someone young and healthy, after all. Psychologically, all these things remind us of death, vulnerability and our lack of control. In some way, this aversion or disgust is understandable and, if we're honest, we've probably all felt it at one time or another. But when you or someone you love is the one being seen as repulsive, it can be quite painful, although only if you "take delivery" as Nisargadatta would say. I've known this pain all my life as a result of being an amputee. I've had children scream at the sight of me. I've been told on several occasions that I make people lose their appetite, that my stump is scary and repulsive, that I should hide it or cover it up. And it's a very similar thing that happens to old people and, on a number of occasions, happened to my mother.

On one such occasion, we were at our favorite diner during the crowded lunch hour. Two young men in suits were seated at the next table. They were telling jokes about old people who smell of urine. "How do you know it's an old folks home? It smells of urine." That kind of thing. Very loud. I could hear them perfectly. I didn't know whether Mom could. She probably couldn't, given her hearing loss; but I was like a mother bear in reverse, feeling protective of my mother who, in her old age, seemed vulnerable to me. I considered getting up and "accidentally" dumping hot coffee in their laps, or asking loudly to be reseated because we couldn't stand the foul smell of the men at the next table, but every plan my mind conjured up sounded hurtful to my mother. In the end, I did nothing. I just seethed and boiled. Which probably did not help my mother have an enjoyable lunch, even though I did my best to conceal my upset.

Perhaps these men were completely oblivious to the fact that an old lady was seated at the next table, or maybe their jokes were targeted at her. I cannot know. Of course, I knew in my head that there was fear and pain and ignorance underneath such jokes, and if I had fully grokked that as an embodied, felt-reality *at that moment,* I might have had compassion for these men, even love. But instead, I felt anger, and under that, hurt and fear.

Mooji once said, "Live as though you have no rights and no entitlements, and you'll appreciate all that comes." And Nisargadatta: "You are free once you understand that your bondage is of your own making and you cease forging the chains that bind you." And Byron Katie: "I am a lover of what is, because it hurts when I argue with reality." She goes on to say, "An uncomfortable feeling is like a compassionate alarm clock that says, 'You're in a dream.' It's time to investigate.... The world is the mirror image of your mind." But in that moment at the diner, I was far from these beautiful understandings. I had taken delivery. I felt threatened, wounded, hurt and outraged.

Without denying the reality that there is prejudice and aversion at times toward old people and those with disabilities, it can be seen how I ended up suffering over my reactions and interpretations of what was happening. Byron Katie would invite me to ask of each of my thoughts: Is it true? Can I absolutely know that it's true? How does it feel when I believe that thought? What would it be like if I didn't believe that thought? Can I see a good reason to hold onto that thought? Feeling into each of those questions is a valuable journey beyond suffering. And Katie would offer turnarounds: instead of, "They are treating us badly," it might be, "I am treating us badly." And she might ask, "Is that just as true or truer?"

Finally, is it possible just to feel what I feel, the raw energy of it, knowing that this, too, is part of how reality is? Life *is* painful at times. There *is* cruelty—intentional or unintentional. We don't have to deny any of that or paper it over with some spiritual story. It's all here—the insensitivity, the cruelty, the pain, the hurt, the rage, and also the impulse to question and transcend and open the heart, to find the love and the compassion hidden inside. And in a way, all the painful and troubling events that the world offers so abundantly are opportunities for this breaking through of our suffering and delusion into an ever-fresh discovery of the light and wholeness of everything, just as it is.

My Buttons Get Pushed Again

Our regular mailman is a sweet guy who always smiles a lovely smile and says "God Bless you." He and I have had many friendly exchanges at the mailboxes and on the street in the years since I moved here. He is someone who has always warmed my heart—a friend.

At the mailboxes one morning, as I was on my way out and he was distributing the mail, he told me how bad he felt for the future of the children of this country now that the courts in Massachusetts have legalized same-sex marriage, thus opening the door to the destruction of marriage. I felt my heart stop. I told him I'm gay. I told him about the many social and economic privileges of marriage and how we gay people only want the same basic human rights, like being able to visit our partner in the hospital or share their health insurance or have the same immigration and inheritance rights and the same social recognition and support that heterosexuals take for granted. I told him religious groups could still do what they wanted, but that civil marriage was a civil right.

"You don't understand," he said. "These people want to re-define marriage so that it's okay to have sex with ten-year-old children."

What!? And had I not just told him I was one of "these people"?! Patiently, I explained to him that having sex with children wasn't about being gay or straight, that having sex with children was a separate issue altogether called pedophilia, and that plenty of ten-year-olds were molested by heterosexuals.

On that line, enter the old Polish lady downstairs who loves to gossip about everyone in the building. I exit out the front door as she asks the mailman what we were talking about.

Once out the door, I was filled with pain and anger. A torrent of appallingly backward, spiritually and politically incorrect thoughts popped up uninvited in my mind. In one of these, I imagined telling my mailman, who happens to be a person of color, to "get out of my country" and "go back to where he came from." *What!?* Where did *that* thought come from?! Such a thought is utterly abhorrent to my conscious mind, the complete opposite of everything I consciously think, feel and believe. But in that moment of anger and hurt, I wanted to lash out, meet insult with insult—and that was what my lizard brain coughed up. Thankfully, it was only a flash of thought inside my head. I didn't *actually* tell the mailman to "get out of my country." But I saw how easily hurt turns into hate and rejection triggers rejection, how the oppressed becomes the oppressor and the terrified becomes the terrorist—how hate spreads like a virus. It's that old Biblical idea of an eye for an eye, a tooth for a tooth, which, it has been observed, will soon leave the whole world blind and toothless.

Eventually, I came home and sat quietly for a long time in the big armchair that I refer to as my bliss chair, that isn't always blissful, and just sat there in the fire of these feelings, burning. It was a very old, very deep, very human pain. It felt so huge, this wall of hurt. I could feel the tears in my chest all clogged up inside me. I wanted to open my heart and break through to love and peace. But in that moment, I couldn't really penetrate it. I couldn't find the love, the open heart, the perfection in the imperfection. I knew all the answers—I dispense them, after all. But right then, no answer would relieve this pain.

Waves of anger, self-pity, despair, grief, fear and heartbreak were passing through, and soon my inner Nazi started turning inward on me, berating me for being so upset, telling me I was over-reacting, that Byron Katie and Ramana Maharshi and all those spiritual super-heroes would be feeling only love and joy, whereas I was still stuck in some backward form of egoic resistance, an obvious sign of my failure to be fully enlightened. "What *real* nondualist would be upset by finding out her mailman is homophobic?" my inner Nazi demanded. I noticed the desire for something comforting, something to grasp, something to numb the pain—a spiritual feel-good idea, a glass of wine, a guru to gaze upon me with love and tell me all is well. But meditative inquiry invites simply being present, aware of *all* of this without trying to explain, judge, analyze, or change any of it, without trying to get into a happier state of mind, simply being right here, present and awake with this whole turbulent, sticky, unpleasant mess of emotion-thought, just as it is.

Counterintuitively, this kind of inquiry—being just this moment—doesn't lead to wallowing in escalating misery, but rather, through the transformative power of awareness, to the vast freedom and relief of simple presence along with insight and compassion for all of us being as we are in each moment. But I hesitate to say that, lest it become a goal or an expectation—a desired result. The freedom and relief, the open heart of love, the resurrection after the crucifixion, are the fruit of giving up all hope of improvement and the willingness to simply *be* this mass of pain. It is a surrendering, an opening, a dissolving, a letting go that cannot be forced or achieved by will. It comes by grace. And sometimes, it doesn't come nearly as fast as we would like it to. That day it came very slowly for me and not with the complete release I would have liked.

Sometimes, it feels as if we will be betraying a whole group of people if we let go of our upset, as if the only way to arrive at the full acceptance of LGBTQI people is to keep this hurt and anger alive. But my heart tells me there is another possibility, one I saw embodied in Martin Luther King Jr. during the Civil Rights Movement, even when so much hate was thrown at him—he didn't succumb to hate, cynicism, self-pity or the kind of rage where you shoot yourself in the foot, the way I often do. He just kept going, one step at a time. It's a great challenge to meet hate with love, bigotry with openness, setbacks with courage and faith, to remain optimistic even when faced with violent hatred and disappointment and finally, in the case of Dr. King and so many others, assassination. You can't get to that openness and love by willpower. It's a kind of surrendering or melting—the very heart of awakening—dissolving that tight self-protective knot. And this is rarely, if ever, a one-time event.

The Lady Who Called Me the Devil

The first time I saw her, she stepped off the elevator in my apartment building just as I was stepping on. She was dressed like the caricature of a society lady from the 1950s, with heavy makeup, a wig of long red hair, and an absurd hat. She was carrying a bouquet of plastic flowers. She reminded me of that group of leftist comics in San Francisco years ago called "Ladies Against Women." They used to dress up exactly like this and then show up at progressive demonstrations with picket signs that had slogans on them like, "A Woman's Place Is On Her Back," "Stand by Your Man," "White Sugar, White Flour, White Power," "Menstruation is Murder." They were a wonderful parody of the ultra-right that brought humor to many progressive events. And for a moment, I thought maybe this woman was in some kind of theater group like that, that this was a joke. Then suddenly, she stuck out her tongue at me, gave me a nasty look, and called me the devil. I still couldn't tell if she was serious or if this was some kind of camp performance piece.

The next time we met, she told me my tail was dragging. It took me a moment to understand that she was again calling me the devil, and this time I realized she was dead serious. In the elevator, if I got on when she was in it, she would turn her back on me and face the wall. Wow! What was it about me she found so appalling? Why did she hate me? Why did she think I was evil? Could she tell that I was a fundamentally imperfect, flawed and basically disgusting and unacceptable human being—as I sometimes secretly fear I am? Did she hate lesbians? Amputees? Spinsters? Had I forgotten to pluck my chin hairs or shave my legs? Was it the way I dressed? Had she read my books and found my views horrifying? Did she know about my drunken past? What was it? On the one hand, I assumed she was crazy. I wasn't the devil. But then again, maybe she was seeing the real truth about me.

My conscious overt self may fully believe that being gay is perfectly fine, that older women are beautiful, that having one arm is
perfect, that being unmarried is totally acceptable; but somewhere in
the shadows of my mind, down in the basement in the lizard brain,
another set of ideas and images linger like ghosts, ideas that I absorbed
by osmosis from the culture in which I grew up, reinforced by such
things as religious leaders calling me an abomination against God and
blaming me and my fellow queers for hurricanes and terrorist attacks,
or by my mother's Republican friends telling me that gay relationships are totally okay but just not worthy of being fully recognized in
the same way straight relationships are, or by my mailman suddenly
revealing that he regards folks like me as child molesters.

In fact, we all have these socially-conditioned prejudices in the
basement of our psyches, these unconscious ideas that are racist,
sexist, heterosexist, ageist, and so on. Even if our own parents were
unprejudiced, open-minded types as mine were, and even if no one
overtly told us such things as, "Blacks and women are inferior" or
"gays are sick perverts" or "cripples are scary and creepy" or "old
people are disgusting" or "alcoholics and addicts are weak-willed,
irresponsible, immoral, bad people," nevertheless, we absorbed these
ideas through our skin from the larger culture. We may have rejected
these ideas in our conscious minds, and we may live our lives according to a higher set of ideas and values. But deep down in the primitive
parts of the brain, conditioned by genetics and survival impulses,
mired in what the Buddhists call our "ancient twisted karma," these
phantoms linger, even in those of us who belong to the group in
question. Deep down, we harbor a shadowy fear that we *are*, in fact,
inferior, sick, creepy, disgusting, unworthy, unclean, evil, imperfect,
and not okay.

These phantom ideas about ourselves and others tend to come
bursting out in moments of stress or extreme upset, like that xenophobic thought-tirade from my inner Nazi that passed unbidden through
my head after my mailman unleashed his anti-gay ideas on me. In my
conscious mind, xenophobic and racist ideas are utterly repugnant
to me.

Many well-meaning progressives deny that this kind of ugly, politically incorrect stuff exists in their minds. I've heard many a white person say, "I don't have a racist bone in my body," and some of them totally believe it. And, of course, there is a huge and important difference between the deliberate, intentional, overt racism of people in the KKK and the more subtle, unconscious and unintentional kind I'm talking about here, the kind that we all probably have whether we're aware of it or not. We may not think of ourselves as racist, sexist or homophobic, but look closely, with relentless honesty, or take up meditation and really listen in on your thoughts, and I'm guessing you'll find these unsavory shadows.

Hitler had Jewish blood and set about exterminating Jews to purify the race. Many closeted gay men have spent their entire political careers as right-wing conservatives fighting against gay rights or persecuting gay people. It's an old story. I can find all of these different groups within my own psyche, the oppressor and the oppressed, the terrorist and the terrified; and they so easily switch roles and morph into each other.

There is an interesting psychological study where people are given something called an Implicit Association Test that measures split-second, automatic (pre-conscious) word associations. It finds, for example, that the vast majority of those taking the test are more likely to associate crime with Black people than with white people, and more likely to associate business skills with men rather than with women. And this applies not only to white people and men taking the test, but to Black people and women taking it as well. The conditioning is there in all of us. Eventually, as society changes, the conditioning will change. It already is changing. People my age have more of this conditioning than millennials.

There is another interesting test, an empathy bias test, where subjects are shown photographs of a large needle being jammed into the back of a person's hand while brain wave censors measure the viewer's level of disturbance. It turns out, we react much more strongly when the hand resembles our own. If it appears to be a different race, for example, we have less empathy. This may even have biological roots beneficial in some way for our survival as hunter-gatherers on the savannah many centuries ago. Recognizing that something may have biological roots doesn't mean it can't change or that it is inevitable, but it does show us that much of our behavior operates at a level below conscious awareness and intention.

It's great to be able to openly acknowledge our internalized, sub-conscious, unintended prejudices, rather than trying to hide or deny them. We can't erase our conditioning with an act of conscious will, but we can certainly take steps in a helpful direction. My mother, for example, made a deliberate effort to befriend people of every race, social class, sexual orientation, ethnicity, religious and political per-suasion; and by doing that, she opened her heart and mind and broke down the conditioning she had grown up with. And certainly, the more we see people of all different kinds in positions of authority and power and in every conceivable role in the cultural mirrors such as television and movies, the more the old conditioning will disintegrate and be replaced by entirely new conditioning. But this doesn't hap-pen overnight.

In the America where I grew up back in the 1950s, every presi-dent and almost every member of Congress was a white man, almost always a Christian, usually Protestant. News anchormen, doctors, lawyers, judges were almost all white men. When my mother was born, women didn't even have the right to vote in this country. On TV shows when I was growing up, the lead characters were almost always white and heterosexual. People like me never saw ourselves reflected in the cultural mirrors. It was as if we didn't exist. On TV shows now, you routinely see a cast that is racially mixed and more and more likely to include LGBTQI people and people with disabilities. Several out-lesbians and gay men are now hosting talk shows and cable news programs, as are more and more people of color. Things have changed. Racism, sexism, heterosexism, anti-Semitism, and ageism are not gone, but conditions have dramatically improved.

It was mildly unnerving, my encounters with the lady who called me the devil, even though I was sure she was crazy, because I took her attacks on me personally. I also felt a bit frightened. She seemed quite wrathful, venomous and genuinely mad, and I began to wonder if she would murder me one day in the laundry room or on the elevator.

Eventually, through talking with others in the building, I learned that she behaved this way with everyone, and I was told that she was indeed seriously mentally ill. Perhaps she was psychotic and also had some form of Tourette syndrome. Immediately, the whole thing was no longer personal, no longer about me at all. All traces of uneasiness and upset disappeared completely. I'd see her sticking out her tongue and saying outlandishly hateful things to other people—cab drivers bringing her home, even the police who tried once to arrest her out on the street.

Yesterday, as I came into the building, she was going out. I held the door open for her.

"Don't go into my apartment, shitbag!" she spat out.

"I won't, don't worry," I assured her pleasantly. "Have a good day."

Now I knew she was insane. And more importantly, I knew it wasn't about me at all. So I no longer felt threatened. Afterward, I watched from my window as she stood on the street corner below trying to hail a cab. She was gesticulating wildly, and I could see her unleashing her hostile tirade at passing pedestrians. Most of the passing pedestrians were Black, Hispanic, African or Arab, and I wondered if any of them assumed this white lady was a racist, that she was attacking them because of their color, ethnicity or religion. I wondered how many of them felt hurt, wounded, or angered by her attack. Maybe for some, her words left them churning in unhappy, hurt, angry, fearful, traumatized, upset feelings, as my mailman's words had left me. And maybe those feelings would spill over into kicking the dog or yelling at their kids later that evening. Maybe someone would eventually yell back and call her a nasty bitch or something. And yet, from my vantage point in the window above, I knew that there was nothing personal in these attacks, that this was utter insanity. This woman was living in hell. She was fighting ghosts in her own mind. And, of course, so was my mailman. And so was I.

One day I came home to find police cars, a fire truck and an ambulance in front of the building. The crazy lady had flooded her apartment and barricaded herself inside it. She was carried out kicking and screaming in a straight-jacket. She never returned.

The Observer-Independent Reality that Doesn't Actually Exist

Is it that there are various ways of seeing one object, or is it that we have mistaken various images for one object?

—Dogen

Even if we know better intellectually, we are all in some way convinced that there is a single objective reality "out there" apart from us, and of course, we all deeply believe that our own view of this reality is correct. But what if there really is no objective, fixed, inherent reality "out there" that we are all seeing, more or less correctly? What if each of us is seeing and participating in our own completely unique movie? What if *nothing* is "out there" apart from the seeing itself? What if we are all waves in one ocean of Consciousness simultaneously dreaming a multitude of dreams?

It's fairly obvious that the Palestinians and the Israelis are each seeing completely different movies, as are progressives and conservatives, as are those who believe in the importance of a woman's right to a medically safe abortion and those who believe that abortion is murder. Is it possible that we're all in some way equally right and equally wrong?

On some level, every well-educated twenty-first century person knows that their viewpoint is one of many. This understanding is reflected in physics, neuroscience, postmodern literature, and throughout the global culture. We may even realize it on a deeper level through meditation or spiritual inquiry. But even then, the illusion of a solid, objective reality "out there" is so convincing and deeply imbedded that it tends to re-form itself, as does the deeply-rooted conviction that my way of seeing this reality is the correct way. And, of course, it *is* correct *as my way of seeing*! The only problem is that we each assume that we are all seeing the *same thing*, and that what we see is objectively and inherently real, and that therefore, we can't all be right.

We are given a name, and we learn to think of ourselves as a certain gender, race, nationality, age, social status, and so on. This may all be relatively true—we can't ignore or deny these realities—but we take them for something much more solid and inherently real than they actually are. We identify with them. We fight wars over them.

Our very identity and survival seem to get wrapped up in our particular subjective view of things. When our views on hot-button topics are questioned or contradicted, we humans tend to become easily upset, angry, wounded, defensive, hostile and perhaps underneath all that deeply fearful. We feel that our very survival is somehow at stake along with our whole perception of reality. The very ground on which we seem to be standing is thrown into question. And when you have something like the Palestine-Israel conflict, where people on both sides have had their lives disrupted and damaged over many decades—loved ones killed, land taken away, homes destroyed—it's easy to see how this can escalate.

I identify with all the women I knew who went through horrible, sometimes near-fatal, back-room abortions before abortion was legal, and I don't want to see that happening to young women ever again. And because I don't believe in the notion of an individual soul that enters the body at conception, I don't feel that stem cell research or having an abortion early in a pregnancy are in any way the same as murdering a baby. I don't even feel that terminating a pregnancy late-term is wrong if the fetus is found to have no brain, for example, or if the life of the mother is at risk. Those who oppose abortion seem, on the other hand, to identify with the unborn "person," the absolutely unique, unrepeatable, lost soul they believe is being deprived of its one and only God-given chance for life, condemned instead to an eternity in purgatory. And indeed, every snowflake is unique, and every fetus is potentially a unique and utterly precious, one-of-a-kind human being. Of course, that view could be carried even further, as Ladies Against Women did with their absurdist slogan, "Menstruation is murder." Every egg and every sperm is a potentially unique and utterly precious, one-of-a-kind human being. So it comes down to where you draw the line, and that will always be arbitrary, because you cannot actually find a place where anything begins or ends. "Pro-choice" and "pro-life" are two different pictures of reality, both equally valid within the conceptual construction they have each accepted as true.

I attended a workshop once on nonviolent communication, and on the last day, we were paired up with another participant who had the opposite view from ours on a hot-button issue. I was paired with a woman who wanted abortion to be outlawed. Our assignment was to take turns speaking, first one of us, then the other. The speaker would tell the listener why she held the view that she did. Notice that this is not the same thing as arguing for our view. The listener would simply listen, not interrupting. When we finished, we would switch roles. At the end, I had a deeper appreciation of the other view, and I think my partner did as well. Neither of us changed our opinion on the subject, but in some way, we were both more able to understand the opposite view and to have compassion for those on that side of the issue. And, of course, there *is* truth on both sides of this issue. No one is really *pro*-abortion, after all, as if abortion were some wonderful and desirable thing. It's a last resort, a way to end an unwanted or unplanned pregnancy, and/or to in one way or another spare the life of the mother or to spare the potential unborn future person from a life of needless suffering.

If I look closely, I can see that none of us chooses the particular construction of reality that we accept as true. None of us sits down one day and *decides* what our political leanings will be or what sources of news and information will seem trustworthy to us, any more than we "choose" our sexual orientation or "decide" who we will fall in love with or what things in life will interest or upset us. The way each of us sees things is the result of infinite causes and conditions. People with different conditioning see things differently. As in the famous old story where one blind man feels the elephant's trunk, another feels the elephant's leg, another the elephant's ear, another the tail, and then they argue over what an elephant is like. But no one has seen or felt the whole elephant, and in the case of totality, no one ever can. The eye can never see itself.

How does seeing the relativity, subjectivity and conditioned nature of all perception change my response to people on the other side of hot-button issues such as abortion, marriage equality, female genital mutilation, factory farming, climate change, or Palestinian statehood? Do I decide every view is equally true? Do I stop caring or distinguishing between what feels right to me and what feels wrong? No. It seems that I still care about what life moves me to care about. I still have judgments, preferences and opinions, some of which I may even be willing to fight or die for. But perhaps there is a greater openness and willingness to question my own beliefs and ideas, to hear where the other side is coming from, and maybe to see the other side in the light of compassionate understanding, even when they are doing something I regard as utterly horrific.

I was the offspring of two very different people. My mother was a progressive who loved Noam Chomsky and did a lot of social justice and civil rights work, and my father was an Eisenhower Republican and a small businessman who read *The Wall Street Journal*. My father was a determinist who believed free will was an illusion, while my mother believed in the power of positive thinking and felt you could do anything if you put your mind to it. My father was an introvert and my mother an extrovert. My father, a very sensitive and once idealistic man, tended toward a slightly cynical disillusionment, while my mother was a beacon of optimism and possibility. How two such different people managed such a happy and loving marriage is a great mystery, but they never fought and clearly, they loved, appreciated and respected each other immensely. They were one of the happiest and most compatible couples I've ever seen. And I often feel that I've spent my life in some way trying to reconcile these two very different, and seemingly irreconcilable, strands from my childhood, both of which I carry within me.

In our world today, things are getting more and more polarized. People listen to different sources of news, some of it on all sides prone to exaggeration and omission, much of it strongly biased, and we all tend to have knee-jerk reactions—if the politician we hate is saying something, it must be wrong. We won't even listen. If our beloved spiritual teacher is saying something, it must be right. We lose all critical discernment. We scan an article on the internet to see if it agrees with our point of view and, if it doesn't, we won't even read it. Our thinking is easily muddied by such distorting factors as confirmation bias, false reasoning, inferring causation from correlation, magical thinking, and a human tendency to overestimate our own knowledge and understanding. Many people have never had even a single course in critical thinking skills, and people who have never done any kind of insight meditation or psychotherapy may be utterly unaware of how their buttons are getting pushed or how there is fear or hurt underneath their anger. Even when you've been educated in critical thinking and done years of meditation and therapy, as I have, you're still greatly prone to delusion. Speaking for myself, I still tend to get easily polarized, defensive, argumentative, and prone to confirmation bias. At least I know it, so perhaps that's a very small step in the right direction.

Clearly, there is real value and truth in *both* conservative and progressive perspectives. Conservatives emphasize individual responsibility and freedom, survival of the fittest, the value of tradition, strong boundaries. Progressives emphasize collective responsibility, equality, innovation and inclusiveness. Clearly, both sides of the gestalt are important in some way. The totality relies on a balance that includes both, just as it needs both the optimists and the pessimists, the cautious worriers and the risk-takers.

When faced with something that pushes my buttons or raises my hackles, can I find the place in myself that thinks or acts in a similar or even identical way? How have I behaved in a similar way, albeit perhaps on a smaller scale or in a different form? In what ways, for example, have I committed genocide in my own mind? What groups of people have I wanted to wipe out?

When is memory a useful function—learning from history and not re-inventing the wheel—and when is it not? When are thinking and storytelling useful, and when do they just keep old injuries alive, so that they happen not just once but, in the mind, again and again and again? How does our identification with certain groups and causes turn issues into identities, so that they seem personally threatening?

It's wonderful to begin to notice what happens to us when we come up against the "evil" in the world, the suffering, the bigotry, the prejudice, or when we encounter disappointment and disillusionment in any form, big or small, when life isn't the way we want it to be or think it "should" be.

Hating racists and sexists is not the same as being opposed to racism and sexism. Hating the people who have these prejudices is rooted in the false idea that we are all freely choosing to be the way we are. By hating them and acting out of that hatred, we tend to drive them further and further into those views. When we feel loved, heard and understood, we are far more likely to be willing and able to question our views and see things in a new way, whereas when we feel hated and attacked, we are more likely to defend our positions to the death. Of course, this openness is easier said than done. One moment, my particular viewpoint seems impossible to question and essential to defend. My very survival seems to be at stake, and maybe in some instances it is, at least on the level of the bodymind. But isn't it amazing how this defensive bubble can pop in an instant?

Our so-called egoic fears and desires, such as wanting to be liked and accepted or fearing rejection and disapproval, may be rooted in something biologically and instinctually real. We're not crazy or evil. We're just conditioned. Our survival as an organism *depends* to some extent on being accepted by our parents and our tribe. As infants and children, we depend totally on our parents for everything and, as adults, if the tribe or the community shuns or exiles us and leaves us behind, alone on the tundra, we starve, physically and emotionally. Psychological insults or threats can trigger real survival fears for the organism. If *everyone* really thinks we're worthless, we actually *can't* survive, because in fact, we *are* interdependent social animals. We exist in communities, tribes, nations, families, workplaces. Of course, this survival reflex gets carried over into areas where it doesn't really apply. Someone tells me I'm worthless and I feel threatened, defensive, outraged. I fight for my survival. I attack my attacker. We argue. We're both angry, hurt, defensive, fearful. And neither of us is seeing anything but projections in our own imagination. We're battling phantoms in our heads. We're each in a totally different movie.

Is it possible to love the people on the other side, and perhaps most challenging of all, to love ourselves with all our warts and imperfections?

Disappointment and Regret

There comes a time in your life as a person when the peak of your physical and mental powers are behind you. Your greatest achievement, the pinnacle of your career, your most dazzling love affair, your most powerful moment of sexual ecstasy are all long gone. The only thing up ahead is disintegration and death. From the perspective of the separate self, this can seem very dismal indeed. It's not uncommon in old age or on one's deathbed to have thoughts of regret and disappointment—a feeling of failure, of not having accomplished what one should have accomplished.

From the perspective of the person in the story, life rarely turns out the way we once imagined it might. Many of us never met the love of our life, made a million dollars, or reached the degree of enlightened freedom we saw manifested in some of our greatest teachers. For some of us, our child turned out to be a disappointment, our novel was never published, we never made it to India, we didn't get a chance to tell our father how much we loved and appreciated him before he died. And faced with all this, as we approach death, there are often feelings of regret, or even shame and guilt if we believe we actually *could* or *should* have done it differently, or perhaps a last blast of blame and resentment if we imagine that we *could* have gotten the brass ring *if only* we'd had better parents, more money, a different skin color or gender, a better body, or whatever. And in some way, that may actually be quite true.

Imagine all the elements that come together to produce a Mozart, an Einstein, a Shakespeare, a Martin Luther King Jr., a Ramana Maharshi, a Stephen Hawking, a Toni Morrison, a Babe Ruth, a Steve

111

Jobs, a Meryl Streep, or any of the people we consider great innovators, successes, or geniuses in their field. There has to be some kind of innate talent, a gift of nature, along with so many favorable circumstances and opportunities, conditions in which to develop the necessary skills, a certain amount of self-confidence, energy, drive, passion, restraint, impulse-control, discipline, faith, trust, willingness to take risks. There must be a certain degree of health and physical stamina or resilience, a certain level of intelligence and sensitivity, and some combination of supportive friends or family or colleagues or the right connections or the right opportunities or the perfect lucky break. Being born in a certain year, or at a certain time of year, or at a certain moment in history, or in a particular geographical location may make all the difference. Take away one essential element and there would have been no such expression.

Imagine how many people have some of these things, but not all. They have the gift, but they lack the favorable circumstances, the right opportunities, the physical stamina, or the necessary discipline. Or they have the stamina, discipline and passion, but they lack the gift. Imagine the frustration of having the music of Mozart inside but no way to bring it forth, or the disappointment of being a scientist or an inventor working hard with tremendous discipline to reach a breakthrough that never comes. Very few of us will be remembered as a genius in our respective fields.

Most of us turn out to be one of the supporting cast, one of the many so-called "average" people whose lives are forgotten completely after they die except by a few friends and family members. And some of us may not even achieve that. We may spend years lost in addictions, in prison, stuck in a bad marriage, or suffering a debilitating illness—perhaps never entirely breaking free from our greatest forms of delusion.

By age fifty or sixty, long-held fantasies and possibilities dissolve with the realization that they are no longer possible. Going to medical school or law school is no longer an option. We look back and see the ways we failed certain people, the various character defects that have not all been magically cured or erased as we had hoped they would be, even after years of meditation, psychotherapy and awakening. Our lives are still messy and imperfect. The hope that this will all one day be resolved is no longer viable.

Years go by very quickly as you get older. Time speeds up. An entire decade vanishes in the snap of a finger. And it becomes abundantly clear that life is indeed like a flash of lightning or a bubble in a stream, over before you know it. Impermanence is now viscerally real. This is actually a great blessing because you begin to wake up more and more to where you actually *are*. "Someday" is rapidly disappearing. And, of course, in reality, it never existed!

Many people have a so-called bucket list of things they want to do before they die. What is it we hope to do before we die? Maybe we think we want to make it to India. But when we get to India, we're still Here-Now, in this timeless presence that never comes, never goes and never stays the same. No-thing lasts. But when we finally discover the wellspring, the source, the still-point Here-Now, we find that we *are* happiness, peace and love.

Do we think Emily Dickinson would have been happier if she'd married and had six children, that Van Gogh was worthless as an artist because his work was unrecognized during his lifetime and he died penniless, that Ramana Maharshi was a slacker who should have gotten a job instead of sitting around in his underwear all day? Probably not. And yet it's easy to shame ourselves for being "too introverted" or "too extroverted," "too poor" or "too rich," "too quiet" or "too busy," "too ambitious" or "not ambitious enough."

In fact, we are as we are, and there is really no such thing as an average person. On the level of form, life is fundamentally unsatisfactory and imperfectable. If we are obsessed with ideals of perfection or self-improvement, this will sound very pessimistic or disappointing. But maybe this imperfectability, this unresolvability, this way that everything is always disintegrating and falling apart, is what makes life worth living.

Suzuki Roshi once said, "Just being alive is enough." That feels so true to me now. Just taking a walk, drinking a cup of tea, exchanging a few words with the checkout clerk at the Co-op—just these simple moments. Often, it is precisely the wonder of these simplest and most ordinary moments that becomes more and more obvious to people as they age and their life on the level of form becomes increasingly limited.

As for regret, it seems to me that there is a healthy kind of regret and a more deluded kind of regret. When I hurt someone, I regret it in the sense that I'm sorry I caused pain. That seems like a natural and healthy kind of regret. It brings forth an apology or amends and hopefully learning something and maybe a resolve to do better in the future. But if I'm lost in a story about what a terrible person I am for having done that, and if I am going over and over what I did in an endless looping form of self-torture, then it feels unhealthy and deluded. I'm not helping the situation or the world or the person I hurt or myself by doing that. It only creates more suffering and more delusion.

We do hurtful things because we don't see what we're doing, or we can't stop ourselves. At that moment, the possibility of a different choice isn't there. It is a conditioned reaction of the whole universe, an act of nature like a thunderstorm or an earthquake. And ultimately, we can't separate the light and the dark. Our pain and apparent misfortunes are often the seeds of our redemption. So we can't ultimately say that the hurt I inflicted was a "bad thing" for me or the other person.

Once we get into regretting things that cannot be changed, it becomes a form of pointless self-torture—someone who is now eighty years old might regret not going to medical school, not marrying a certain person, not having children, or yelling at somebody thirty years ago, and none of this can be changed, so the regret is pointless.

Someone in a private meeting asked me half-jokingly if things get better. I said that some things do get better but other things get worse, and maybe the most important way in which they get better is that we are more at peace with them not being better.

This Is the End: No Heirs, No Descendants, No Future

Friends with children and grandchildren have a sense that they will live on in their children. They can pass on their family photos and family treasures to their heirs along with their genes. When you can pass those things on, there is some illusion of survival in that. In some way, your memories will survive, and *you* will survive. But I am an only child with no children. My only living relatives live very far away. It occurs to me that my photo albums will be taken to the dump by my executor when I die. All the photos of Mom and Dad, of me as a baby, of my childhood, of me at different times in my life, of all the people and dogs and places dear to me—these will all go to the dump. It can be a strangely painful thought, as if my mother and father and my childhood and everything dear to me will be dying all over again with even more finality.

And yet, what will actually be going to the dump? Bits of paper with old images on them, photos I almost never look at of people who have dissolved into the mists of history but who also live on in some way in my heart.

The real continuity, what we truly love and cherish, is not confined in the forms. And perhaps there is something infinitely freeing in letting all these relics go. Perhaps holding onto our family treasures is actually painful. Because we know deep down that we are holding onto dust. We are clinging to nothing at all. And yet, at the same time, it is beautiful to have things in my life now that were there in my childhood, things my mother and father cherished and touched, things they found beautiful.

Sometimes people feel obligated to keep family treasures that they don't actually want. My mother was great that way. She told me repeatedly, "These are my things, from my journey, and you don't need to keep any of them you don't want."

CHAPTER NINE: The Banquet of Life

A Wild Amusement

The world tonight is green and wet, waving its branches in the wind. Thunder rumbles, leaves toss, lightning flashes. Everything cracks open. Gold is running in the streets, trees sparkle with diamonds of liquid light. The warm darkness is full of water, the sounds of water, the sweet smells of rain and rain-drenched earth. Everything is a flashing, dissolving appearance without substance or continuity, a beautiful display, with no more purpose than a child's finger-painting. A wild amusement.

In the morning, I watch squirrels eat and play, groom each other, sleep and work on the branches of the tree outside my window.

Later, in the park, I see a great blue heron and a black-crowned night heron. The light from the water ripples on the leaves of the trees and on the neck of the night-heron.

The great blue heron strikes the water, comes up with a frog, legs dangling. I watch the great blue eat the frog. The night heron also watches, perched high in the willow tree. An old woman in a wheelchair rolls up beside me and we talk for a while.

That night, ladybugs appear on my wall, and a large green grasshopper sits on the window glass for a long time.

A few days later, I take Mom out in the wheelchair to enjoy the first little green leaves and flowers. A woman out gardening calls out to us and brings Mom a flower. After enjoying the emerging spring leaves and flowers, Mom wants to go to Subway for a sandwich. "I want a big one with everything on it," she announces. In recent years, she eats very little, so this is totally unusual. She wants turkey, ham, cheese. *Everything!* She keeps saying, *BIG!* She is wearing her purple hat with the visor. The woman from the drug store is in there also ordering a sandwich and she gives Mom a kiss. Mom gives her the flower.

I was invited to Boston to give a weekend of events, and so I went. At one point, a mother spoke about the death of her child. The response that came up here was simply silence. There was no impulse to say, "Your child was an illusion. Birth and death are illusions." When I look deeply, everything does dissolve into thin àir. And yet, it also appears. And the child dying hurts, probably one of the deepest of hurts.

A Night Out with the Republicans

Several of Mom's closest friends are Republicans, including Penny, a very feminine, upbeat saleswoman in her forties who wears short skirts and high heels and seems like the exact opposite of me in so many ways. She has a beautiful spirit and a heart of gold, although she voted twice for George W. Bush, thinks marriage is between a man and a woman, and is utterly clueless about why that feels anti-gay, hurtful or insulting to me. Mom and Penny met each other at church, and they went on a bicycle trip across Bali together when Mom was eighty and Penny was in her thirties. Penny has been a dear friend of Mom's for over a decade, and she is one of the most generous people I've ever met.

And there were the Log Cabin Republicans in my mother's church. Log Cabin Republicans are an organization of gay Republicans, a kind of oxymoron, if you ask me. And yet these men were lovely people who cared deeply for my mother.

Last night a bunch of us, including Penny and the Log Cabin men, went to hear some jazz at the church. After the concert, we went to a restaurant for dinner. The Republicans spent the whole dinner ripping apart Democratic politicians, some of whom, admittedly, deserved it. Mom is blessed with near-total deafness and is thus spared the conversation, which I unfortunately was still able to hear. I focused intently on my rainbow trout and mashed potatoes. I wish I had more ability to talk to these good-hearted Republicans about the issues in a non-reactive way, but I get easily triggered and become hot-headed and reactive. I write books about open listening but, more often than not, I fail. My mother has one essential message these days that she repeats over and over: "We need to love each other." She walks her talk much better than I do. But I'm not a total failure.

Penny and I are walking down the street together afterwards to get the car, our arms around each other, laughing.

"I love you," she says.

"I love you, too," I reply.

And we really mean it.

I remember listening once to a German Jewish survivor of the Holocaust, a friend of a friend of mine, as she recalled how on *Kristallnacht* many of Hitler's men who had to demolish the Jewish homes were in fact their neighbors. In many cases, they only *pretended* to destroy things, carefully and tenderly turning some beloved piece of furniture on its side, pretending to carry out their orders and destroy everything. I've always been fascinated by these ambiguities. In hindsight, it all looks so black and white. But in reality, it never is. In reality, we are all some strange mix of oppressor and oppressed, darkness and light, capable of amazing acts of love and horrific acts of cruelty.

The next day, I was out walking and passed a man with a leaf blower. I hate leaf blowers. They are incredibly loud and offensive machines blowing leaves temporarily from one side of the street to the other—an absurd cosmetic undertaking that wastes fossil fuel, creates noise pollution, and accomplishes absolutely nothing of value as far as I can see. I was instantly filled with aversion. Then I *saw* this happening, and suddenly it was comic—this Mexican immigrant with his incredibly loud hose doing this utterly absurd task to feed his children while on the other side of the street this middle-aged, white princess out for a walk fumed in self-righteous rage. The comedy of life. The banquet that includes Republicans, Democrats, racists, xenophobes, people with loud machines, people with chemical and biological weapons, people who think George W. Bush is a good man, people who think he is an evil man, people who are billionaires, people who dig their graves for minimum wage. What a banquet. What will we be served? The vegan entrée or the veal?

119

Not knowing if this banquet has any purpose. Not knowing anything except that you have mysteriously been invited. And apparently, so have all these others. And there is no way to leave the table. Here you all are, the infinite faces of God, finding your way toward love.

Any true meditation practice is humiliating and disappointing because you can no longer believe that you are better, that if you had been in their shoes, i.e., if you'd had the same conditioning, the same nature and nurture, the same life experiences, *you* would never have voted Republican, bombed Iraq, gassed the Jews, driven the Palestinians off their land, tortured a prisoner, abused a child, or engaged in factory farming. You know that you've played all the parts and you still do.

We've had tornados and thunderstorms and floods and then sudden gorgeous clearings; and these amazingly colored warblers migrating through have been flitting about in my tree.

Dark Days

My mother's doctor, who is also my doctor, urges me to get away, take a break. So, I am going to Springwater for a retreat. Springwater is the retreat center in northwestern New York state founded by Toni Packer, the place where I lived and was on staff for five years in the late 1980s and early 1990s. My mother's friend Penny agrees to keep an eye on Mom while I am away. I arrange to meet one of my dearest friends at Springwater, someone I haven't seen in several years, my friend Jean. She is one of the people Toni has asked to carry on the work, one of the new teachers who will eventually be taking over from Toni.

A week before I am to leave, Jean's husband calls me. He and Jean were eating breakfast that morning, she got up to get more coffee, fell down the basement stairs, hit her head, and is in a coma. They don't know if she will ever wake up.

It has been a very busy week with Mom needing more and more care, and I feel like I'm never caught up, like I'm drowning—and then this darkness came, feeling totally lost and alone. I'm sure my friend Jean being in a coma and Mom hovering at the lip of death must have something to do with it.

Mom called me yesterday in her sleep. She has only to push one button on her phone to get me. She asked me, "Why are my bones frozen?"

As it turned out, Jean never regained consciousness. Her husband told me that "Jean stopped being Jean" on Monday. Tests showed there was no brain activity. He disconnected the life support and moved Jean to hospice to die. She is making that last journey now.

Only Silence Remains

Jean died just before I left Chicago for Springwater. Her husband called it the "Pooooooffff Effect." Here one minute, then *pooooooffff*, gone the next. I reread her last email to me: "It all boils down to the presence that we are. How simple can this get?" Arriving in Springwater, her picture hangs by the front door and her words: "When the lover of silence dies, only silence remains." Hard to believe I will never see this face again. I sit at the little cascade where she and I once sat side by side in the moonlight listening together to rushing water, and I listen again to water running over rocks and to this immense silence that is her final word now in our conversation without end. And I discover that what I loved in her is everywhere: the presence, the silence, the love, the wonder.

In her prime, Toni Packer was one of the most energetic and vibrant people I'd ever met. She used to stride through the fields on her walks. But by the time of this retreat, she had been having serious health problems for a number of years involving severe chronic pain and an increasing loss of mobility. She made her rounds in the sitting room on this retreat in big shoes that clumped as she walked, unsteadily now, slowly, carefully.

I remember one of the first talks of Toni's that I heard here at Springwater. She ended it with the word *"nothing!"* I can still hear her saying that word with great force, followed by this immense silence in which the word seemed to unfold itself endlessly. That silence, so alive, so infinitely vast. *Nothing!*

121

That was what Toni gave us—nothing. And *nothing* is the greatest of gifts.

Bowel Control

In her last year, Mom started losing bowel control. Often it happened at night, but it happened once when she and I were at a bookstore together. And the worst time for her was one Sunday when Mom went out for brunch with a bunch of young gay men from her church, Log Cabin Republicans, and they were at a crowded restaurant having Sunday brunch when Mom lost bowel control and had an enormous outpouring of diarrhea. These young men handled it with utter grace. They escorted her back to the bathroom, a journey during which she had to pass, smelly and shit-covered, by tables of people, so it was utterly humiliating for her, but these young men escorted her back there. One young man went to his apartment nearby, got some clean clothes for Mom to change into—sweatpants, socks—and they got her changed and escorted her out of the restaurant and took her home—these beautiful, gracious, loving men. And one of them gave me a heads-up call, so that I would know what had happened.

I went over to her apartment and found her staring, rather blankly, straight ahead at the TV, shell-shocked, humiliated, stunned, broken in some way I'd never seen before. I gently reminded her of the large box of Depends I'd put in the bathroom months ago that she had so far ignored.

"I'm wearing one," she said. Staring blankly ahead, expressionless.

I found her soiled clothes in the bathtub and began rinsing the poop off of them, getting them clean enough to put into the laundry basket. I had poop on my hand and arm. We were down in the nitty-gritty now, the places no one wants to see or know about, the dark side of growing old as the body begins to lose control in more and more ways. On her penultimate day alive, she would pee on herself. This is what happens. We go back to where we started as babies—pooping on ourselves, allowing others to clean up our shit and piss. Only back then, as babies, we were totally innocent. We felt no shame or humiliation, until we gradually began to absorb those feelings from our caretakers as we learned about toilets and what things are unmentionable. But at first, as babies, we thought poop was something fun to play with or even put into our mouths and taste. We were innocent. But in our old age, we've learned that this is shameful, undignified, bad, wrong, ugly. We have soiled ourselves, wet the bed, broken the social covenant we entered with toilet training. Our children and our friends are cleaning us up. We are broken. This is painful. It is painful for my mother, and painful for me to see her pain. This is hard. And at the same time, it is all strangely okay. I watch myself washing her clothes in the bathtub with her shit on my hand and arm, and it all seems oddly beautiful. In reality, there is nothing shameful about it. Nothing ugly, undignified or wrong. It is simply life, doing what it does.

Summer Gets Hotter and Death Comes Closer

My mother is in the hospital—effects of congestive heart failure—fluid leaking out of her swollen legs. The skin is so thin it breaks open. The doctor says she's only going to be in the hospital for a few days, and maybe they can get her legs in better shape, but I am definitely watching the body disintegrate before my eyes. Her roommate, another old lady named Nellie with fever and pain, fell on the floor yesterday in a pool of urine while trying to make it to the bathroom, forgetting that she was hooked to an IV, with me trying (and failing) to catch her and the IV. The room seems to have no air conditioning or even any air. Turns out Nellie is turning it off because her side of the room is freezing cold. Mom's side is boiling hot. Chicago is in the nineties now, Fahrenheit, sweltering and humid.

I spend every day at the hospital sitting in bed with Mom or in the chair beside her bed, being together. At night, I go home alone.

After several days, the doctor is discharging Mom. I arrive at the hospital at eight a.m. to find Mom fully dressed, out of bed and sitting up in the chair, her bags packed, ready to go. Nellie says Mom was up at six packing. Mom was like a little kid, her face was so happy and gleeful. Her doctor showed up an hour later and officially released her, and I took her home. She is much better. So, for a moment, it appears that once again death and disintegration have been vanquished.

Adventures in Absurdity

Once a partial bridge containing a row of teeth came unglued and dislodged itself from my mother's mouth. She put it in the machine that cleaned her hearing aids overnight and turned the machine on. In the morning, she re-inserted the bridge in her mouth, but of course, it was not glued in, so it kept falling out. When I discovered the situation, I feared she might choke on this row of teeth or lose it, so I managed to get it away from her and decided to take it home with me for safekeeping until the dentist could see us the next day.

When she realized what was happening, Mom didn't like it one bit. "Give me my teeth!" she demanded. I held firm, clutching them in my hand wrapped in a Kleenex, on my way out the door. "I want my teeth!" she repeated with considerable anger. I told her she might choke on them. She looked at me with disgust.

"You have to trust me on this, Mom," I said. "I love you." And off I went with her teeth.

She used to call me up sometimes in the last years and say, "I can't remember how to turn the television on." I'd have to go over to her apartment and turn it on for her.

There were times, not often but occasionally in the last couple of years, where I found myself on the verge of blurting out, "Come on, Mom. Get it together. Snap out of it!" This person was my mother after all. She was supposed to be in control and taking care of me, not the other way around.

Then she would lose her hearing aids or her glasses. She'd drop them or put them someplace she couldn't remember, and it was my job to find them. The hearing aids were smaller and more challenging. But I was always able to find them until a few days before she died. They went missing one last and final time. I searched. And searched. And searched. No hearing aids. It was weeks later, long after she died, when I was cleaning out her apartment, that they turned up in one of the small decorative silver pill boxes on her dresser. It was as if she had been playing hide and seek with me, and she had finally outwitted me. *Gotcha!* I heard her say in my mind, laughing gleefully.

The Man Who Walked in the Rain

There is a man in my neighborhood here in Chicago who always walks in the rain. Whenever there is a torrential downpour in the summer, one of those magnificent storms with thunder and lightning and pouring rain coming down in sheets, I'm usually at the windows enjoying it, and I always see this man walking aimlessly back and forth on the sidewalk in front of my building, obviously out there enjoying the rain. He is a middle-aged man with a balding head, wearing Bermuda shorts, a T-shirt and rubber flip-flops. He carries no umbrella and wears no raincoat. He clearly wants to be drenched by the rain, to be out in it, engulfed in it, reveling in it. He is a very ordinary-looking man, someone who looks like he might work in a cubicle in some downtown office selling insurance. By all appearances, he's not a hippy or a nature freak or somebody stoned on weed. He's just a lover of rain. You might expect this behavior in San Francisco or Berkeley, some old acid freak out dancing in the rain; but this is gritty, Midwestern, down-to-earth Chicago, and here he is, this very ordinary-looking, middle-aged man in his rubber flip-flops and his Bermuda shorts, unabashedly doing something that is utterly useless—enjoying the rain. I love him. He makes my heart sing.

Beyond All Ideas

In the summer before my mother died, I watched movies about the Holocaust. I don't know why I did this; it just started happening. Maybe I was interested in looking deeply at the worst imaginable suffering, and discovering how we survive it—"Going to the heart of the world's sin and pain," as Maggie Ross, an Anglican solitary, described her vocation. Not that my mother's impending death was in any way

125

comparable to the Holocaust, but for me, it was going to be a huge loss. And the world seemed to be going in a darker direction in so many ways. So, I watched all nine hours of the Holocaust documentary *Shoah*. I watched *Schindler's List, Sophie's Choice, Bent, The Pianist, Paragraph 175*. Watching those movies, looking deeply into the Holocaust, I had no desire at all to say, "All is One, everything is perfect, nothing real is really being hurt, it's all just a dream." That kind of response just didn't come up. At the same time, as I watched these horrors unfold, I didn't feel the anger and outrage I might once have felt, the hatred toward the perpetrators, the bitterness and despair. I watched these movies with a kind of equanimity and peace that I could never have manufactured. It just happened by itself. There was a deep sorrow, but not despair. There was no urge to put a spin of any kind on what I was seeing, as any such overlay was clearly about moving away from the raw actuality. I was simply completely present with it. The only way to truly be with something that huge and that unfathomable is silently, wordlessly, openly. And I learned that it is possible to come through the fire with an open heart. I saw that some who had survived these unimaginable horrors were filled with love and not with bitterness. I certainly don't always come through every fire in my life with an open heart, but I saw and tasted the possibility. What makes the difference between being caught in bitterness or open and free in love? This isn't a question to answer with an ideology or an explanation. It's a question to live with and to explore directly in our own lives.

CHAPTER TEN: Death Comes

Autumn 2004: Death Closes In

I'm at home drinking a beer. The fire department calls me. They're at Mom's apartment. She's fallen. The people living below her heard the crash and called 911. I rush over. I take her to the ER. They hospitalize her. In the morning, her doctor tells me it's time for hospice and live-in nursing care. I hire a live-in nurse. We sign the forms for hospice. I post bright orange "Do Not Resuscitate" signs all over Mom's apartment. Still, I tell myself that maybe she could last another year, who knows?

"I can't believe she's still breathing," the hospice nurse said to me after her first visit to Mom. "There's nothing left of her lungs." The hospice nurse couldn't believe anyone had lasted this long and been this functional with lungs as compromised as Mom's apparently were.

As Mom drew closer to death, Sailor Bob showed up in Chicago. Bob is a contemporary nondualist from Australia, then in his seventies, who had spent time with Nisargadatta Maharaj in India years ago. My friend Tom and I met him at the airport and hung out with him, and he did a number of wonderful events. It was great to be with him. Bob's simple message is that there is always only undivided intelligence-energy, which vibrates into different patterns. Everything is this presence-awareness, this Consciousness or unicity from which no separation is ever possible. He speaks as Consciousness to Consciousness, not as one person to another person. I found him to be a very generous, kind, unpretentious, awake being.

We had an interesting conversation about evil. Bob asked me, if everyone who died in the Second World War—the soldiers on all sides, the civilians on the ground, the people who were gassed in the concentration camps, those who died in the two atomic bombings—if all those people had survived and reproduced, what would that do for climate change and dwindling energy resources? Of course, Bob was not trying to justify or defend the Holocaust, the atomic bombings, or the war. He was only pointing out that we can't isolate so-called "good" from so-called "bad," that what looks horrible to us at one level may be beneficial in a larger sense, that nature always restores balance one way or another, and that, ultimately, all forms will perish. *All* of it is a dance of intelligence-energy in which nothing real is ever destroyed.

Bob went home to Australia.

Mom was in a wheelchair much of the time now. Many times during these last four years in Chicago, I had thought to myself, "God, I hope I don't live to be ninety-five," because it really looked hard. But as Mom entered her final weeks, I came to see the beauty of being ninety-five, that she was so completely stripped of everything, everything that seemingly defined her as a person. And yet, she still had this love, this spirit, this wonder at life. She'd look out the window, and the view out her window is nothing really extraordinary, just buildings and some sky, and she'd say, "I am so blessed to have this wonderful view, to be able to see the sky. It is so beautiful to be able to see the sky."

Dying to Everything

The closer things get to nonexistence, the more exquisite and evocative they become.

—Leonard Koren

My friend Valjean and I took Mom on an outing to the nearby Lincoln Park Zoo. Valjean is the friend my age who would be dead in a few years from a fast-moving lung cancer. We wheeled Mom around the zoo in the wheelchair. Mom was mostly interested in the little children that were there, much more than the animals. She stopped and talked to lots of little toddlers and had these wonderful interactions with them and with their parents. She kept saying, "This is such a treat. This is such a blessing. This is such a wonderful day. Thank you so much."

It became so clear that, in interactions with people, the content isn't really important. It's what's under the content. Mom can't always hear the words anymore, but she feels the love. The content is like an excuse to be together, and what matters is the love. Like the words of that old Louis Armstrong song, "What A Wonderful World"—under all the small talk, what we're really saying is, "I love you." That's the main thing my mother has always talked about, that everybody needs to love each other, that I should love myself, that love is the most important thing.

She's very proud of me, so she loves to tell people that I've written books, and when they ask what the books are about, my mother says, "They are about being who you are." And she says, "That's really important, to be who you are."

In one sense, of course, you can't *not* be who you are, on every level, relative and absolute, personal and impersonal. But "How am I not being myself?" is an inquiry, an invitation to notice if there are ways that I am not being true to who or what I truly am, whether that might mean pretending to be straight when I'm really gay, or pretending to be sweet and loving when I'm really feeling enraged, or pretending I'm just a neurotic little person when I'm really this vast boundless *no-thing-ness* that includes everything, or pretending I'm a fully enlightened somebody who knows how the universe works when I'm really just another clueless bozo on the bus. The question can be heard on many levels. It's an invitation to stop, look and listen.

I felt as if I were in this stripping process, being with death, being stripped of so many things I've been holding onto—my mother, my sense of entitlement, my ideas for how the world should be—and I was feeling more and more deeply that what's real is only the absolute simplicity of everything just as it is. I felt like this whole spiritual journey had been a stripping process, one in which I kept uncovering new and subtler layers of grasping, clutching, holding back, seeking outside myself. And the deepest truth is not to find an answer, but to live with the answer-less-ness.

Any urge to sum everything up in some neat and tidy formulaic package just wasn't there anymore. I didn't want any conceptual answers, any feel-good philosophy, any nondual or Advaita-speak coming from the head.

I flew to Massachusetts to do a long-scheduled weekend of events. Penny would once again keep an eye on Mom while I was gone. I arrived home afterwards to discover that Mom had gone on oxygen and morphine over the weekend. I realized that this was it. She was actually dying. It was happening. It was happening now. Several times before this in these last two years, I had *thought* Mom was dying, but this time, I *knew* she was dying. Driving to Mom's place from the college where I work, tears came pouring out.

Her pain got pretty severe toward the end. She was in a wheelchair all the time by the last week, and the morphine made her a little loopy. At one point, she was trying to make phone calls with her water bottle, which she had mistaken for the telephone, holding it first to her ear and then to her mouth, talking into it, listening to it, and then expressing tremendous frustration when the person she was calling failed to respond to her invitation to come down for a martini. "This phone isn't working!" she said with great exasperation.

Dorothy Lifts Off

Her last days were an ongoing, spontaneous party. "Dorothy's Last Party," I called it. Her friends kept coming by in a steady stream for a final visit. People were laughing and crying, telling stories, being with her. At one point, there were so many people that we were out of furniture, so Penny and I were squished together onto one tiny hassock.

There was so much joy being in her presence, so much love and delight in life. I've watched her lose so much, but her attention is never on what has been lost. It is always on what is here now. She still has enormous strength and spirit.

The night before she died, hospice delivered the hospital bed. I had them put it in the living room by the windows she loved. My high school friend Lola flew in from Santa Fe and a beloved second cousin arrived from England—both of them were very close to Mom. I slept on the couch next to Mom that last night.

There is a groundedness that comes from dealing so intimately with the body as it breaks down. Cleaning up her shit, holding her teeth in my hand. It gets very earthy. It's like the other end of what mothers do with babies. We find ourselves making more and more decisions for that other person, just as mothers must do for their children.

I remember the home health nurse asking me on that last night that Mom was alive how much morphine I wanted her to give. "We'll ask Mom," I replied. And the nurse said to me, "She can't decide anymore. You have to do that now." A sobering moment.

There were snow flurries in the forecast that night and the sounds of dry leaves blowing over the pavement.

The next morning, Mom looked quite different. Her eyes were closed and her mouth was hanging open. I leaned over her and said, "I love you." She opened her eyes and said, "I love you too, very much." Those were her last words to me. She closed her eyes and didn't speak again while I was there. She was basically unconscious on morphine for the rest of the day, but maybe on some level she was still conscious and listening.

I was slated to bring her oldest friend Charlotte over that day. Charlotte is also in her nineties and has struggled all her life with serious mental illness. She's strong but fragile. She and Mom have known each other since they were single young working girls. They go back a long way. I was nervous about bringing Charlotte over because Mom didn't look too good. She had stuff dripping out the side of her mouth, which was hanging open, and her eyes were closed. I thought, "This could be really upsetting for Charlotte." But Charlotte wanted to come, even though she was fearful about seeing Mom on her deathbed. Until she got there, I don't think Charlotte fully believed that it *was* Mom's deathbed, because Mom had always revived. But this time, I knew Mom was not reviving.

While I was bringing Charlotte over, my friend Lola had gone out and gotten bubbles. And we were blowing bubbles over Mom, the Lift-Off Bubbles. We were all laughing and joking, bubbles were floating through the air, and as soon as Charlotte caught the spirit of what was happening, she got really happy. She was radiant.

131

"I was afraid of dying," Charlotte said, "but Dorothy is teaching me how to do it. I want to die just like this. This is so beautiful."

Hospice had brought a portable commode and we were using it with the lid down as the table for our lunch. Friends of Mom's were coming and going. It was an extraordinary day, full of love and joy, laughter and tears.

Finally, Charlotte said she was ready to go home, so I leaned over Mom. "I'm going to take Charlotte home," I told her. "I'll be right back." I kissed her. And then off I went with Charlotte. I thought Mom might die that night or the next day, but it never once crossed my mind that she would die while I was taking Charlotte home.

I didn't have a cell phone in those days, so I was out of reach. After getting Charlotte home, I stopped briefly at my apartment to pick up a change of clothes and send off some material to the substitute who was going to be covering my classes at the college. And then, while driving from my place back to Mom's, just as the sun was setting and everything was bathed in that marvelous reddish-golden light, what seemed like a very peculiar thought came to me: "Driving the car is part of Mom's dying." It was as if I were getting a message from the universe that driving was as perfectly a part of the whole event as holding Mom's hand. I felt a deep peace and calm come over me. It was quite a remarkable moment.

They told me when I got back to Mom's apartment that Mom had taken her last breath at the very moment when that reddish-golden sunset light filled the room. They told me that soon after Charlotte and I left, the pain had come back and Mom's eyes had opened. She was agitated, she pushed away the oxygen, she refused the nebulizer. "Get me out of here!" she said—her last words. Then she laid back peacefully, closed her eyes, and her breathing came more and more infrequently, until she stopped breathing. I arrived back very soon after she died.

Friends who are doctors or hospice workers have told me that people often die when the family leaves the room. My father died when my mother was out of the house. Maybe Mom needed to die when I wasn't there. She had said that the hardest thing was going to be leaving me, and I wonder if perhaps my presence might have pulled her back. In any case, that's how it happened. She slipped out when I wasn't there, surrounded by loving friends.

We all stayed with her body for several hours, and more people poured in. There was an amazing presence in the room, an energy. I felt what I can only describe as bliss. I kept touching Mom's hands, her face, her hair, her ear—that body that was so familiar and so precious. I took her "You Go Girl!" pillow and laid it on her. I asked the cremation society to wait a couple of hours before coming. And we all sat there with Mom, laughing and crying and joking and loving her. Saying goodbye. In those hours I spent holding her hands and touching her ears after she died, I was seeing both the absolute preciousness of the body and the utter ephemeralness of it.

Finally the Cremation Society arrived with their gurney. "You probably want to leave the room now," they said, "because you don't want to see this." I remembered years ago when my friend Michael Bumblebee died of AIDS, and our mutual friend Micky was with him when he died, and she was telling me about it on the phone afterwards, how she dressed him and put flowers on him, and then the Neptune Society came and put him in a black bag and zipped it shut over his face. "And that," she had said, "was a very clear lesson." I wanted that lesson. I wanted to see everything. And so I watched as they very gently picked Mom up out of the bed and put her in this black bag and zipped it shut over her face and strapped her onto the gurney. And I walked her out to the elevator and saw her off. The doors closed. She was gone.

The party of tears and laughter continued until past midnight—all these people in the apartment, and more kept arriving. Earlier, when I was driving Charlotte home, Charlotte was saying to me, "Oh my God, how am I ever going to explain this?" Charlotte lives in a retirement home. "They all know I was going off to spend the day with my oldest friend who is on her deathbed. And I'm going to come back and tell them that we had this really happy, wonderful day and we blew bubbles! There's no way I can communicate this to anyone. I'm so happy! And they're not going to understand."

Mom had told me to take a walk in nature after she died, so in the morning, I walked by the lake and the pond in the park. She is everywhere now—and yes, Dorothy, it's a beautiful world. The feeling of bliss continued for several days, sad and grieving at times, but strangely filled with this radiant bliss. It was a very powerful experience.

In the lobby of her building, they had a photo of her on the front desk now with a sign that said, "Toodles to Our Beloved Dorothy," because Mom always said, "Toodle-ooo." In the photo, she's wearing this wild fuchsia and orange outfit, and she looks like a Buddha.

She died the way she lived, surrounded by love and full of joy. She was a generous, strong, open-minded, fun-loving, passionate woman. She loved art and music. She loved parties. She loved people. She wanted to see the whole world. She reached out to people who were outsiders, people who were different from her. She worked hard for peace, social justice, civil rights for minorities, equality for lesbians and gays, fair housing, and against police brutality and racism. She believed in positive thinking and love. She said it's a beautiful world. Love yourself, love life, love everyone. That was her message. She was full of wonder and delight. She had an exceptionally good marriage to a wonderful man whom she loved deeply. She was a loving and proud mother who encouraged me to follow my dreams. She loved gardens and animals. She loved life. She would want us to celebrate her life and all life, not to mourn. She would want us to love one another and to love ourselves and to enjoy every precious moment of life to the fullest. As she always said in her favorite toast, "Here's to love."

She left me a note that she'd written long ago that I was to open when she died, and it said, *"Dear Heart—Don't grieve for me... know that I've had a wonderful life... I consider each year a special gift... my life is a joy... have a party when I'm gone... I love you with all my heart."*

I imagined that I would feel this immense devastation when Mom died because we were very, very close and I love her so dearly, and my whole life had been so completely focused on her for the last four years. But it wasn't like that. It wasn't the horrible devastation I had imagined. I cried a lot, but there was mostly this immense happiness and joy. Her last few days had felt so celebratory, so loving and joyous.

It left me with a great deal of peace.

Death is a very grounding thing. Everything is dissolving, groundlessness is being revealed and, paradoxically, that is very grounding. Of course, I was blessed to have a mother whom I loved dearly, and who loved me. I realize that many people don't have that kind of wonderful relationship with their mother. I was very blessed to have those four years with her at the end of her life and to be part of her disintegration.

Disintegration is a word we don't usually think of as being very positive. But actually, disintegration is beautiful.

I spent many hours in Mom's apartment in the week after she died, just being there, absorbing her spirit, her absence and her presence. The apartment was filled with all these colorful things she loved—clothes, chairs, paintings, little objects like sculpted elephants and turtles and all kinds of things that have her spirit in some way. Things she loved. Certain smells lingered there that reminded me of her. Being there was like being in this big heart, her heart.

I had given my mother *Tuesdays with Morrie* a number of years ago, and that book was in her mind as the end approached. Two copies of it were sitting by her bed when she died. Morrie died of ALS. Mom had emphysema and congestive heart disease, but it's a similar kind of ending where you can't breathe. If I have a bad cold and can't breathe, it brings up this feeling of panic. But Mom never seemed panicked by that air hunger, which really amazed me.

Her worst fear in life was to be dependent. She always said, "I want to run my own ship." She was very big on that. And yet, she went through her worst fear, the loss of her independence. And she met it with incredible grace and surrender.

Ashes

I asked her before she died, "What should I do with your ashes?" She said, "I don't care what you do with them. Throw them in the trash. Whatever you do, it's for you. I'm outta there."

One week after she died, I went to the Cremation Society and they handed me a small cardboard box labeled "The cremated remains of Dorothy Tollifson." It was drizzling, a mild November day, and I carried her in my arms, all that remained of her. I stopped for lunch at a diner and began crying. The college where I teach sent me flowers. Cards arrived from friends. One week without Dorothy.

In the tree outside my window that morning, the cardinal was singing his beautiful song, the gorgeous red of his body against the gray sky and the bare trees.

Life after Death

If everyone is up in heaven, it must be getting pretty crowded up there.

—Dorothy Tollifson

Nothing whatsoever is to be clung to as I or mine.

—The Buddha

It's astonishing how many people believe Mom is in heaven now, or floating around the room somewhere as a disembodied spirit, or that she's been reincarnated in a new body. People around me all have their different theories and beliefs about what happens after death. The wonderful homecare nurse who lived with Mom for the last month told me, "Dorothy is up in heaven now having sex with your father." She believes this literally. According to her, everyone is restored after death to how they were when they were young. Mom could be pregnant right now, and I could still have that tiny right hand, not yet amputated.

There is a feeling here right now that all these ideas about an afterlife are beautiful stories, beautiful for what they are trying to express. The nurse's belief that Mom was up in heaven now having sex with Dad was her way of understanding the wholeness of life and the okayness of death, and I didn't have any urge to say to her, "That's a load of crap." It felt beautiful to me that she was expressing something about what doesn't die, and I could hear it as poetry or metaphor. Even though, of course, I don't believe Mom is up there in heaven with my now forty-year-old father about to give birth to me.

We imagine that after death, we'll still be here, buried alive as it were, unable to turn on the TV and see what happens next in The Story of My Life. Or we imagine that we will be looking down on the show from a distant heaven, forced to live on in perpetual exile from our loved ones. This attachment to the experience of being "me," and at an even more primal level, to *experiencing* itself—to consciousness, to *being*, gives rise to all our desperate efforts to live forever. But is there anyone in deep sleep who is desperately trying to get back to waking life or worrying about not waking up again?

This experience of disappearing completely, which we all dissolve happily into every night, far from being bleak or dreadful, is deeply peaceful and rejuvenating. The dreaded "nothing" that we scare ourselves with is actually *something*—a mental image, an idea, a story, a subtle form—and not the actual *reality* of what remains in deep sleep. In deep sleep, no story, no mental image, no fear survives.

Whatever remains really can't be put into words, because it is nothing perceivable or conceivable. It is more subtle than any experience. It is invisible, like space. It has no content, no form. It is prior to waking or dreaming consciousness, more subtle even than the first impersonal sense of being here. When you enter deeply into silence, stillness and presence, there can be a dissolving into that vast emptiness, for it is always Here-Now, at the very heart of everything. Out of this infinitely subtle pure potential, the world of apparent form emerges, unfolding itself with increasing degrees of apparent density and complexity, and then withdrawing itself again and returning to the unfathomable depths.

What has actually died? It *seems* like something very precious and real has come to an end in a very undeniable and irrevocable way, but what exactly *is* it? After all, there were many times when she was alive that my Dorothy disappeared—whenever she went into another room, or I was in another city, or my attention was elsewhere—so what's *actually* different this time? Maybe it's nothing more than the *thought* that, "I'll never see her again." And who was she anyway? I knew many different Dorothys over a lifetime or even in the space of an hour, and Dorothy undoubtedly did too! Which was the *real* Dorothy? What exactly *is* this "Dorothy" who seems to have disappeared forever? *Something* has ended, that cannot be denied, but when we try to pin down exactly *what* it is, we find nothing graspable. It is like trying to grasp smoke or water or clouds.

When scientists look closely at any form, they seem to find mostly empty space and subatomic particles or wavicles that flash in and out of existence in a quantum world where apparent solidity seems to be contingent upon observation. Nothing ever really forms or congeals into any enduring *thing* that stays put. In Buddhism, emptiness is not the *opposite* of form or the *container* of form. Emptiness *is* form and form *is* emptiness.

Form is not a *distraction* from emptiness. This movie of waking life is not a problem that needs to be solved, or some kind of cosmic mistake that needs to be transcended. It is more like a dance or a painting or a song to be enjoyed, sometimes in the way a comedy is enjoyed, sometimes in the way a tragedy is enjoyed, sometimes in the way a mystery is enjoyed, sometimes in the way turning off the TV is enjoyed. The body and this whole amazing world of apparent form is so beautiful, so precious. And so utterly fleeting. And the more deeply you enter into any apparent form, the more it dissolves into formlessness.

The vision of my mother up in heaven, young again, having sex with my father, is in some sense just as real as the room you think you're sitting in right now, the book or reading device you think you're holding, and the whole world you seem to be living in. *All* of this—the supposedly imaginary and the supposedly real—is made of the same radiant presence, the same formless consciousness, the same infinite potential, the same indivisible and mysterious dancing emptiness.

This Instant, Alive and Vanishing

I've been busy with memorial celebration planning, estate settling, talking to all Mom's friends. I go back to work Monday and have my group Sunday. Tomorrow I have to clean my own apartment which looks like a tornado went through it—papers everywhere, and Dorothy in a cardboard box.

This morning my car door was frozen shut. I had to scrape ice off all the windows.

Death has a way of erasing everything. And it's not just something that happens at the end of a long life or a short life. It's actually the nature of every single moment, of *this* moment. Death has a way of bringing you very quickly to what's really essential, what really matters.

I had my twelfth moon, the twelfth month without a menstrual period, the same month Mom died, and thus officially became post-menopausal. I feel the changes in this body acutely.

In Zen, the transcendent is not beyond the world, but right here in the midst of daily life. In Mom's dying, there was a deep seeing that transcendence is not separate from the body. It is not something other than changing the diapers, giving the morphine, hearing the traffic— *that* is the absolute, all-embracing Holy Reality.

Part of what is beautiful about that bird flying past the window just now is that it is only there for an instant. And yet we have this instinct to try to hold onto things, to freeze things in place, to keep everything alive forever, to prolong our lives as long as possible, and to make everything we like last as long as it possibly can.

Dorothy's Memorial Celebration

It was a dark, wild day with pouring rain and gusting wind. Traffic was unbelievably backed up. Those who made it to the memorial celebration in downtown Chicago had indeed braved the elements to get there. Several who were older and frailer and whose health was compromised were kept away. But in spite of the weather, the church was filled with friends of Dorothy, people of all ages, races, social classes, sexual preferences, political persuasions, and walks of life. Lots of people were wearing purple or other bright colors. My boss from the college turned up and one of my students was there and several of my own friends.

On a table, I had assembled photos of Mom from her childhood through the day she died, along with memorabilia—her silver shoes with the silver bows, her martini glass, her purple baseball cap with the purple jewel, the newspaper clipping from when she testified to the Illinois legislature decades ago in favor of lesbian and gay rights. Mom loved jazz, and we had gone together several times to hear the Franz Jackson Jazz band, and she loved them, so they provided the music for the memorial. Franz is in his nineties and has been playing jazz in Chicago since the 1920s. My dear friend Dan DeLorenzo, whom I first met at Springwater, plays the bass with them. At the end of the service, at my request, they played "What A Wonderful World," the old Louis Armstrong song that Franz does so beautifully, a song that seemed to me to perfectly express my mother's spirit.

As we crossed the hallway into the party room, Lola blew bubbles. She had found some kind of giant bubble blower that she was using, and she was blowing these enormous bubbles, at least twice the size of watermelons.

It was a beautiful celebration that continued later in Mom's apartment, where several of the guests from out of town were staying, long into the night. Finally, long past midnight, I headed home. I think Dorothy would have liked her party very much. And I guess that through all of us, she did enjoy it.

The next morning, when my alarm went off at five a.m. for work, I don't even remember turning it off. I awoke at six-thirty, the time when I usually leave my apartment, in bed, holding my alarm clock in my hand. I jumped up, took a shower, got dressed, ate some breakfast, made my lunch, gulped down a cup of tea, and was on the road at seven a.m. For those who know me and my leisurely, reflective, slow-paced, meditative morning routine, this will astonish and amaze you as much as it did me. In fact, I'm not sure how I did it. But I do know I don't ever want to do it again. I missed my morning office prep, but I made it by the skin of my teeth to my first class.

The World without Mom

The biggest earthquake in forty years strikes under the Indian Ocean setting off a tsunami that kills over 150,000 people and leaves thousands of others injured and homeless, their towns, homes and livelihoods swept away in an instant.

Clouds blow across the sky, a flight of birds sweeps past, the breath moves, the Mars rover inches along in the red dust. Without the words, without labels, without the story, what *is* all of this? Not to answer that with some word or idea, but simply to be open to the wonder of not knowing.

The TV News shows a house raid in Iraq. The camera zooms in to a close-up of a little Iraqi girl's face—her lip is visibly quivering and her teeth literally chattering in fear. Her father is being dragged away by American soldiers. What would that have been like for me when I was a little child, to see my beloved father brutally dragged away in the night by foreign soldiers, maybe never to return? And then we see other American soldiers being carried out of an explosion. Apparently, one of the most common injuries that US combat troops are experiencing from improvised explosive devices is the loss of both legs and the genitals. These are called "genitourinary" wounds. Another program on TV shows a mother whose son came home from Iraq as a paralyzed vegetable, his face burned off and his cognitive faculties wiped out, an empty shell whom she must take care of for the rest of her life. And all of this for these pointless and ill-conceived wars in which so many Americans have died or been hideously wounded and God only knows how many Afghans and Iraqis have been killed, maimed, orphaned and displaced.

All the pain in this world—the genocides, the wars—and the inner turmoil that may be imaginary but is still excruciatingly painful to so many people. I've been reflecting on how "spiritual practice" *is* in some way not always effortless and easy and full of warm and fuzzy blissful feelings. It's a long, hard slog sometimes. It takes perseverance and endurance. Life is challenging, even for those of us who are immensely privileged in so many ways—I have ample food and water, a very comfortable place to live, good medical care, no bombs falling regularly on my neighborhood. For so many people on this planet, life is so much more cruel. And even for the most privileged, being human can be just plain hard.

My mother began every day with prayer. Since she died, I have taken to morning prayer along with quiet sitting, not prayer to any God in the sky, but simply to voice aloud, and to hear, and thus to attend to gratitude, caring, and intention. I give thanks for all that I am grateful for. I name whatever comes to mind that morning: the sunlight, the time and space to be quiet, my warm apartment, my parents, teachers, friends—whatever shows up. I listen to what shows up. Then I pray for all suffering beings. Again, I name them, whatever emerges that morning—those in natural disasters, famines, epidemics, wars, those in prison, those being abused or tortured, those who are sick, those who are suffering emotional and mental pain, those who are oppressed. Again, I listen. For that moment, I give attention, simple attention, to each one that I name. I pray for particular people I know who are ill or grieving or going through some difficulty. And I express my intention to dedicate this life to waking up. I pray for guidance.

I enjoy this practice of starting the day by consciously reflecting on and giving attention to my blessings, the suffering in the world, and my intention. Perhaps I have picked up the work my mother was doing, taken on the job, stepped into her shoes. I have started wearing her well-worn deerskin slippers around the house and wrapping her purple shawl around my legs when I'm sitting down, as she did.

I wore her slippers until they disintegrated.

I have finally dug in for real cleaning out her apartment. It is exhausting and emotional work. The emotional part is not devastating or horrible, but more a sense of being very opened up. Mom's spirit is so present in the space and in all the objects she touched with her hands and her gaze. It is a peaceful space, and working there is meditative and healing. A family friend I've known since we were children has generously offered to help me and is with me through it all, and sometimes other friends pitch in as well, so I am not alone.

At night, when I get home from Mom's, sometimes I sit quietly or do a Feldenkrais lesson. Sometimes I watch *Six Feet Under* or a movie. Sometimes I drink wine and listen to Leonard Cohen or Bob Dylan and feel like I am grieving not only my mother, but my lost youth. Sometimes I read a Tim O'Brien novel and revisit Vietnam. Sometimes I read Nisargadatta or some other spiritual book. Sometimes I talk to a friend on the phone. Sometimes I bite my fingers until they bleed. Sometimes I draw pictures.

I got a massage with a Tibetan monk who chanted over me as he worked. And I've been walking in the park between spurts of activity at Mom's. I am learning that this clearing out can't be done in steam-roller fashion. There is too much deep feeling.

In the morning, my bare tree branches are full of snow-covered mourning doves. Recently there has been a peregrine falcon in my neighborhood who has been swooping in and eating the pigeons and doves. But this morning, the doves are cooing in peace when I leave for Mom's.

Being with Grief

I remember when Toni Packer's beloved husband Kyle died, she spoke very openly about her grief and the depth of it. She said that, although many other people in her life who were dear to her had died, she had never experienced anything like this grief. She definitely wasn't denying it or trying to push it away. But she was also exploring it with the open curiosity and spirit of scientific inquiry that she brought to everything. I remember her saying during a retreat talk that when she was on retreat, and energy was totally gathered in presence, the grief wasn't there, but when she'd go home, back to the house they had shared, it would return. She noted the connection between thoughts and emotion, or how she'd want to share something with him and then realize he wasn't there anymore. These triggers can be very subtle.

When my mother died, I did a similar exploration, and it was fascinating. Sometimes grief was triggered by seeing something of hers, or maybe even a smell that reminded me of her, maybe even a smell I wasn't consciously aware of, and then immediately a thought like,

143

"I'll never see her again," and then the flooding in again of grief, that empty feeling in the pit of the stomach, and the heartache.

Plants

Yesterday I gave away Mom's plants. Gwen and Luke, a younger couple in her building whom she loved, took them all. There were a lot of them. It took three or four loads on the dolly to transport them all. When it was over and done, the apartment looked suddenly very bare and unoccupied. It was a huge disappearance, a major turning point. They come unexpectedly, these turning points.

I told Luke and Gwen a story that Mom told me often. It was one of those stories from her past that I heard more and more frequently as she got older. Some stories would be repeated weekly, even daily. I came to regard these stories as liturgical events, something to be heard again and again, each time freshly. Acts of worship or attention. This story was about the Great Depression when my mother's family was thrown out of their apartment because they couldn't pay the rent. They were walking down the street carrying whatever possessions they could carry. My grandmother Hattie insisted that my grandfather Billy had to carry this huge rubber plant. Struggling under the weight of it, he asked her why they had to take this plant. "Because it's *alive*!" Hattie replied. My mother told this story over and over. In her final year, when she got a little more confused, she actually came to believe that the rubber plant in her living room was the very same rubber plant that her father had carried down the street. Gwen and Luke have named the rubber plant Dorothy.

After that walk down the street carrying whatever they could carry, my mother and her brother and sister and their parents all lived in one room. Mom supported them all. On Luke and Gwen's wall is a picture of Luke's ancestors. His father, I know, was a doctor. But these are farther back. They are rural Black people who look very poor standing in front of a run-down building, each holding a cherished possession.

After I gave away the plants, it was sunset, and I walked around the pond in the park near Mom's building and then went home and watched a movie.

Mom once told another story about taking me to a fair at the Village Green in our home town when I was very little. There was a little children's train ride around a circle, and I went on it. Mom said she watched the little train take me away as she waved goodbye, and suddenly she was weeping, because it foreshadowed the time when real trains would take me out of her world into a future she would eventually be unable to enter. It foreshadowed the day I would leave home, and the way my generation would be thrown into a whole new universe from hers, and the moment of her death when she would finally have to let me go forever. Of course, she was young then, much younger than I am now, and we had our whole life together ahead of us. She was the caretaker, and I was the child. It was another lifetime, a split second ago.

Life is like a firework display. Its beauty is in its brevity, its bursting quality. It would be no fun if it stuck in the sky, static and frozen, or if it went on for sixteen hours, like that TV commercial for one of those popular new drugs for erectile dysfunction where they say that if your erection persists for more than four hours, seek medical attention. Form is a magnificent expression of emptiness, bursting with love if only we can wake up and realize it.

Aftermath

The whole process of emptying out Mom's apartment was not the nightmare I had long feared it would be. In fact, like Mom's death, it was unexpectedly full of joy and even fun. It was a way to be with her and her life, sifting through her possessions, all the things she loved and treasured, and it was a further unfolding of the dying and grieving process as she faded out of her apartment, while simultaneously coming in over here at my place. I have some of her furniture, six paintings, lots of colorful pillows, several pots and vases, various little carved animals and birds, some quilts and blankets and shawls including the colorful Mexican blanket that my Dad had over him at the end, and then Mom had it over her on her last day, and now it is here in my place, warming me. Never in my life have I been this tired, this utterly exhausted. But my spirits are mostly good. I still cry, but not every day anymore. Spring is coming, and soon I will scatter her ashes.

Several people have told me that the worst grief can hit long after the death, when you finally finish all the tasks and there is nothing more to do. I'm going to a retreat in Springwater in April. It will be good to have a period of silent retreat to sink into the deep waters, for it does feel that death opens up a deep and fertile place, not a bad place by any means, although it can sometimes feel scary or empty.

I plan to scatter Mom's ashes at Springwater. I'd love to scatter them here in Chicago, on her home turf, in the park or at the beach, but in this post-9/11 urban world, I fear it might bring forth the HAZMAT team and the police and perhaps land me in prison. So, Springwater will have to do. After all, Mom did say that whatever I did with them was for me, not her, and scattering them there is like scattering them in my heart.

First Day of Spring

It is Easter Sunday, the day of rising from the dead, and on my morning walk, I see crocuses in bloom—the first—pushing up out of hard earth, and tears fill my eyes as I stop to gaze at the new life emerging from the dead world. The long winter is over. It is spring. The first spring without Dorothy. This week I will close her apartment, turn in the keys, never see it again. The rooms are quite bare now, although her purple jacket still hangs in the closet, and her wild fuchsia pants suit. These last few items will all be carted away tomorrow.

CHAPTER ELEVEN: Loving What Is, Letting It Go

Releasing Mom's Ashes

I have Mom's ashes with me on the plane flight to Rochester, in my backpack. It is a heavy load. Arriving at Springwater Center on an April evening, there is the sound of peepers—those small frogs whose chirping chorus is the welcome sound of emerging spring. Their peeping brings a rush of joy to the heart.

On an early morning before the retreat begins, a morning of immense quiet, blue sky and sunlight, I walk around the land, feeling out where to scatter Mom's ashes. After lunch, huge clouds arrive in the sky, giant white boulders. I load Mom's remains into my pack and head up to the north woods.

I am suddenly exhausted and achy, carrying this heavy weight on my back. The sun is disappearing and then reappearing. It is a long uphill walk to the northernmost part of the woods. When I get there, I am trembling with exhaustion. I see a butterfly—the first I've seen this spring.

I find a spot off the trail and drop to the ground. I pull the plastic bag containing her cremated remains out of my pack. I can't get it open. I finally cut it open with Mom's Swiss army knife, which I have inherited and brought with me. I dip my hand into the bag, feeling the texture of what is there, taking a handful of it, scattering it on the earth, dipping into the bag with my hand again and again, sifting out handfuls of ash, fragments of bone and teeth, scattering them on dirt, logs, lichen, moss, stones, scat and leaves.

I sit on the nearby bench afterward, my hand covered with traces of ash, the last traces of mother. I see the butterfly again darting around me. I breathe in the immense silence, the songs of chickadees.

I walk back finally through the woods, no more weight on my back. Light. When I emerge from the woods into the open field, huge white clouds float now in the blue sky, immense clouds. Looking back across the field toward the north woods, there is a ring of light—an eye—in the clouds, and tongues of white light rising from the woods where Mom is, and the eye above, and these huge clouds like boulders.

In the pond, I wash my hand. I see sacs of frog eggs and a few tadpoles under the water. Coming back down the hill to the house, Chippie the chipmunk is out for the first time, bright yellow birds are feasting at the feeder, flowers are blooming. Spring peepers are chanting and the sun is on my face, bathing me in warm light.

The next day, I visit the site where I scattered the ashes. There is dappled sunlight on the ashes. Chickadees are calling and answering. Mom is merging into leaves, moss, wood, scat, blue sky, air, sunlight—riding perhaps on the hooves of deer, the feet of raccoons and squirrels, the boots of retreatants who venture off the trail, the wind.

Retreat begins. I take evening walks after dinner with Toni up past the pond and into the north field. Toni walks slowly using two walking sticks. It takes a long time for her to get ready, to put on hat and shoes—like my mother in her last years. We talk of my joining the teaching staff, the people she is asking to carry on, and in the end, we come to a mutual decision that I'm better off on my own.

On our final walk, after the retreat, deer are everywhere in the red light, a blood red sun is visible between the dark trunks of the trees, sinking into the earth. Wood thrushes are singing. We sit in silence by the pond.

In the morning, I fly home to Chicago. Rain is predicted for Springwater, maybe washing Mom's ashes into the earth more and more. When I next return, perhaps they will be invisible, no longer separate in any way from the environment.

The trees in Chicago have exploded into green during my absence, and everything is in blossom—magnolias, redbuds, forsythia. Squirrels are building nests.

I visit Charlotte, Mom's oldest friend, who was there at Mom's deathbed. She has been moved out of her apartment in the retirement home and placed in a tiny room in the assisted living facility. It is very institutional. She is sitting on the bed. She says she feels lost.

She speaks of Mom's death and how it was the end of everything for her. Charlotte was an artist, now going blind, with a history of schizophrenia. Like the brilliant mathematician John Nash whose life was depicted in the movie *A Beautiful Mind*, Charlotte works her way every day through difficult states of mind with amazing courage, and now she has dementia as well. Mom's death hit her very hard. Now she is in this final End-of-the-Road terminal place, about which she can still joke in her wry and penetratingly honest way. I love her dearly. We have a heart connection I cherish. Although the situation sounds sad, every time I visit, when I leave, I feel this great joy and lightness, a buoyancy and clarity, as if I've been on a silent retreat. Proximity to death is truly a sacred time, and being close to it is a gift.

The Nursing Home Turns into the United Nations

It was hot and steamy in Chicago that summer, and the apartment building where I lived was sold. The old owner, who was Hispanic, never rented to Black people. There was the Mexican maintenance man and his family and, for a brief time, an Asian woman who was a psychiatrist. But otherwise, the tenants were all white. Most were elderly and had been there for many years. I was fifty when I moved in and, aside from the maintenance man and his family, I was the youngest person in the building. During the years I lived there, many tenants died. The fire department ambulance often pulled up out front responding to heart attacks, and many tenants were carried out on stretchers, some already dead. Others left for retirement communities and nursing homes. The building itself often felt like a nursing home, with all these old people, many using walkers. It was a quiet building. The only noise problem was from radios and TVs turned up extra loud for deaf ears. We had a number of Catholic nuns and ex-nuns in the building as well, and also a retired cop who drank himself to death.

When the building sold, the new owner began renting to people of color, to younger people, and families with children. A large family from Africa moved in down the hall from me, and other African

149

families were elsewhere in the building. There were people from India and Pakistan. There was a woman who wore a full burqa covered in black from head to toe except for a thin slit for her eyes. My next-door neighbors were a young Black couple with a rambunctious child and a loud stereo system. There was a Cuban lady downstairs who smoked cigars, and a large Hispanic family who seemed to be running a catering business out of their apartment. The smells of cooking food and cigar smoke permeated the building along with the screaming of children and the pounding rhythms of super-sized, surround-sound stereo systems. It sometimes seemed as if the whole world were contained in that one apartment building, bumping up against each other in the laundry room and on the elevator. And of course, until she was finally evicted and carried away, we had the crazy lady as well. It was no longer a quiet nursing home. It was a lively United Nations potpourri from all over the world with shrieking children, multiple languages, cigarette and cigar smoke, loud music and weekend parties. I was still, as far as I could tell, the only gay person who ever lived there. When the Black people and the people from all over the world began moving in, one white lady who had been there for many years was totally freaked out.

"They didn't used to allow them in this neighborhood," she told me in a whisper.

I told her I didn't care what color people were or what country they came from, as long as they were good neighbors. This white lady was actually good-hearted and deeply religious, and she performed incredible acts of generosity and kindness for many people in the building including me. But she was also a racist, and she voted for Bush, and I always prayed she wouldn't start talking about gays, because I was sure she was probably anti-gay, and then I would have to come out and stand up for us. But thankfully, she never did. Maybe she suspected. After I moved to Oregon, she wrote me letters for a while and I wrote back. We had a real fondness for each other.

Chicago was like that. I became deeply connected to many people I would never have imagined myself connecting with. My mother, after all, befriended people of every race, sexual orientation, political persuasion, religion or no religion, age, social class. She had the most amazingly diverse mix of friends you can possibly imagine. And there were the people from all over the world living in my apartment building after she died. The neighborhood where I lived had Hispanics, Blacks, Arabs, Indians, Pakistanis, Orthodox Jews, and Eastern Europeans. On one street, everything was in Spanish. On another, everything was in the languages and scripts of India and Pakistan. On another, it was all in Hebrew. There were Islamic centers, synagogues, churches and Buddhist temples within blocks of each other. And there was my job at the college, where I had students from all over the world and from low-income families and gangs. And there was Chicago itself, probably one of the most diverse and cosmopolitan cities on the globe. And while that wasn't always pleasant, it was something I loved.

Why not always pleasant? Because people from other cultures have different ideas about things. Sometimes other cultures have very backward ideas about people with disabilities, for example—we are thought to be a curse—and many cultures are deeply homophobic or patriarchal. I sometimes experienced people looking at me with disgust or aversion. One African man, who came to look at the apartment when I was preparing to move out, fled as soon as he saw me, without even coming in.

And of course, I didn't like the cigarette smoke, the loud noise and the now densely populated building with extended families crammed into one-bedroom apartments. I didn't like being in a world where many of those around me probably would have thought I should be stoned to death if they knew the truth about me. So, it wasn't always easy being in a multicultural environment. But I loved it at the same time, all these cultures rubbing up against each other, the energy and vitality of it. Sometimes the experiences were very positive. I got on wonderfully with the young Black couple next door and their daughter. And there was the Pakistani cab driver with a limp who would sometimes brush all the snow off my car early in the morning when he left the parking lot before me, and his wife, who studied English with me a few times and brought me dinner one night.

Grieving and Aging: The Dance Continues

I've been feeling a deeper wave of grieving over Mom. These waves come unexpectedly. This one has tears and sadness and also that desolate, empty, frightening feeling that hasn't been there in this grieving process before. It comes in the middle of the night sometimes.

Death, I realize more and more, comes in waves and layers. People die slowly. Not all people, of course. Jean died very fast, falling down the stairs. But Mom died in stages, as Toni and Charlotte and my friends Fran and Ed in the Bay Area are doing now. Grieving is a long, slow process that occupies much of the second half of life.

As friends and family members age, certain conversations and activities are no longer possible. Charlotte, who was a visual artist and jewelry maker, is losing her vision to macular degeneration and large parts of her mind to dementia. I am seeing my own friends losing things more and more. Several can no longer drive for one reason or another. Several have had serious memory loss. Several have hearing aids now. Tom has a serious heart condition that makes severe strokes more likely. The hands of another friend, also a jewelry maker, are getting increasingly arthritic, and another had to end his massage practice because of the pain in his hands. Another friend is finding it hard to keep working in construction. Oddly, the nation, the human species and the entire planet seem to be on a similar journey, as the climate heats up, species go extinct and human civilization threatens to crumble. What I notice again and again is that all of this can be very scary if I think about it, but without thinking, the problems vanish.

Toni emails me:

Hi Joanie dear,

Am convinced that humanity will not survive as we know it or would like to see it continue, unless a massive awakening (or "mutation in the brain cells") takes place, and that seems highly improbable. But then—what do or can we know? Plays have beginnings and endings, but the present one simply remains present, in whatever shape or form—forever present. Stop thinking and what is left? (Vast emptiness is a concept, and playfulness as well as seriousness are pleasant images... so what are we holding in head and hands.....

Love,
Toni

A hot green morning, dense and humid, the fan whirring, hot tea steaming in a cup, the birds silent and a single piece of Kleenex waving just slightly in the breeze from the fan. When I called Charlotte to see if I could visit, she sounded terrible and said I couldn't visit because she had run out of money and was being transferred to the county hospital, a fear I've heard her express before. I didn't think that sounded likely, so I called the nursing station, and they said no, she's just confused. So I went over in the afternoon. Found her in not great shape—the most fragile I've ever seen her.

She took my hand, led me into her room, and we sat side by side on her bed holding hands, as we often do, and she said she was having a very hard time. She said it was hard to breathe. I assured her she was not being moved to the county hospital and that she was okay. She seemed glad I had come, although she didn't want me to stay more than a few minutes.

The cicadas are buzzing and clicking away at an unbelievably loud volume. Fireworks are popping, the fourth of July is approaching. Middle Eastern music drifts up from the street in the evening along with the heat from the pavement. As I head out for a walk, two Muslim women are sitting on the front steps of the building talking and watching their kids play. I smile at one and she smiles back, a radiant smile.

Day after day, night after night, there's a vast open space into which I have been sinking in a very delicious way. Deep presence.

I dream about Mom all the time now. In one dream, I'm bringing her to the hospital—she's dying—and in the entranceway to the hospital, she collapses in my arms and says, "Don't take me in there, just hold me," and I do. And she dies.

First Anniversary of Mom's Death

As summer's luscious extravagance turns to fall, there is an especially bittersweet quality this year, because it was at this time last year when I knew in my bones that the end was coming fast. There will be Mom's birthday in October and then the first anniversary of her death in November. My beloved trees out front are full of tiny migrating warblers darting and hopping about, the leaves are beginning to turn yellow and gold, the air is suddenly cooler, the cicadas and grasshoppers that click and buzz in the late summer are silent now, almost entirely gone. The days are growing noticeably shorter. Soon the trees will burst into flame and then the leaves will blow off. The vibrant colors of summer and autumn will dissolve into the stark black and white of winter. The snow will come, the bitter cold, the long winter—and eventually, I will leave Chicago—stepping into my own old age and death.

The Chicago White Sox won the World Series. People sprayed each other with champagne and lit up enormous cigars. It hit the News the same night it was announced that Rosa Parks will lie in state in the Capitol rotunda, the first woman in US history to do so. It is an honor reserved mostly for dead presidents. I cried when I heard that. I remember when she wouldn't give up her seat on the bus, back when the Black folks had to sit in the back of the bus. I remember the world as it was back then. And now, some fifty years later, she is receiving the nation's highest tribute. Slowly but surely, one way or another, things do change.

On a gorgeous late October day, I go to the park. My friend Sandy is there. We talk. We traveled together, he and I, just before 9/11, to attend a retreat in California with Tony Parsons. Colored leaves are falling from trees. The sky is blue and empty. I don't know it yet, but in just a few years, Sandy will be dead. A slow procession of Asian Buddhists is winding down the path toward us, some in robes, coming from the Thai temple around the corner.

Last night we had a fierce thunder and lightning storm. The first explosion jolted me awake. My first thought was a terrorist attack. Then the sky flashed. Again, I thought bombs. Then another crash.

Another bomb? Finally I made the connection. Rain! Terrorism penetrates the brain in this post-9/11 urban world.

On the anniversary of Mom's death in early November, on the little table beside my bliss chair, I put a photo of her on her deathbed with the bubbles floating over her, and next to it a photo of her as a young woman all dolled up in a stylish coat, and a card she sent me years ago telling me she'd love me always, even after she died. A little anniversary altar.

Springwater: November 2005

In the north woods where I scattered Mom's remains, most of them have been absorbed into the soil or carried away on the wind. But in a few spots, they are still visible—a trace of ash, a few pieces of bone. I pick up one tiny fragment—a last trace of Mom's body. Hard to fathom that it was once alive as my mother. The owl cries out. Sunlight floods the woods, vanishes, comes again. I toss the fragment back into the leaves on the ground and look up to see a single leaf falling through the air.

In the middle of the retreat, I am sitting outside at dawn. The woman from Mississippi who survived Hurricane Katrina is sitting in the garden. We are the only ones outside. Dark ominous clouds are gathering, and then the rain comes, gentle at first, the blessing of a few warm drops, then hard. The woman from Mississippi and I both run for cover. Water sounds are everywhere now, gurgling, trickling, hissing, tapping, washing, splashing.

Chopping vegetables during the work period. Snow falls outside the window, the first snow of the season, floating down so gently.

Toni struggling down the stairs. Snow blowing past the windows. Pileated woodpeckers hammering the trees. Gunshots from hunters in the woods. Reflections rippling in the pond, and sudden squalls of darkness skirting the surface. By evening, the ground turning white.

I wake from a dream about my father. My roommate is snoring as if crescendoing toward an orgasm, then in wild arrhythmic bursts. I toss and turn.

The next day, feeling at loggerheads with Toni in a group meeting. Feeling this deep wound, this desire to run, contract, give up, slide into self-destruction and despair. Feeling how I want to throw a tantrum like a two-year-old—yell, scream, cry, stomp my feet. And then seeing how I do a subtler, more "adult" version of the same tantrum by not closing the door of my room quietly and carefully as we are encouraged to do, mindful that others may be sleeping. Instead, as a gesture of anger, I let the doorknob make this tiny clicking sound. Such a subtle gesture. I don't slam the door. Just this tiny barely audible little *click*—but I can feel the anger it in, like giving the finger to the whole universe. The middle-aged meditator's temper tantrum on a silent retreat.

Then at dinner, all this has dissolved, and I feel a huge soft tenderness for Toni and the ache of imagining her no longer here.

Toni reads Mary Oliver's poem about the empty hospital bed on the last day's reading. Tears come. Toni is saying goodbye. The retreat is over. People are leaving, the place emptying out. The little community is dispersing.

I spend an afternoon with Toni a few days later in the deep peace of her home. I read Mary Oliver while Toni naps and look out at the snowy dark fields. Toni emerges and announces we will go for a walk. We suit up. She provides me with a red sweater and a scarf knitted by a mutual friend. It is dusk, freezing cold and windy. She leads us out across the snowy, partly frozen lawn, over the icy driveway, and onto the road, walking with her two sticks like ski poles. Up the road we walk in the darkness, a freezing wind blowing through us. I am praying she doesn't want to go too far, but onward and onward we go, until finally she takes pity on me and turns us around. Afterward, we sit at her dining table. She light the lamps, and we talk over scones and tea. Where will I go? What will I do? she asks.

I tell her that I still sometimes imagine being at Springwater, and she encourages me to go forth, be on my own, be free. She says she hopes people will take the work elsewhere, to new places, not just have it only at Springwater. She tells me it is a blessing in many ways not to be named, not to reference anyone as your authority.

It was very close, tender. We are friends, Toni and I.

My last morning at Springwater I wake early and walk a last time into the north woods. Mom's remains are completely blanketed now in snow. Completely hidden. Vanished. Out of sight. Come spring, I wonder if any will still be discernible. Sun is coming through the trees, and the falling snowflakes are glistening with light, like millions of tiny jewels falling through the air.

Shock

I arrive home from the airport at dusk to find that both my beloved trees out front have been cut down while I was away. Totally gone! I moved into this apartment in large part because I loved those trees. They were right outside my fourth-floor windows, full of birds and squirrels and beautiful colored leaves every autumn, and it made my apartment feel like a tree house, as if I were living in those trees.

There is a huge empty hole now where they were. My wonderful little nature world of leaves and birds and squirrels is gone along with my privacy, my summer shade and the year-round buffer from the busy street traffic. It is a different world here, naked, bare and empty. I feel utterly devastated.

These two trees were dear friends, as were all the squirrels, doves, cardinals and migrating birds who nested and roosted there; and now they are all gone away. My mother is dead, Springwater is a world I've discovered I can only visit. Toni seems to be in that long process of saying goodbye, and my beloved trees are gone. Darkness comes and an awful grief.

But then I notice that a new view of the sky has opened up. I'll see the moonrises now. It's quite beautiful, the sky, as long as I don't think of my missing trees. In a way, it's the perfect way to celebrate the first anniversary of Mom's death.

But the grief comes again and again, the worst I've been through since Mom died, and the snow begins to fall, gently blanketing Chicago. The darkness is rather scary and immobilizing when it gets intense, and the grief is sometimes gut-wrenching. I feel rootless and lost.

Something one has deeply loved is suddenly irrevocably gone. It could be your mother, or a tree, or a family of squirrels you've grown to love as neighbors. It could be your own youth. This is the mystery and the gift of death. The grieving, when it comes, can neither be bypassed nor wallowed in. Cling to the disappearing forms—mother, tree, squirrels, youth—and you suffer. Avoid loving the present forms fully and you miss the gift.

Beyond the heartbreak, the empty spacious sky, the falling snow, the unreality of all problems. And then, in another moment, the wound is re-opened, the ache comes back, tears well up in the eyes, a host of scary thoughts erupt in the mind. It is a delicate dance, this breaking open. Loving what is, letting it go.

Toni emails me and gives a brief description of walking with her neighbor's dog Bailey, whom she dearly loves and with whom she has developed quite a rapport:

> *"I walk up the hill almost every evening, and Bailey is running with me for a while, then ahead, then left into the fields, then right, then back to me, always somehow in touch."*

I felt it was a metaphor, consciously or unconsciously on her part, for my relationship with her.

Disintegration

I visited Charlotte today. She'd been moved to the Alzheimer's unit on a different floor, the unit for advanced dementia, and she was pretty disoriented. But she knew me, and she kissed me and held me. She is the last person still alive who knew me when I was a baby and who knew my mother before my mother was married, the last person who will ever tell me I'm just like my father. But she may already have forgotten my father. She does remember Mom. She said she'd been dreaming about her.

"Mom's waiting for you," I told her. Did I say that? Yes, I did. After all, it's true in some bigger way, and although this survival of the personal self is a child's version of the truth in my view, it's the version most people still believe, so I offer it spontaneously, as comfort.

Charlotte is in a shared room now, which I had feared would be awful, but it really isn't. It's big and nicely divided into two very private spaces, and her roommate is utterly silent, motionless and almost invisible. Charlotte has the side with the windows—big beautiful windows and lots of light, so it feels quite spacious and open.

I cried once, when she wasn't looking, but otherwise did okay. She smiled faintly, took hold of my arms and leaned forward to kiss me before saying, "I need to escape now. Where should I go?"

My task now is to remember the code I have to punch in to get the elevator when I leave. The patients can't get on unattended from this unit, hence the code. Charlotte had taken to wandering from her previous unit and was found once in the basement, huddled in a corner, terrified and lost. So I must remember the code to be able to leave. No small feat.

Outside my apartment, the pigeons are sleeping on the window ledge as I write this. The trees across the street are bare, their branches waving in the wind. The naked empty space where my beloved trees once were is full of light and blue sky and clouds. Life rolls on.

Days on end below freezing. Snow pours through the air, a soft curtain. Months go by.

I found Charlotte a bit more confused when I visited one day. She told me Mom had visited earlier in the day. Mom looked great, she said, and Charlotte was relieved to see her because Mom hadn't visited in a long time, and Charlotte was beginning to think Mom was mad at her. Charlotte also expressed fears of being moved to the basement. She said it was hard to tell dream from reality. Sometimes what she conjures up is quite amusing. For example, she told me that she's being cared for by a tribe of Africans who live in the US now. We attended a sing-along together. She walks with more difficulty and says her legs hurt, but she smiled a few times, finished a bowl of ice cream after the sing-along, and let me stay for a whole hour, much more than she usually tolerates. And she's very loving. Sadly, after she died, I learned from her daughter that Charlotte thought I was stealing from her. Such paranoia often comes with dementia. It happened to Mom once, too, when she became convinced that two of her close friends were out to get her, a thought-form totally out of character for her.

A friend from California tells me on the phone that my friend Ed, of Fran and Ed, the couple who hosted my meetings in California, was on the floor again after yet another fall. He couldn't get up because his legs wouldn't move. He slept on the floor beside his bed for several hours. He refused to let Fran call for help. Eventually, after Ed dies, Fran herself will end up stuck on the floor for several days after a fall—discovered, luckily, by the gardener just in time to save her life. From there, she will go into a nursing home and be bedridden for the remainder of her life. But for now, they are both still alive and living at home, but from what I hear, they are crumbling.

The trees are still bare, but they are budding now. The forsythia is ready to emerge. There are the first tiny green leaves on the hedges. Everything is poised, hovering, ready to explode. All we need is a week of warm days and a good thunderstorm and spring will burst into blossom. But for now, it is still a bare landscape and the earth is still brown. The Canada geese in the park are wildly excited over something, honking madly, and the ducks are swimming around amidst the garbage that humans have thrown into the pond.

Another day and Charlotte was very happy—and amazed—to see me. She was amazed I had "found" her. She asked me how long it took me to get to her. I said twenty minutes. She looked incredulous, smiled wickedly and said, "How fast were you driving!?" It gradually became apparent to me that she thought she was in Kansas, her childhood home. "Wherever I go, you manage to find me!" she said incredulously. She told me that she needed to find Angela, her long dead sister, because they had to get packed—they were going home tonight. I played along, wandering around the nursing facility with her in search of Angela. We attended a party in the common room, a lively affair with music (Vivaldi), little plates of cheese and watermelon, and semicomatose Alzheimer's patients nodding off. Although one lady was quite chipper and verbal and discussed the arrival of spring with me. Charlotte had several gashes in her forehead that had been treated, and she told me she'd had a fall. Charlotte is slipping away, but still walks around with her walker, manages a bit of conversation, and plots her trip home with Angela.

In the park, ducks are mating. Standing on their heads. Jumping on top of each other. Sunlight sparkles on the water. Spring is coming. A squirrel is drinking from a drain pipe.

Yesterday they planted four small blossoming trees far below my windows to replace my beloved old locusts that were cut down last November. New life takes root. Things change. Life goes on.

I dream of Josette, the therapist with whom I sobered up in the 1970s, and in the morning I google her and discover she died on Christmas, 2002. The brain tumor finally got her. She was only a year older than I am.

Chicago Spring

Baby ducklings the size of half dollars shoot through the water in the pond like little rockets, while slightly larger goslings are trailing their mother out on the grass. It is warmer but still deliciously cool, sparkling with light, and these marvelous newborn ducklings are cheeping and speeding thru the water.

When I saw Charlotte and mentioned Mom, she looked blank. She thinks her husband and her sister, both of whom are long-dead, are somewhere nearby, and she keeps searching the hallways for them. A table of old ladies, all with severe dementia, were gathered in the dining room, across the room from us, whispering to each other in loud booming whispers that I could hear perfectly, talking about me, saying what a lovely man I was, with such a nice smile. When I left, as I waited at the elevator, I could hear one of the aides telling them in a loud booming voice, "She's not a man, she's a girl. That's Charlotte's daughter." So, if Charlotte weren't already confused enough, she should be even more confused now. I guess those old ladies in their dementia could see right into this transgender, non-binary soul of mine.

On TV that night, Oprah was doing a documentary with Elie Wiesel, the two of them together at Auschwitz talking about the

Holocaust. On a commercial break, rather unbelievably, there was an ad for a cream that heals scars, with a beautiful young woman demonstrating it on her flawless skin. This struck me as rather emblematic of the dissonance so common in our culture—one moment we're hearing about the latest mass shooting or the urgent, life-threatening crisis of climate change, and the next moment we're hearing about the exciting new iPhone or the new season of *The Bachelorette*. We're at war, but unless you happen to be in a military family, you'd hardly know it.

Springwater in June

Toni is clearly in terrible pain much of the time. It is poignant to see this person who was once so amazingly vigorous slowly and painfully shuffling along with her three-pronged cane. On the retreat, she is barely audible in group discussions. Being around Toni nowadays is like being with Mom in those final two years—it's being in the presence of death, disability, disintegration and loss, watching the body and mind of a beloved teacher and friend crumbling away, disappearing. Not surprisingly, this scene is not drawing big crowds, so retreat attendance has fallen. It feels to me like the whole place is dying.

The retreat lasts a week, but it all occurs Now. And what is it? Sensations, smells, tastes, textures, sounds, the rise and fall of breathing, the flickering thought-movies that come and go, the shifting weather, outer and inner, the baby raccoons I see running up a tree, the pieces of Mom that have survived the winter, the wild turkeys flushed suddenly from a field, the fragrances in the early morning, the blinking fireflies at night that light up the dark fields, the turtle whose head pops up periodically from the skin of the pond, the twanging frogs, the humming buzzing insects, the singing chipmunks. There's no holding onto any of it. Nothing can be grasped, all of it disappears instantly, utterly inconceivable and ungraspable. And everyone there is on a totally unique and different retreat, each with our own movies of what is transpiring, and yet, at the same time, mysteriously, we are all one whole happening, One Mind, One Body.

Back in Chicago afterwards, the cab driver from the Sudan who drives me home from the airport talks about Africa, and on my answer-ing machine is the news that another friend in California has died.

Another Goodbye

Back from the gentle, delicate, soft, tenderness of Springwater, here in Chicago, I see children being smacked in the head and bullied by their over-worked, over-wrought mothers, homeless people with twisted toothless faces, crazy people yelling at the wind. My apartment smells awful, like a bar, from traffic exhaust and the secondhand smoke of other tenants. But I also see the wonderful diversity and mixing of cultures that urban life in a large cosmopolitan city affords. Driving along, I see a small band of Hare Krishna people in their orange robes coming up the street in a largely Hispanic neighborhood wholeheart-edly singing bhajans and beating their tambourines, and no one even seems to notice them.

Back to the News of the world—the wars, the posturing, the insanity, the playing out on a global scale of all the things one sees in oneself on a retreat.

In the park in the morning, teenage boys, loud and violent, pass through on skateboards yelling obscenities. The signs that the park district has posted telling about the wildlife have been graffitied over with gang symbols. Trash litters the ground. Still, the leaves sparkle with light and there is beauty everywhere.

And then Charlotte's daughter calls me to tell me that Charlotte died in the night. Luckily for her, she died before reaching the final and more comatose phases of the disease. I'm sad that she is gone. I had planned to go see her that day. But she is no longer there. She has vanished like so many others, and yet, she lives on in my heart and in my memory.

Grieving really does take a couple years. You think it's over and then another wave hits. I'm grateful for those friends who encouraged me to go on silent retreats, get massages, take walks in nature, and otherwise nurture myself. Grieving is a special time. It's like an open window or a door, a door that keeps opening it seems.

CHAPTER TWELVE: Closing the Book

The Woman in the Flag Scarf

I watched a movie called *Forgiving Dr. Mengele,* a documentary about Eva Kor, a survivor of the Holocaust from Romania. When she was a young girl, after a seventy-hour train ride without food or water, Eva and her family, including her twin sister, arrived at Auschwitz. On the selection platform, the twins were spotted by the SS and immediately taken from their mother, whom they never saw again. They were both used by Dr. Mengele for his horrific experiments, such as being injected with potentially lethal strains of bacteria and not given treatment. The movie is about Eva's decision, very controversial in the Jewish and survivor communities, to forgive Dr. Mengele and the Nazis. She's also engaged in dialog with Palestinians.

She is now living in the US, selling real estate, and often wearing an American flag scarf, the very same one a dear friend had sent to me once as a joke, since I'm no fan of flag-waving patriotism. As I watched Eva selling houses wearing that scarf, I realized with pain in my heart that she is someone I might have judged rather negatively if I'd seen her on the street, viewing her perhaps as a foolishly patriotic old lady. To realize what her life had actually been like and what she has been through and survived, and what she's doing in her life now, was to see this person in the flag scarf in a whole new way—one of those powerful moments when you suddenly see someone in a totally new light, seeing below the costume and your own interpretation of it. I saw all my own prejudices about that costume and how those prejudices would have misled me.

Closing the Book

*Keep on
dissolving like
ice in warm water.*

—Mooji

In September, I'm back at Springwater. Toni is like a fierce Zen master on this retreat, like Nisargadatta—ruthless. Anything you pick up, she says, throw that away. Anything she describes—wholeness, presence, whatever—she immediately says, throw that away, too. Don't hold onto anything. She speaks of closing the book on the past, on the encapsulated little self. "Stop holding to this little thing," she says. "You are vast. Close the book on this little thing, and in that closing, there is an opening—the empty page." Freedom. Space. Vastness. Stop following the *"yes, but's"* in the mind, she says. Close the book. Be the vastness you are.

The silence is so palpable, the immense quiet, the natural world so vibrant and full of depth. This fresh page, this empty mind *is* God: "A way of seeing in which everything is perfect," as Toni put it. That *seeing*, that infinite intelligence, that unconditional Love, that vast awaring presence beholding it all—accepting everything and clinging to nothing—*that* is God. It's not that the cruelty and horrors in the world are perfect as they appear to us; the perfection is in the way of *seeing* them, the unconditional love beholding them, the no-thing-ness of them, the seamless unicity in which everything goes together perfectly, the non-clinging to any viewpoint, any idea, any memory, any interpretation. Closing the book on all our ideas, not holding to anything, not knowing what anything is—*that* is God, that vast open presence, which is actually all there ever is. That vastness is free to take any shape, and no shape endures.

We are here together learning to close the book. We can't really say how we do it, any more than we can say how we ride a bike, drive a car, lift our arm, open our hand, swim or walk. And closing the book is a newer, less familiar movement, like those we learn in Feldenkrais. We are learning slowly to open. The old habits return—grasping, clinging, controlling, defending, seeking, resisting—but the new possibility is also there, and gradually, over time, the balance shifts. And, of course, "we" aren't doing *any* of this. It is all happening by itself. Ever-fresh. Ungraspable.

The fields are full of goldenrod and wild flowers, milkweed, buzzing insects, delicious fragrances. A few pieces of Mom remain on the wet earth in the north woods where I scattered her ashes, a few tiny bits of bone still discernible. But slowly, she is dissolving back into the earth, like a dream.

At night, sitting in silence, the delicious sounds of rain, wet and playful, soft, delicate, cleansing, opening the heart.

On the last day, Toni reads from Nisargadatta: *"There is no progress in reality...the source of light is dark...seedless and rootless...without cause, without hindrance."*

Words, like the hands of a skilled bodyworker, can draw your attention to something previously unseen or overlooked. Something is illuminated, touched, revealed by the word as by the touch of the bodyworker—awareness floods the area, light comes into the previously darkened room, a flame is ignited in the heart. And then, throw that away, too. Don't hold onto anything.

Whenever I get the urge to drop the whole spiritual thing altogether, which I periodically do, it seems to be one of those little dharma bells—*ding ding*—waking me up to the fact that I'm lugging around *something* that would best be dropped, and it might not be spirituality, but rather the *ideas* I have about it. After all, the real heart of spirituality, at least as I mean it, is about dropping everything, moment to moment. Not clinging to anything. So when I'm feeling fed up with the whole thing, perhaps it is a good time to ask myself what exactly I'm thinking "the whole thing" is.

The Jewel in Disillusionment

I dreamed that Mom and I were dancing together, ballroom dancing, and we knew the end of her life was very near. In fact, it seemed as if the end of the song was going to be the end of her life. So this dance was incredibly precious. And it was infinitely tender and sweet and a little sad. I also dreamed that I was setting up house in a new place, I'm not sure where, but I remember realizing that it was okay to move.

A friend gave me a CD of Gangaji called "The Jewel in Disillusionment" from a retreat she gave not long after it was revealed that her husband Eli, who is also a satsang teacher, had been having an affair with one of his students, after which he developed a serious cancer. On the retreat, Gangaji pairs people up and has them take turns asking and answering a set of questions to see what comes up. One question was, "How do you want things to change?" I found myself saying that I want to be confident and sure of what I'm doing, and I want to be openhearted and not hurt and defensive and angry and depressed and fearful. I want the war in Iraq to end, and Islamic and Christian fundamentalism to disappear, and all their adherents to wake up. I want the world to deal with climate change and factory farming to stop, and on and on. And then Gangaji asks, "What if *none* of this ever changes as you want?"

I'm sitting with that, realizing how freeing that is, to accept myself and the world as it is with all the contradictions and unresolved problems and horrors and upsets—not needing it to be any different. That doesn't mean not trying to make changes. But at the same time, being at peace with the way it is—imperfect, unresolved, often painful and unjust.

Meanwhile, a gigantic green grasshopper is climbing slowly up the glass outside my window, the biggest grasshopper I've ever seen.

Depression

I listened to a talk by Zen teacher Ed Brown that someone gave me, and it touched my heart. Ed speaks openly of being depressed and about being a spiritual teacher with depression. And he doesn't bring it all to some inspirational conclusion but ends with the simplicity of being here in the unresolved rawness of life just as it is.

It was a relief to hear a talk by another teacher who was openly acknowledging depression. Thankfully, more and more teachers are beginning to disclose these kinds of things and talk about them openly.

People who have never experienced depression often think it means you feel sad all the time, and you just need to be cheered up. But that may not be it at all. For one friend, it manifests as irritability. For me, it manifests mostly as feeling overwhelmed by life. And for most people, it includes a variety of symptoms such as fatigue, loss of appetite, trouble sleeping, and so on.

I've had waves of mild depression off and on over much of my adult life. I've never had major depression—the kind where you can't even get out of bed and you feel seriously suicidal. I've had only what they technically classify as mild depression, but it doesn't feel particularly mild when I'm in the grips of it.

The worst it ever got was probably in Chicago, several years after my mother died. Imagine that you have five-pound weights strapped on all over your body, but you don't know they're there. You just know that the simplest activities seem to take enormous effort, that you are exhausted, that everything feels heavy, difficult and overwhelming. You sense that it is not like this for everyone else. That's how I felt.

There was a sense that I was going under, that I was drowning, that life was sweeping over me. I was often fatigued. I was having a hard time eating. I'd feel hungry, but I had a hard time cooking—it seemed too overwhelming—and then whatever I tried to eat seemed unappetizing once I started eating it. More and more of my once-favorite foods were nauseating me. I'd gag trying to eat them. Nonessential mail was piling up unopened in bags in my closet. It was unimaginable to me how I would ever be able to leave Chicago—the logistics of packing up my apartment and my storage unit seemed utterly overwhelming.

I was eating at least two and usually three meals every day of reasonably healthy food. I was getting up in the morning and making my bed. My bills were all paid on time. My rent was paid. My emails were answered promptly. I was holding meetings. I was writing. I was keeping my apartment reasonably clean and tidy. I was seeing friends. I wasn't suicidal. But it definitely felt as if I were walking around with heavy weights.

At some point, my doctor suggested I try Zoloft, an antidepressant. I'd never taken an antidepressant before. For many years, I was totally against antidepressants. I felt they were being overprescribed and overused as a way to avoid difficult emotions that are part of life. I thought that Big Pharma was pushing them on the public for profit. I'd seen my schizophrenic aunt ravaged by psychiatric medications and shock therapy all through my childhood, so I was wary of psych meds in general and concerned about the side effects. I'd even been active many years ago in an organization called Women Against Psychiatric Assault. In addition, I had the belief common among many spiritual people that we "should" be able to rise above depression, anxiety, addiction, compulsion and all psychological and emotional problems through meditation, insight, awareness, being present, and "being here now." Certainly, if you were "awake," you wouldn't have such problems.

Toni Packer was much more open to psychiatric medications, perhaps because she came from a family of scientists, and her husband Kyle had been a chemist before becoming a school principal. Toni felt it was quite reasonable to think that neurochemistry might be involved in our moods and psychological states. During my years at Springwater, my mind had opened up to these medications a bit more, and I'd heard from a number of retreatants who told me that antidepressants made it possible for them to engage in meditative work. I came to see that sometimes, before we have the energy, the will and the ability to even begin this kind of practice or exploration in any sustained or effective way, a certain level of neurochemical smog must be cleared away first. So, in working with Toni and listening to others who used antidepressants, I had become more open to this possibility; and when my doctor in Chicago suggested Zoloft, I agreed to try it.

It was amazing! Taking Zoloft was like having the weights removed. I felt full of energy. Nothing seemed overwhelming anymore. I zipped through those bags of unopened mail in one day. The kinds of thoughts that bog me down when I feel depressed or anxious were completely absent, and if one of those thoughts *did* pop up, it was *instantly* seen through, transparently absurd—*it had no sticking power*. My appetite improved. Food tasted good again. I felt free and unbound, energized and alive. It was as if some inner—psychological or perhaps neurological—muscle that had been paralyzed was set free. It was truly wonderful.

But I began to experience serious neck and arm pain, and then muscle weakness in one of my arms and in my only hand. It turns out this muscle weakness is an uncommon but reported side effect of Zoloft. I had to go off the drug. I wasn't on it very long at all.

But amazingly enough, it jump-started me. A few months later, I moved to Oregon. In reflecting on how this jump-starting happened, I thought about how the process of change is described in Feldenkrais, a form of somatic awareness work I've studied. They say in Feldenkrais that, through the Feldenkrais movement lessons, the body discovers new ways of moving, and once discovered or brought into awareness, these new ways become more and more available to us. In times of stress, the body may revert back to the old constricted ways of moving, but the new possibility is there and, over time, it becomes more and more stabilized. That had always seemed to me like a good description of the awakening process as well, and now it seemed to me like a good description of what Zoloft had done. The antidepressant had shown my bodymind and my nervous system a new way of functioning and, once that possibility had been discovered, brought into awareness and embodied, it became more and more readily available.

I had a similar experience some years later when a somatic therapist I was working with called my attention to my posture as I was talking about feeling like a failure. I noticed I was somewhat slumped over, curled in on myself and shrunken. My therapist had me shift my body to the way I hold myself when I speak of feeling strong, free and happy. When I did that, the body opened and straightened up. Next, she had me go back and forth between the embodied posture of failure and the embodied posture of feeling joyous and strong. She had me move between these two postures more and more rapidly, over and over. My therapist commented that she could feel the difference in the room with each one, that it affected her as well. Of course, we know that intellectually, but it was profound to hear it.

Not long after that session, I was feeling overwhelmed by a task that seemed completely impossible, and I suddenly remembered this exercise. I noticed I was slumped over. I deliberately moved my body into the powerful posture and, to my surprise, I was immediately able to engage the task, no longer feeling overwhelmed. It seemed that what the whole bodymind had learned from that exercise was that I had a choice. It felt very similar to how Feldenkrais works—it opens up a new possibility.

In the end, I was grateful I had those side effects from Zoloft, because otherwise, I might still be taking it. I've learned since then that many therapists now use antidepressants very conservatively and sparingly, as a last resort, prescribing as low a dose as possible for as short a time as possible, on the very jump-starting principle that seemed to inadvertently work so well for me. Of course, some people may need to be on psych meds permanently, and that's fine too when needed. There is nothing wrong with needing medication.

What happened to me on Zoloft was a visceral, direct lesson in how powerful biology and chemistry can be. By simply changing my serotonin levels, certain thoughts no longer popped up, and on the rare occasions that they did pop up, they had no power, no believability. Of course, many other things have also been helpful: meditation, psychotherapy, The Work of Byron Katie, Feldenkrais, Zen, Advaita. I'm sure they've all helped immensely. But clearly, a change in serotonin levels had a huge impact. And it makes sense. In my view, the mind affects the body, and the body affects the mind—it goes both ways. Bodymind is one whole happening, not two separate things.

Years later in Oregon, my dentist suggested I might have sleep apnea. Dentists often alert people to this now because they can tell by the features, shape and size of your mouth, tongue and airway, and by asking a series of questions, that it's a likely possibility. For example, I have a large tongue and a small mouth, I snore, and I have experienced both fatigue and depression—all common indicators.

Sleep apnea means that many times every night your airway closes and no oxygen goes to your brain. While this can lead to death, that's rare, because usually the body finds a way to wake the person up, often without the person even realizing how many times they've been awakened. But if it goes untreated, the brain is oxygen-deprived every night and crucial REM sleep perpetually disrupted, perhaps for decades. Apnea can result in fatigue, depression, brain fog, digestive problems and a greater likelihood of developing dementia, stroke, heart disease, diabetes, and a host of other problems.

At the time my dentist suggested this to me, I didn't follow-up since my health insurance at the time wouldn't have covered it, and I hated the thought of being on a CPAP machine, which I imagined was huge and noisy and would entail wearing a giant face mask—none of which is actually the case anymore.

Some years later, after I was on Medicare, my urogynecologist suggested I might have sleep apnea. I got tested. I've slept ever since with a CPAP machine and these sweet little "nose pillows" in my nostrils shooting air into my nose. It has changed my life significantly for the better. I definitely feel it further alleviated my tendency toward depression.

Who would imagine that the size of your mouth and tongue might be a cause of depression? What I've learned is that many factors play into our inner weather—genetics, neurochemistry, enzymes, hormones, brain injuries and abnormalities, trauma, childhood conditioning, socio-economic conditions, life experiences, sleep apnea, the hormonal changes of menopause, and so on. And if we ignore all of these and think that meditation or awakening or "being here now" can cure everything, we are missing something.

Just as Seattle has more rainy and cloudy days than Tucson, some bodymind organisms have more depression or anxiety, a greater tendency to addiction and compulsion, less impulse control, more ADD, or whatever it might be, than others. And, as with Seattle and Tucson, it's simply a difference in conditions and conditioning. It's simply weather. It's not personal.

Certain conditions have been stigmatized and personalized for too long, the cause too often attributed solely to lack of insight, failure to "be here now," false identification as a separate self, or even failure to "suck it up" and "be a man" (or a woman). It has sadly often been assumed by many in the counterculture that the only acceptable cure for depression or anxiety is spiritual or psychological work, or maybe acupuncture, homeopathy or herbs—anything other than allopathic medication.

I'm not arguing for or against antidepressants or other psychiatric medications. There are clearly many different and conflicting views on the efficacy and safety of these drugs and, as with any medication, there are almost always—if not always—side effects to weigh in the balance. If you can avoid medication—given the side effects and the expense associated with it—it is certainly preferable, but not at the expense of being perpetually miserable or unable to function. So if you need medication, please don't think it is a sign of spiritual failure. I continue to urge all of us to keep an open mind, ready for new discoveries, not just defending our favorite tired old ideas.

My Last Winter in Chicago

Ed, of Fran and Ed, the couple who hosted my meetings in California, died on Christmas Day. My friend Valjean in Chicago was diagnosed with lung cancer. She is my age. Our mothers were friends who lived in the same building, and we went through their deaths together. Valjean was at my mother's deathbed, holding one of her hands when she died. Valjean is a writer and a Zen student in the lineage of Joko Beck, so we have much in common. We both had pain on the same day not long ago that we each thought might be the symptoms of a heart attack. Mine was pain and numbness going down my left arm, and hers was chest pain. We both went to our respective doctors to have it checked out. Mine turned out to be the side effects from Zoloft; hers was lung cancer.

I got an email about a retreat with both Gangaji and Eli in Ashland, Oregon in January called "Facing Everything: Realizing the True Capacity of the Heart," and I immediately felt this urge to go. I was a student and devotee of Gangaji back in the 1990s, early in her teaching career. This seemed like a perfect opportunity to see her again, be on a retreat, and explore Ashland as a possible place to live. A friend had told me about it, and it sounded promising. I signed up quite spontaneously, without thinking about it for more than a few seconds.

It was snowing like crazy after I pushed the button on the computer to register, big huge white flakes pouring down, really magical.

Facing Everything

The retreat was wonderful, and I loved being in Ashland. There was a huge snowstorm and the city was buried in snow all week. Every morning, before the first satsang, I'd walk in Lithia Park, a beautiful park in downtown Ashland that runs along a rushing creek through woods, and it was a winter wonderland in the snow. It was as if I had found the place I had dreamed about since childhood.

Ashland is a small city in southern Oregon, right over the California border, inland from the coast, in a valley surrounded by mountains. It's a rural area, so as you drive around town, you pass fields with horses and cows grazing. There is a lot going on spiritually and culturally, people seem to be progressive, openminded, educated, intelligent. It has acupuncturists, naturopaths, satsang teachers, a Zen Center, a Tibetan Buddhist temple with lesbian lamas, organic farms, art galleries, a university, and it's the home of the Oregon Shakespeare Festival, which is nearly year-round world-class theater, not just Shakespeare, but three different theaters with plays of all kinds. There are four distinct seasons but not as extreme in winter as Chicago or Springwater, and lots of sun, not overcast and rainy like Portland and Seattle and what people usually think of as Oregon weather. And it's not too far away from all my old and dear friends down in the Bay Area, only about six hours by car. It has a great food co-op and wonderful independent bookstores. It seemed like a good fit. So, right there in Lithia Park one morning, I knew. At long last, I was making the move out of the Heartland.

Leaving Home / Returning Home

I returned to Chicago to pack up and say goodbye. I watched a movie one night that Toni had recommended to me recently, *Nowhere in Africa*, about a Jewish family who flee from Germany to Africa to escape the Nazis. When they first come to Africa, it's a strange land. But when they leave Africa at the end of the film to return to Germany, they have grown to love Africa, and it is hard to say whether they are

175

leaving home or going home. In fact, they are doing both, as I am doing now. I am leaving my mother, my childhood, my birthplace and my youth behind me, going home to the West, into my old age and finally my own death.

My Chicago friends were magnificently generous in helping me pack up, and finally the movers came and emptied out my apartment. I would drive my car, loaded with a few of my most vital things, across the country.

It was a cold, rainy morning when I left Chicago. My dear friend Tom came to wave me off, and I watched him disappearing behind me in the rear-view mirror. And then I was on the open road, heading into the future.

Part II: Oregon

2008 – 2019

CHAPTER THIRTEEN: The Beauty of Everything Falling Away

Returning to the West

Driving across country is an epic journey. It gives you a visceral sense of how far you're going. You feel the ground covered, the prairie turning to mountains, the open spaces, the continental divide, the salt flats, the desert, and ever-changing weather—sun, wind, blinding snow.

I had rented an apartment in Ashland sight unseen over the phone with some help from a friend in Ashland and, when I arrived, it was as wonderful as I had imagined. It was a small one-bedroom apartment above the office of a hand surgeon, with windows on all sides looking out on the mountains and blossoming trees. After weeks of packing, weeks of unpacking.

The Downward Slope

The distance between the Joan who moved to Chicago in 2000 and the Joan who left Chicago in 2008 is immense. In that stretch of time, so many people dear to my heart had died, and I had watched up close as bodies and minds disintegrated before my eyes. I had gone through menopause and begun to experience my own bodymind aging in a much more palpable way. Soon after arriving in Ashland, I turned sixty. Suddenly the future, that vast and seemingly infinite place of possibility that had always stretched out ahead of me, that place where my real life would finally happen, was no longer there, and instead, the future seemed to promise only the gradual disintegration of mind and body, the long slow process of loss and decline that I had watched my mother live through. It is an interesting stage of life, this doorway to old age. You're still relatively intact and functional, but things are beginning to give out, and you know what's ahead, although there's still an astonishing capacity for denial.

Fran, who once hosted my weekly meetings and accompanied

me on long hikes in the East Bay hills, is now totally bedridden in a nursing home with the shades drawn. She declined very quickly after Ed died. My friend Heather had a stroke, can't handle too much talking, has difficulty reading, and can no longer track TV shows or movies with complex narratives. People in our age group always seem to be dealing with some injury or medical problem. Knees and hips are giving out, bones are growing more fragile. We're all noticing varying degrees of cognitive decline and problems with memory. Physical pain, to one degree or another, seems to be a feature of old age, as does a decline in energy. Things we did effortlessly in our twenties and thirties now seem to exhaust us completely. Many of us have survival concerns about money and whether we'll have enough or be able to earn enough in our later years. And we all know in an ever-more visceral way that this vulnerability and loss will only increase. We're not getting younger, we're getting older.

Late middle age, on the cusp of old age, is a strangely liminal time. I can feel both the desire to die, to relax back into the darkness from which I came, and the will to live both present within me. The movie of waking life is like the ocean's play on the surface, while at its depth, the ocean is dark and silent. We love the adventure of being a wave, roiling and dancing, moving this way and that, especially in our youth, and then, more and more as we age, we love relaxing back into the deep, melting into shapelessness, dissolving back into the vastness that we have never actually left.

Unlike my youthful future fantasies of a new and improved me, my ruminations about the future these days are more likely to be focused on strokes, dementia, cancer, broken hips, and how I will manage if one of these things befalls me. Back then, in a new place, I'd be checking people out to see who might be a potential lover, and now I'm checking them out to see who might make a good power of attorney to pull the plug on me and settle my estate. After my mother died, I realized I was next in line. When I arrived in Oregon, I bought a prepaid cremation plan, spelled out instructions for disconnecting my life support, purchased a copy of *Final Exit: The Practicalities of Self-Deliverance and Assisted Suicide for the Dying*, should it be needed, and in many ways prepared as best I could for either the slow disintegration or the sudden ending that lay ahead of me in the no-longer-too-distant future.

I'm on the downward slope now and I know it. Even if this downhill course contains a few more exhilarating and triumphant uphill moments, I know in my bones which way this train is headed. The signs are unmistakable—my hair is getting whiter, memory is becoming less reliable, the plumbing is leaking, the joints ache, the bones are thinning, the hearing seems not quite as keen, digestion is sluggish, my vagina has dried up and is disappearing, the enamel is slowly wearing off my teeth making it sometimes surprisingly painful to eat, sleeping through the night is a distant memory. The body is sagging, drooping, bulging, wrinkling and drying up. Death is coming closer, beginning to track me. I can feel it.

Valjean Dies

My friend Valjean in Chicago was on oxygen and had gone into hospice last I heard. Then one night, I knew she had died before I got the news the next day. It was just six months since her diagnosis. Another one down.

Barack Hussein Obama

When I was growing up, it would have been unimaginable to think a Black man would be president in my lifetime or that gay marriage would actually be legal in America when he left office eight years later. Even in 2008, it seemed questionable whether enough white folks would actually vote for a Black president, especially one with a name that sounded like a cross between Osama Bin Laden and Sadam Hussein. But he didn't let that story of impossibility stop him.

Watching Obama accept the nomination, and then eventually be elected, was amazing for someone my age who grew up in such a different era. It was beautiful to see the diverse, multiracial, intergenerational crowds that showed up. It was beautiful to realize how much has changed in my lifetime around race, gender, sexual orientation, disability and old age. Not to say we still don't have a long way to go, but this event would have been utterly unimaginable when I was growing up.

I didn't imagine that Obama could or would solve all our problems. I knew he was no radical socialist, and that in many ways it would be business as usual. I knew he had to walk a delicate tightrope as the first Black man in the Oval Office. I knew that the forces of bigotry, ignorance, class privilege, racism, patriarchy, homophobia, nationalism, imperialism, disaster capitalism, greed, delusion and dualistic thinking were still alive and well, and it soon became clear that the Republicans would block and undermine him in every way they could. I knew that Obama would disappoint me in many ways, and he did. But still, to see a Black family moving into the White House was something breathtaking, just as it was to see the White House lit up in rainbow colors a few years later after gay marriage was legalized. And it was wonderful to see a president who seemed to be an intelligent, well-educated, openminded, thoughtful and nuanced person.

Fighting for Your Limitations

I attended two small weekend retreats with Gangaji in the first years after I moved to Ashland. On the first night of the first one, she called everyone up one at a time to be introduced and to say something about why we were there. When she called me up, she said to everyone, "Joan is also a satsang teacher." Suddenly, with all eyes upon me and with those words unfolding in my mind, it seemed that "I" contracted down and became "Joan," rather than the boundless presence that I had unselfconsciously been moments before when I was not thinking about myself, or being looked at and talked about as "Joan the satsang teacher." At first, there was a rush of pleasure at being recognized by Gangaji as a fellow teacher, but then instantly, my body contracted in fear. Thoughts came flying up. Now I would be scrutinized as a satsang teacher and could not just be another anonymous person at the retreat. "I'm not good enough to be a satsang teacher," the thoughts told me,

"I'm a fraud, I shouldn't be doing this." I wanted to disappear.

The next day, at one of the satsang sessions, a woman was talking about her very harsh internal critic. Gangaji suggested to the woman that she agree with her inner critic—agree with everything it says. This is not the usual approach, but I began to try it out on myself that night, and I found it amazingly liberating and hysterically funny.

I went up during satsang the following day and told Gangaji what had happened when she introduced me as a satsang teacher and how I'd been playing with agreeing with my inner critic, and how liberating that was. I began telling her, with absolute relish and glee, "I'm a fake, I wasn't ready when I started doing this teaching thing. I started way too soon, and I'm still not ready. I have no idea what I'm doing, it's obscene that I'm doing this, I'm a totally fucked up mess!" Everyone was laughing, I was laughing, Gangaji was laughing. She said that *I'm a Totally Fucked Up Mess!* would be a great title for my next book and that she was looking forward to reading it. It was wonderful. Agreeing with one's inner critic in this way reveals how absurd and irrelevant those critical voices actually are. When we embrace the darkness, it turns into light.

At the second of these small retreats that I went to a year or two later, Gangaji challenged me to stop endlessly confessing my flaws. As she said, it's great to be able to see them clearly and know what they are—that's very important—and it's wonderful to share them openly as a way of helping others to feel more at ease with their own imperfections and less inclined to idealize me as a teacher. That's all great. She has always loved my honest self-disclosure, so I didn't take this in any way to mean that she thought I should stop revealing my human side. But as my friend Chuck Hillig once said, "You are fighting for your own limitations, and there are no limitations."

In the past, I'd often heard Gangaji say, "Tell the Truth." And by that, she didn't mean confessing our sins and imperfections. She meant telling the deeper truth that we are this totally free, empty, boundless presence that is not limited or imperfect in any way. She would say that it was safer to be "just little ol' messed up me" than to tell this bigger Truth. Why? Because being "little ol' me" sends out a certain protective message: "Don't criticize me, I'm already criticizing myself. Don't hit me, I'm already down. Don't expect too much, I'm a mess. Say something kind to me, I need it." It's a way of hiding and staying safe, keeping ourselves small.

When confessing my imperfections becomes a way of identifying as the little "me" and reinforcing some deficiency story about that fictional character, I'm only cementing those old stories of failure, lack and not being good enough. I'm cementing a false identity and hiding out in the safety of being "just little ol' me." It's safer to be a fucked up mess than a satsang teacher. The latter carries the risk of being criticized or challenged, whereas, if you confess your flaws, people won't expect too much. You'll be safe. As in my slumped over posture—small and protected, curled in on myself, incapacitated.

Honesty about our humanness is important, to not deny our humanity or make the false claim that no me-thoughts, troubling emotions or delusions ever arise anymore, because that's pretty much always bullshit. But we don't need to make ourselves small either. And we can always notice, with any thought or anything we say, whether we are speaking as the little self or as boundless presence. Where are we locating ourselves, in other words. Sometimes it's appropriate to speak as Joan. But sometimes, it's a way of hiding and denying the bigger reality.

As soon as I imagine that *Joan* is giving satsang, holding meetings, writing books, giving talks, or anything else, things tend to go badly. Because, of course, Joan isn't doing any of it. When there is simply unbound, open presence, there is no problem, no me, no better or worse. Things flow. They emerge from wholeness rather than from apparent separation.

Remembering to Breathe

I've been crewing on a local access TV show, working the big TV camera, and also writing and holding meetings and watching movies and reading books and taking walks and biting my fingers and taking photographs and drinking tea and tinkering with my website and sitting quietly and doing laundry and eating and sleeping and so on.

Squirrels have been cavorting and having wild sex on my balcony. Tiny buds have been unfurling.

High above the earth in the International Space Station, American, Russian, European and Japanese men and women work together as they circle the planet once every ninety minutes. Americans fly there on Russian spacecraft, launching and landing in Russia. We've come a long way since the Cold War, although before long, we'd be told once again that Russia is our enemy. But for a brief moment, the Cold War seemed to have ended.

Yesterday a large asteroid narrowly missed hitting the earth. It was closer to us than the moon.

On the local news last night, I learned that there is a statewide neo-Nazi group based in a small town just up the road from Ashland, between here and Medford. Apparently, they call for White Pride, deny the Holocaust, and want immigrants, especially Mexicans, out of Oregon. It is chilling to see people wearing swastikas and waving huge swastika flags right next door. The white supremacist right wing seems to being growing more menacing. Hate groups are on the rise, fueled by their distress over the election of Obama.

And then Dr. George Tiller, a beloved doctor in Kansas who ran a women's clinic that performed abortions, was shot in the head in church by one of these radical "pro-life" folks. Dr. Tiller had been shot before and had recovered, his clinic had been firebombed, and the death threats and harassment were unending. But this time it was fatal.

I look out the window and see white clouds floating in blue sky, spring blossoms, new green leaves. And I remember to breathe.

Jekyll and Hyde

I flew to Toronto to give a weekend event, and before the events, the organizer and I drove down to Springwater for a visit. I had two meetings with Toni in her bedroom, where she is in bed almost all the time now.

It was like Jekyll and Hyde. On the first day I visited her, she was a cantankerous old lady with a bit of dementia, a wildly exaggerated version of her worst tendencies—incredibly negative and judgmental, her face screwed up with a look of utter disapproval, complaining about everyone who was helping her.

The next day, she decided to hold a bedside group meeting, and we all gathered around her bed. She was Toni at her best—open, loving, clear, transparent, luminous, right on the mark. And luckily for me, that was the last Toni I saw in person.

To her credit, Toni was always aware of these two sides in any human being, herself included. I'm told that she once read aloud to the staff a letter that she had received from her niece, a letter in which her niece expressed disbelief that the author of these books about awareness and open listening could be so controlling, picky and critical in person. Toni apparently told everyone on staff that this was very important, that when there is awareness, there is clarity and love, and when the thinking mind takes over, there is the conditioned personality. Her husband Kyle had insisted that she always attend post-retreat dinners so that people could see her as a regular person.

This is actually a huge part of the teaching, and I feel very lucky I got to live with two of my teachers, Mel at Berkeley Zen Center and then Toni. Otherwise, when you only see teachers at their best, leading a retreat or giving a satsang, it's so easy to idealize them and make them into idols. In many ways, I did that anyway! I had Toni way up high, and then periodically, I'd have to knock her down a bit. Poor Toni, alternately revered and then toppled, never knowing which side of *me* might appear next, Jekyll or Hyde. We *all* have both sides.

We start out with the idea that the spiritual path is about becoming perfect, and we have all kinds of ideas about what that would look like—no more unwanted thoughts, no more emotional upset, no sense ever again of being the separate self, no more suffering, a perpetual good mood, always radiating love and joy, a continuous sense of oneness. And we project that imaginary perfection onto teachers and gurus, and sooner or later, they disappoint us, which is actually a great thing if we don't immediately run away and start seeking a new perfect teacher. In our attempts to perfect ourselves, we fail again and again, which is also a great thing. Of course, some people claim to have succeeded, which usually means they are the most deluded of all. Eventually, gradually, evermore-deeply, we seem to realize that this journey of waking up isn't about becoming perfect in the ways we had imagined, and we realize that no human being is beyond human foibles.

Darkness and Light

I google an old friend in New Mexico thinking that I'd like to get in touch, and her obituary comes up. Liver cancer. The dead are mounting.

On the anniversary of Mom's death, I wake up in the middle of the night laughing out loud in my sleep. I dream I'm in the town where I grew up and I'm carrying my mother's body, which is the size of a child, to the bed she shared with my father in the home where I grew up. I place her on the bed, which is now her deathbed.

I've had many strange dreams lately, dreams about dying. Sometimes I'm up drinking chamomile tea in the wee hours with energy coursing through my body.

On the Winter Solstice, the darkest day of the year and also the day when the light begins to return, the cat across the street and I, both in our respective windows, are watching the snow falling between us.

In the spring, Joko Beck died. And I heard from a friend at Springwater that Toni was bathing in an inflatable rubber tub on the bed now, singing, with a yellow duckie.

Everything Falling Away

My first lover and I both moved to Ashland at the same time, unbeknownst to each other. Lydia was the woman I came out with while we were in college in New York during the 1960s. We had stayed loosely in touch ever since and had seen one another a handful of times when we both lived in California. But during the years that I was in Chicago being with my mother, Lydia and I lost touch. As it turned out, she had been in a serious cycling accident—she was a triathlon competitor—had gone through multiple surgeries, could barely walk, had been in a wheelchair for a while, got melanoma and almost died from the last treatment option, which left her in a coma for weeks.

When we finally discovered each other in Ashland, the melanoma was in remission, but she told me that if it came back, they were out of treatment options. Lydia and her partner of the last twenty-some years, a doctor named Theresa, had bought a condo in Ashland, initially so that they could come here for theater getaways, but now they were moving here full time. Theresa, who was quite a bit younger, had found a job as a hospitalist in Medford.

For a brief time, Lydia and I had a wonderful renewal of our friendship. But then the melanoma came back, and I spent the winter of 2011 and 2012 being with her as she died.

When she knew beyond any doubt that she was dying and that the cancer was in her brain, Lydia signed up with the organization here in Oregon that assists people in legally terminating their own lives. She asked me if I would be there with her when she drank the medicine that would end her suffering, because Theresa didn't want to do that. I agreed, and I filled the prescription for her.

I drove her to her radiation treatments in Medford on many mornings, palliative radiation to the brain. And on that drive one morning, she said to me, "It's so interesting how everything is falling away."

As her illness progressed, she said many times again, "It's so interesting how everything is falling away." In the end, she never drank the Magic Brew that would have ended her life. And everything did fall away.

The former triathlon competitor was using a walker, and then we were feeding her, and then she was in bed unable to get up. The brilliant woman who had been a writer couldn't always find words anymore, and the words came less and less frequently. Eventually, the Foley catheter was put in, and she could no longer swallow. In the end, she was completely unable to move, unable to speak. It was not unlike being with Mom in her last years, watching them both lose one ability after another, until all semblance of independence and control had been stripped away. And strange as it may sound, both times, as this process unfolded, my own fear of this loss of control fell away. As in spiritual awakening, you lose everything. And you discover there is nothing to lose.

It was an amazing circle to go from first love—that passionate, fiery, erotic love charged with desire and jealousy that Lydia and I had back when we were in our late teens and early twenties—to this love at the other end of life that needed nothing and that embraced everything. It struck me how both these forms of love were equally earthy and fleshy and full of body fluids and physical intimacy, and yet, in such utterly different ways.

The last week before she went into active dying, Lydia wanted lobster, so Theresa had lobster flown in from Maine, and we all sat around eating lobster dipped in warm butter with asparagus. Theresa and I were feeding Lydia at that point, because Lydia could no longer feed herself, but she could still swallow. Lydia was in total bliss eating that lobster. As we devoured the lobster, some especially grisly crime program was playing on the TV. Lydia and Theresa both loved *Weekend Crime Mysteries* and old reruns of *Law & Order*. It was a scene I never could have imagined, and yet it was so beautiful.

During the daytime, MSNBC, a cable TV channel with mostly progressive political news and commentary, played constantly. It was the season of the Republican presidential primaries, so all the shows were focused on that. I am someone who cannot stand to watch TV in the daytime, especially in the morning, so this was a big adjustment. I would never have imagined that nonstop TV featuring grisly crime dramas and endless political commentary on the Republican presidential primaries could be a peaceful backdrop for someone's deathbed, or that I would actually grow fond of it, but it was surprisingly perfect and peaceful. I would even say, it was totally spiritual, because really, what isn't?

The spiritual world is full of ideas about how you should die and how you should deal with pain. Many spiritual people think you should die with harp music playing and candles flickering softly, and some believe you should avoid palliative care or antidepressants and deal with all forms of physical and mental pain only with meditative awareness. But Lydia died with MSNBC and *Weekend Crime Mysteries*, both of which she loved, and with morphine and expensive wine that she sipped from a water bottle.

Theresa cared for Lydia with great tenderness, occasionally affectionately calling her a douchebag. Their two beloved cats, known as The Horribles, slept in the bed with Lydia, their faithful dog curled up on the floor beside the bed. Hospice workers came and went, and the room always felt exceptionally peaceful and full of love, MSNBC and all.

Lydia was in active dying for an entire week, mostly unconscious, with long pauses between breaths and blood moving through the catheter tube as her kidneys failed. Having been a high-performing athlete, her heart and lungs were in great shape, so as everything else failed, it took these vital organs forever to shut down. As Theresa joked, there are advantages to being out of shape.

On the day when Lydia finally died, I had gone home for lunch, and Theresa had gone to the Co-op to do some shopping—the first time Theresa had left the house in days. The hired nurse was the only one there when Lydia died, and strangely enough, that nurse died a few weeks later, quite unexpectedly, out of the blue. Theresa and I sat on opposite sides of Lydia's cooling body, her first love and her last love. We cried, made irreverent jokes, and Theresa chanted the Heart Sutra.

The blossoming trees burst into blossom all over Ashland the last week Lydia was alive, and the day she died it was snowing furiously, one of those last spring snowstorms with the big white flakes.

Wanting to Live Forever and Having the Right to Die

We spend our whole lives trying to stop death. Eating, inventing, loving, praying, fighting, killing. But what do we really know about death? Just that nobody comes back. But there comes a point in life, a moment, when your mind outlives its desires... Maybe death is a gift.

—David Gale in *The Life of David Gale* by
Charles Randolph

I see fliers for an "Anti-Aging Workshop" here in Ashland, and in a magazine I read about a person who thinks age is a "disease" that we can "cure," allowing us to live forever. Another article in the same magazine describes someone who wants to keep our minds alive in computerized form. It all sounds grotesque. I'm all for doing reasonable things to optimize health and well-being, but a world of billions of perpetually young humanoids with perfect plastic bodies and computerized brains living forever on an increasingly crowded planet doesn't sound good to me. And looking upon aging as a disease that we should be "against" strikes me as one of the saddest perspectives I can imagine.

I love the seasons of the year, and I love the seasons of life. It seems to me that eternal springtime would completely destroy the very thing that makes springtime so precious and magical. Part of the beauty of winter, or old age, is the very stuff that these people seek to eliminate—the loss of control and mobility, the increasing limitations and challenges, the ending of everything known. Part of the beauty of a flower is its impermanence, its vulnerability, its fragility. A world of eternal plastic flowers and eternal plastic people doesn't sound appealing. Why does someone want to live forever? And why are we so anxious to keep people alive as long as we possibly can? There comes a time when death is a welcome gift and a natural event.

In fact, I'm a big supporter of the right-to-die movement that is working to legalize physician-assisted dying. While I've found real beauty in the limitations and challenges that come with aging, at the same time, I don't see any reason why people should have to endure horrible pain and/or suffer years of dementia or profound disability if they would prefer not to, thus sparing themselves and their loved ones weeks, months, years or even decades of misery and expense. Some people say only God can make such a decision, but I don't believe in that kind of God, and even if I did, the reality is that people wouldn't live so long in the first place, and be in such dire shape, if human intervention weren't making it possible through advances in medicine.

One of my aunts, a brilliant woman who taught school and traveled the world, spent her last years mostly lying in bed in a nursing care facility, moaning in pain, with nursing aides forcing food into her mouth at mealtime and changing her diapers and ostomy bags. She clearly no longer wanted to eat. The bodymind wanted to die. She was ninety-nine and had survived colon cancer and several severe strokes. But they would literally force her to eat. I protested during one of my visits to Chicago—this was long before I lived there—and they told me they were legally obligated to do this. People kept enthusiastically telling my aunt she'd live to be a hundred, as if that were an important and valuable accomplishment. I told her on my last visit that it was okay to die, that she didn't need to live to be a hundred. She expressed gratitude for my saying that. A few weeks later, she was gone.

When you are facing a long process that may include such things as unending excruciating pain or being semicomatose on morphine, regular grand mal seizures, vomiting up excrement or parts of your organs, and/or being terrified because you don't know where you are and you can no longer remember anything, is it really so hard to understand why you might prefer to die? We're often kinder to our pets than we are to our fellow humans in this regard. And is it really so hard to imagine why you might want to spare your loved ones from witnessing that kind of suffering or having to take care of you if it *was* a burden for them? Or why you might want to spare the taxpayers the burden of paying for you to live through this hell?

Yes, I have tremendous gratitude for the opportunity I had to be with my mother and others at the end of their lives. That was certainly no burden for me, and in fact, it was a great gift. In my case, moving across country to be with my mother didn't damage my ability to do the work I do. I was single so there was no partner or family to consider. I fully appreciate that caretaking and being with a dying loved one can be a profound experience, as it certainly has been for me. But I've also witnessed a number of women friends go through a whole decade or more of caring for a mother with Alzheimer's, setting those friends back financially in the process, disrupting their careers and their relationships, and bringing them endless heartache. If I were their mothers, I would have wanted to spare them that. It wasn't the beautiful journey I had with my mother, and it came at a very high cost. If I were diagnosed with Alzheimer's, I'd want to spare *myself* that as well!

My mother had a daughter—me—and she had financial resources. And being an extrovert, she had a host of younger friends. My situation is quite different. As a much more introverted and reclusive single woman with no partner, no siblings, no adult children and very few younger friends, I may very well be relying primarily on friends who are my age or older. If I live to be eight-five, many of them will be ninety or older, maybe already dead. How are we all going to care for one another if one or more of us has a stroke or gets dementia? I don't have the money to hire caretakers and nursing aides for more than a very brief time. If I end up in a nursing home, I will soon be wiped out financially, living at the mercy of what the state has to offer indigent people, which is often not the best. The taxpayers will be footing the bill for me to live in pain. And unfortunately, this is exactly where more and more of us are ending up in our final years. None of us want to end up here, but most of us do now. And we call this prolonged nightmare, the kind my aunt endured, a "natural" death, and we insist that this is somehow spiritually and morally superior to ending your life more quickly, even though in wild nature, without modern medical intervention, no one would ever survive long enough to endure such prolonged misery.

People who want to die and are determined to do so will end their lives anyway, but why make them do it in a dangerous way that leaves a hideous mess for their loved ones to find, or that might leave them still alive but even more impaired? Why not allow it to happen in a way that is medically safe, reliable and comfortable? Why do we think this is "unnatural" or "spiritually wrong"?

Those who feel it is against their religion to end their own lives at a time of their choosing certainly don't need to do it, but must they impose their religious beliefs on civil society? In fact, no one is ever *forced* to do this. *On the contrary,* you have to jump through countless hoops to do it legally here in Oregon. You must be over the age of eighteen and in sound mental health, several doctors must sign off on it, there's a waiting period to insure it's not a passing mood, you must be terminally ill with a life expectancy of no more than six months to qualify, and you must be able to lift the glass yourself and swallow the brew. No one else is allowed to help you administer it. This right to end your own life doesn't apply to teenagers who are terminally ill and who would like to end their lives comfortably, or to people with Alzheimer's or with severe chronic pain or other conditions that are not immediately terminal, or to people with conditions such as locked-in syndrome or a severe stroke that have rendered them unable to administer the drug to themselves without assistance. In other words, it's *very* limited in scope and heavily regulated. But under those very narrow and limited conditions, adults who are terminally ill do have the right in Oregon to choose a quick and comfortable death over a long and painful departure, and it's one of the reasons I live here.

Many people end up doing what Lydia did. They get the drug and have it on hand but never end up taking it, but they are comforted by knowing it's there if they want it. One person I know did use it in the end, after enduring much pain, and it was a very peaceful way to go. Another friend had a terminal degenerative condition that would have meant years of increasing pain, loss of mobility, frequent seizures, serious cognitive decline and so on, but he didn't qualify for the right-to-die here because his life expectancy was years rather than months, so he elected to self-terminate, which was much harder on him and on those left behind. Why do we make it so hard?

In this country, the biggest opposition to physician-assisted dying comes from religion and, very sadly, from the disability movement, in which I was once actively involved. I have thus written articles, speaking as both a spiritual person and a person with a disability, in favor of right-to-die. The doctor who delivered me back in the 1940s gave my father the option of smothering me when I was born without a right hand, so I fully understand the fear that people with disabilities have. But in regard to legalizing physician-assisted dying today, I think it's an unreasonable fear. The right-to-die laws in the United States are incredibly narrow and carefully crafted, and I feel quite sure that it's not going to lead to a mass genocide of people with disabilities. It certainly hasn't led to that in any of the places where physician-assisted dying has so far been legalized.

I worked in the independent living and disability rights movements, and I've known many people with very serious disabilities, including intellectual disabilities and severe physical disabilities of all kinds—people who are living happy, creative, fulfilling lives. I'm obviously not in favor of snuffing out everyone with a disability. I certainly don't feel that Helen Keller or Stephen Hawking would have been better off dead. But each of us will differ in how much pain and disability we're willing and able to tolerate. Why shouldn't reasonable adults be able to make this decision for ourselves? Death is not the great boogeyman. It's a natural part of the life cycle. Since modern medicine keeps us alive longer than we would live in the wild, why not allow it to also give us a merciful death *if we so choose?*

I wish we had the same rights here that they have in countries like the Netherlands, Belgium and Switzerland where these laws are much broader. If I get a diagnosis of Alzheimer's, for example, I would like to have the right to end my life in a comfortable way. But unfortunately, we have too many zealous fundamentalist Christians in this country, not to mention a disability movement that has increasingly aligned itself with the religious right, and a Republican Party that favors individual rights and small government when it comes to controlling guns, but full-on government intervention when it comes to reproductive and end-of-life decisions. And now Trump has appointed a judge to the Supreme Court who wrote a whole book against physician-assisted dying. That does not bode well. America is a strange country indeed. We tolerate people having semi-automatic assault weapons and carrying out mass murders on a fairly regular basis, and we still execute criminals, sometimes wrongly convicted ones, but heaven forbid some senior citizen should elect to die comfortably rather than waste away in a nursing home in pain.

Everything Is Sacred

I attended a weekend retreat here in Ashland with Anam Thubten, a marvelous Tibetan Buddhist teacher who radiates love and freedom.

His talks were all about the beauty of being lost, and how samsara is nirvana. He said, if you don't know you're lost, then you're really lost. He spoke of Mother Theresa as a modern-day bodhisattva and how beautiful it was that her diaries, after she died, revealed how lost she was. He says the freeway traffic, the bad air, the golden arches of McDonald's are all part of the spiritual journey, all sacred.

I flew afterwards to London where I did a number of events. My first event was in the upstairs of a pub, with the sounds of Friday night revelers drifting up from the street below.

I return home to find that my landlord, the doctor whose office is below my apartment, is retiring. He sold the building quite unexpectedly while I was in London. No one has told me if I'll be able to stay or if I'll have to move, and no one seems to know.

Meanwhile, they've started a huge remodeling project downstairs below me, and we have had repeated middle-of-the-night malfunctions of the security alarm—a deafeningly loud, ear-piercing, nerve-wracking, alarming sound going off over and over, night after night. Then during the day we have hammering, banging, loud machines, vibrations, fumes, nerve-shattering noises of all kinds, the alarm being set off again and again, fire trucks arriving, police—generally, noise and chaos and no word on my fate. Ah, the symphony of life! The dance of Shiva!

I went through several months of this, a long stretch of uncertainty and headaches, fumes and noise, and finally they tell me, I have to move out.

New Home

After a long search, I found a place way up in the hills at the edge of town, looking out over the mountains. Moving is a giant adventure in chaos, exhaustion, being uprooted, and going through Kafkaesque scenarios while trying to disconnect and reconnect utilities and so on.

And now I am in my new home. Hawks glide past the windows. Rainstorms sweep through. I hear deer hooves crunching softly on the gravel drive, the morning breeze kissing the leaves, the sounds of quail. I feel the deep peace of the rolling green mountains in my whole bodymind, and the deep silence. I feel very blessed.

CHAPTER FOURTEEN: All for Your Benefit

The Final Word

When I called Toni Packer on her birthday that summer, she sounded faint, and it turned out to be the last time I would ever talk with her. The very last words I heard Toni speak, at the end of this final conversation, were, "I have to go to the toilet now." A perfect finale to a long and wonderful relationship, and the perfect final words from your beloved spiritual teacher. I'm not sure if she was addressing me or the aide, as the phone was clearly slipping from her ear and mouth as she spoke.

Buddha died of diarrhea or food poisoning, and so many teachers have died of cancer—Nisargadatta Maharaj, Ramana Maharshi, Krishnamurti, Shunryu Suzuki, Katagiri, Maurine Stuart, and so many others. Toni's final years have been much occupied with the mundane and painful concerns of a disintegrating body.

I hear soon after that Toni has been taken to a nursing home where she is now in hospice. Last I heard, the pneumonia was not subsiding and could be fatal. Sometimes she can only speak German now, I'm told, her first language, and she cannot use her hands at all anymore. People from the Springwater community are visiting steadily and sitting with her, so she is not alone.

The Dance of Loving and Letting Go

Now all my teachers are dead except silence.

—W.S. Merwin

As Toni was dying, I was on a weeklong silent retreat with Anam Thubten. He is a big fan of Toni, they have met, and he holds her in the highest regard. And oddly enough, there were a surprising number of people on this retreat who had worked with Toni and been deeply touched by her. A friend at Springwater sent regular updates from Toni's hospice room to this small group, and we would all huddle around the phone every day to watch these little videos of Toni and the people gathered at her deathbed. Being on a silent retreat and seeing these videos, it felt like we were in the room with Toni all week, breathing with her. I kept sending her love. It seemed incredibly serendipitous that so many of us who had sat together at Springwater and at Toni's retreats in California were sitting together again the very week she went into active dying. Every day we'd be told by the people at her bedside that this was probably the last day, but then Toni would survive another day. When the retreat ended, she was still alive.

On the retreat, Anam Thubten talked about our humanness. He is so wonderfully down to earth and honest. "I'm distracted all the time during meditation," he says. This isn't about not having any more darkness, doubt or imperfection. And in fact, that's exactly the place where we find the light. Perfection can only be found in the imperfection. Nirvana can only be found in samsara. He spoke of the importance of humor. Love is losing everything, he said. Any states of spaciousness or clarity will come and go. Not to attach to any of it. Non-attachment is not detachment, he says, and he speaks of the dance of attachment (or love) and non-attachment (or letting go, not clinging to anything). Awakening doesn't mean pulling away from life—detaching or dissociating—it means loving fully, but not holding on, not clinging.

We do walking meditation outside as the sun goes down, single file down this country road. A horse gallops excitedly across a pasture to greet us. I feel my love for the beauty around me (attachment) and then letting it go as we walk on (non-attachment)—the dance of attachment and non-attachment, loving and letting go.

When you're on a silent retreat, the group becomes a little community. You become deeply bonded in some way. You are sharing something deep and profound. You are opened up, undefended, unmasked. You are eating together, sleeping in the same building, sitting together in silence, going into deep waters. There is a real intimacy that develops, perhaps even more so in silence, without words, names and all the surface stories. And when the retreat ends, suddenly this little community dissolves—everyone goes their separate ways.

On the last day of the retreat, Anam Thubten weeps as he speaks of communities coming together and dissolving, of the places he's been, here and in Tibet, of his teachers who are all dead now but in his heart. And I think of Toni on her deathbed, Joko who is already gone, my mother and father who are gone.

There are many little deaths in a single lifetime. We leave home to go to college, we leave college to go out into the world, we leave a house where we've lived, we move to a different city or a different country, we leave a relationship or a marriage, our children grow up and leave home, people and animals we love die, our youth disappears behind us, we leave a job or retire from a long career, a retreat ends. Every moment is a little death. The previous moment, and everything that came before it, is gone forever.

Returning to Ashland, making my way through all the emails that came while I was away, I learn that another old friend died. He and I had coordinated many of Toni's California retreats together, a beautiful man.

And then Toni died. She died peacefully on an evening in late August, surrounded by some of her oldest and dearest friends. I'm relieved for her that she is free from her difficult situation, and happy the end was peaceful, that she was surrounded by so many loving friends. I also feel a weight has been lifted from Springwater that will free up the energy there—it has been so focused on her in these last years. Whether they can dance with that energy and survive, given the small staff and all the other difficulties, we shall see. But I am hopeful. I see great potential and possibility.

I spent a week at Springwater, attending the memorial. Members of her family from Europe were there as well as many of us who had been her students, or friends as she preferred to say. We all sat in silence, heard a recorded talk by Toni from one of her retreats, sang and ate together. Later in the day, anyone who wanted to participate was invited to a scattering of Toni's ashes down at the little waterfall, and her son held out the bag of ashes and anyone who wanted dipped in and took a handful. I scattered some. And several people took small containers of them to put elsewhere, at Point Lobos in California, and even in the Ganges in India.

In addition to celebrating, honoring and remembering Toni and her life, the gathering was a wonderful reunion with a great many dear friends whom I hadn't seen in many years, and also with that land which I love so dearly. But above all else, the entire week was a meeting with Toni, realizing all over again how truly marvelous and rare and profound she was, and yet how simple, how unpretentious, how open and ordinary in the best sense of that word.

I've noticed that, however far afield I wander, I always come back to Toni and Springwater and the bare simplicity and openness of presence. That is the spirit that lives on at Springwater Center, where others are carrying on the work that Toni began, holding retreats and providing a space where people can look and listen, alone and together, in an atmosphere that is refreshingly open and free from religious tradition and dogma. It was such a deep joy to be there again, in such wonderful company, absorbing the stillness and silence and warmhearted community that pervades the place.

I needed to leave Springwater to find my own voice and to fully appreciate Toni's depth, and she was amazingly generous in allowing me to go every time I did.

New Year

Every year over New Years, I take three or four days, sometimes a whole week, to be in silence by myself. This year I had a marvelous retreat—lots of quiet sitting, some on my meditation cushion and much of it in my comfortable armchair, gazing out at the mountains and the clouds. I went for daily walks, did some house cleaning—but no TV or computer, no phone, no socializing, no reading, no music.

My friend d (he goes by the initial "d") has been overseeing the care of our mutual dear friend Fran, who is now bedridden in a nursing home. He emails me:

Spent two hours at Fran's bedside with zealous realtor going over papers related to house sale, with Fran's semi-conscious roommate being wheeled in and out. The roomie's 100-year-old husband waiting to feed her, as he does when he comes in every day, after saying a very, very long grace and then singing "Jesus loves you" into her ear, while simultaneously the 25-year-old guy in the room around the corner from Fran, who lives in a wheelchair, continued to vocalize his groans and screams. The TVs in nearby rooms trying to drown it all out... signing, initialing, signing, initializing, and Fran lying in bed trying to follow it all.

These are the Fellini-like scenes you find yourself in during your sunset years.

What Happens to Women after Menopause

I was so thrilled when Jane Fonda and Lily Tomlin started talking openly about vaginal dryness and vaginal atrophy on their TV show *Grace and Frankie*. We are bombarded with articles about how to stay young forever, and there seems to be a huge push to keep people sexually active in old age. The reality is that men can't get it up anymore, and women dry up and lose interest, but God forbid we should stop having sex, so we take drugs and use lubricants and keep on pretending we're still twenty-five. And, of course, some old people do genuinely enjoy and want to have sex, but many older couples are quite content just to snuggle.

The truth is, for most women, life after menopause means osteoporosis, vaginal dryness and vaginal atrophy. Skydiving and passionate sex with penetration are not viable or enticing options. The whole vulva changes after menopause. Things seem to recede and disappear. The vagina dries up. The tissue in the vagina becomes paper thin. Particularly if you haven't ever given birth or used your vagina much in recent years, it begins to close up. Vaginal stenosis they call it, or vaginal atrophy. Suddenly just putting something the size of a regular tampon in there can bring pain and even blood. Some women report no longer being able to reach orgasm. Most notice a steep drop in libido. And for many of us, urinary leakage begins to happen more and more.

If you're a young woman reading this, this may all sound dreadful. It certainly would have to me back then. Leaking urine and a dried-up vagina would not have been a happy thought. And if you had told me back then that I'd lose all interest in sex and be happily celibate for decades, I would have stared at you in utter disbelief. Sex was very important to me. But surprisingly, it's an amazing relief to be free of all that. Many of my women friends who are in relationships with men tell me that they would rather not have sex anymore, but their male partner still wants it, so they do it for him.

I've had vaginal stenosis, atrophy, dryness and urinary leakage since menopause. I had heard about a surgical procedure that could fix leakage, so I went to see a urogynecologist, but she told me there are different kinds of leakage with different causes, and the kind I have, which is caused by the vaginal atrophy, is not fixable by surgery. Instead, I wear leakage pads and use estrogen inserts twice a week to help with the atrophy. I do that not so I can have vaginal sex, but to help with the leakage and to maintain my urinary function. And as it turns out, wearing bladder leakage pads isn't all that bad. You get used to it.

I often think now about my mother and wonder if she had any of this going on. I suspect she did, but no one ever talked out loud about what happens to women's vaginas and vulvas, and I was clueless back then. It also makes me realize the full horror of what happens when old women are raped or gang-raped, as they sometimes are.

Why am I putting such intimate material in a book and revealing such personal things about myself? Because it isn't really that personal; it's very common. It's just been hidden and unmentionable for too long. We're much more aware of the problems faced by men as they age—erectile dysfunction, prostate cancer, enlarged prostate, difficulty urinating. Old age is no picnic for either gender, and feeling it's shameful doesn't help.

Yes, people make jokes about Depends and old people drying up, but then it happens to you, and it might not seem so funny anymore, except when Jane Fonda and Lily Tomlin take it on. But they're not laughing *at* us, they're laughing *with* us.

This disintegration of the body is a great lesson in the transitory nature of physical glamour, sensual pleasure, athletic prowess, cognitive agility—everything to do with form. It all turns to dust. And that's not bad news. It's an invitation to discover what is deeper than form, the presence that is always whole and complete.

Spring Bursts Forth

At the nearby Nature Center, I saw a dazzling array of elegant purple irises and brilliantly colored yellow and orange poppies, a bunch of young bucks grazing in the tall grasses, a muskrat in the pond gathering grasses for a nest, a bunch of big turtles out sunning themselves on the rocks, a mother duck swimming with a bunch of tiny newborn fluff balls, and some little boys trying unsuccessfully to catch a frog. The white seeds of the cottonwood trees are in the air everywhere. The wild grasses are tall and green and abundant, and the wind is making the leaves of the poplar and birch trees dance their shimmering happy dance.

In the dance of existence, there is endless variation—cloudy days, sunny days, warm days, cold days, sickness, health, happy, sad, exciting, dull.

The beauty and wonder are in the quality of the seeing, the awareness, the presence, not in the object being seen.

Fire and Lightning

The whole state of Oregon is on fire by the looks of the fire maps. Days of triple-digit heat, then thunder and lightning. Up here in the hills at the edge of town, it is immensely powerful. Huge lightning bolts flying across the sky, rain pouring down in torrents, wind blowing every which way. It hails, it pours. I think the entire driveway will wash away. It's wild.

One lightning bolt lands in the field right below our house and starts a small grass fire that the rain quickly puts out—luckily it was raining at the time, which isn't always the case when the lightning flies. Several fires are burning near Ashland, and the valley is filled again with smoke. The light has a strange orange tint, the air is painful to breathe and the eyes sting.

A large branch of the beautiful mimosa tree that I look out on was snapped in half by the winds and has fallen into the rest of the tree, greatly changing my view. But the hummingbirds are still enjoying the tree, zipping through the blossoms drinking nectar.

My friend d, who teaches Zen in Mexico, is down there now, and in an email, he describes a beautiful sunset sky and then an old woman at a busy corner crawling very slowly across the intersection on her elbows and knees. "Below her elbows and knees," he writes, "there were no limbs."

All for Your Benefit

All of you undisturbed cities,
haven't you ever longed for the Enemy?
I'd like to see you besieged by him
for ten endless and ground-shaking years.

Until you were desperate and mad with
suffering...

He is the one who breaks down the walls,
and when he works, he works in silence.

—Rilke

There's an old Zen koan about two monks, washing their bowls in the creek, who see two birds fighting over a frog, tearing it apart. One monk asks the other, "Why does it have to be like this?" And the other monk replies, "It's all for your benefit."

What on earth does that mean? Rape, genocide, mass shootings, environmental destruction—all of this is for my benefit?

When I was young, perhaps in grade school or junior high school, I remember reading a novel called *On the Beach,* about the aftermath of a nuclear war, and then several years later seeing a movie called *Days of Wine and Roses.* Both had alcoholic characters, and I actually remember thinking back then, that's what I want to be when I grow up—a drunk. In some way I could never have articulated at the time, that's how I felt I could best embody a certain sense I had about life. And, of course, for a number of years, I did exactly that.

I was a wild and reckless drunken writer, like Charles Bukowski—often violent, often enraged, often abusive, often disruptive. My subconscious role, my message, was to enact despair and outrage, a death howl for humanity, to fly in the face of convention, to disrupt the façade of society that seemed so false to me.

Although I sobered up long ago, sometimes I still want to rage and howl, an urge that is perhaps not entirely negative. I'm still a fan of Charles Bukowski—and of Jesus, who gave us the Beatitudes and told us to turn the other cheek, but who also overturned tables and said, "I did not come to bring peace, but a sword." And Nisargadatta, who lived near the red-light district in Bombay and smoked cigarettes during satsang, even while dying of throat cancer, and sometimes yelled at people and threw them out. And Kali with her necklace of skulls, devouring all things, even her own children.

There is unimaginable suffering and cruelty in this world. It can't be denied. We can hate it, or we can embrace it. To embrace it doesn't mean liking it, or denying the grief or the pain or even the anger we feel. It doesn't mean wallowing in despair and negativity, nor does it have to mean being an abusive drunk. Finding out what it *does* mean is perhaps the koan of a lifetime. It has something to with transcendence, but not the kind of transcendence that dissociates or turns away. It's more the kind of transcendence that comes from entering deeply into what is. Somehow, it's all included in this dance, and in some mysterious way, the darkness is essential for the light. A movie wouldn't be interesting if it didn't have conflict and suspense, and life would offer no way to grow, learn or evolve if it consisted of nothing but endlessly pleasant spring days.

Watching the oil spilling out in the most recent disaster and the polar ice melting is like watching my mother's body fall apart in slow stages, and then Lydia's. In some way, it is *all* a totally natural process. And at the deepest level, all is well. Even the most apparently unwholesome and unenlightened actions, our own and those of others, are *all* as insubstantial and ephemeral as last night's dream.

From the perspective of unicity, the apparent disharmony is all part of a larger harmony. That larger harmony doesn't mean the birds will stop fighting over the frog or that human beings will live in some blissful and utopian paradise. Actually, there is quite a bit of violence and conflict going on even inside the human body on a regular basis, just as the two birds in the koan are engaged in a conflict, probably with some anger, fighting over a meal. The birds have no ideas about "being present" with their hunger, or "taking a time out" from their anger. They are simply doing what nature compels them to do. And so are we!

We imagine that human beings have free will and "should" do better. We find human cruelty more upsetting than the destruction caused by "natural" events such as hurricanes and earthquakes. Nature acts without intention. It simply does what it does. But what may be realized is that humans are an expression of nature as well. The Nazi, the child rapist, the factory farmer, the slave owner, the abusive drunk only have the sensitivity and capacity for empathy that they have. They don't really have a choice, until perhaps they do— but when they don't, they don't.

Commenting on this koan about the frog being torn apart, Zen teacher Susan Murphy writes: "It is a very harsh world; heaven and earth are ruthless... What gives us this amazing life also takes it away...We have to witness and endure things being torn apart in front of us... How do you go about releasing the blessing from the curse? How do you get off the wheel of reactiveness that we all seem to be chained to and convert a cursed condition or situation into a fiercely simple blessing? ...Only by resting completely, right here in the heart of chaos." (Susan Murphy, *Upside-Down Zen*)

We humans *do* have this possibility—not on command or through individual will, but when nature so moves us—to wake up to the damage and the pain we are causing, to repent, to change, to choose love. This is part of our human nature—to transform ourselves. And so, we have political movements and spiritual paths. These are also movements of nature, like the body battling an infection or the ecosystem restoring itself. Both political activism and spirituality have something to do with the alchemy of how we transmute suffering into love. The political world works on the external causes and cures—climate change, economic justice, racism, sexism, heterosexism, the humane treatment of animals, and so on. The spiritual world works on the internal causes and cures—the illusory sense of separation and encapsulation, the dualism of self and other, mistaking the map for the territory, opening the heart, and so on.

Rest assured that, as a child, most of my ideas about what I wanted to be when I grew up were more positive and conventional in nature—a doctor, a monastic or religious person of some kind, a writer, a social worker, an actor. And I *do* have a deep faith in the fundamental goodness of life, a recognition that unconditional love is our True Nature, the nature of awareness, what remains when delusion falls away. Hate is a kind of reactive overlay based on delusion.

But it's easy, on the spiritual path, to start thinking we "should" be other than how we actually are in each moment, that we should be beyond all conflict and anger, and then, when we fail, to feel bad. But our ideas of how we or the world "should be" are just ideas. Even our ideas of how we *are* in this moment are already ideas about the past—imaginary forms created out of formlessness.

Is it possible to forgive the world for being imperfect and to forgive ourselves for being imperfect as well? And is it possible to discover the perfection in the imperfection, not as a comforting idea, but as something we actually open our hearts to and deeply realize? "Right action" doesn't look any particular way. It might be political organizing, it might be social service work, it might be teaching meditation. It might even be Jesus overturning tables, or Charles Bukowski drunk and raging, or Kali devouring her children.

Perhaps, in the end, the greatest contribution any of us can make to world peace and social justice is simply to wake up. Otherwise, our actions come out of a divided mind that perpetuates conflict and division. When our actions flow from awake presence, they are more wholesome in the truest sense, more whole. But there will never be absolute peace and justice in a relative world. There will always be things falling apart and things that we regard as terrible from our human perspective. The frog will always be torn apart, the birds will always fight over it, the savior will always be crucified—somehow it all belongs.

And I have the deep sense that a life of nothing but sunny days and eternal youth would not be nearly as rich as the life we have, the one where things get torn apart.

Autumn

Walking along the trail in Lithia Park, four deer led by a large buck with huge velvety antlers came downhill right in front of me and stepped onto the path that I was on, walking just ahead of me. The five of us walked together, single file, for quite a ways. I felt like one of them.

The wind that evening was clocked at 75 mph. I really thought the windows would blow in or the roof would blow off. It was frightening. Rain was lashing against the windows in torrents. I sat in my bliss chair for several hours watching it—huge wind gusts slamming the house, things blowing through the air, a tree snapping in half, rain battering the windows, the mountains appearing and disappearing, clouds racing past. Quite a show. When the rain stopped and the clouds lifted, the mountainsides out my window were, for the first time this season, white with snow.

Falling

I took a nasty fall yesterday on a hike by myself on a trail through the woods. My foot slipped on loose gravel, and I slid down a small hill, landing hard on cement because the trail crossed a road right where

I fell. I was in a lot of pain, afraid that I might have broken my hip or knee.

Luckily, a couple with a little dog came along at just that moment, and they sat down on the road beside me and stayed with me until the pain subsided enough that I could get up and walk. Their little dog had bonded with me though, and when the couple and I parted in opposite directions, the little dog kept racing back and forth between us, until he was finally convinced to go with his people.

X-rays showed nothing was broken. Given that I now have osteoporosis, no broken bones is a small miracle. The whole incident demonstrated both the vulnerability of these bodies and also the way the universe holds us—that couple showing up and their tiny dog who nuzzled me as I lay on the ground, and who kept running back to check on me when we parted company.

CHAPTER FIFTEEN: Descent

Early Warning Signs

Down in California, my dear friend Fran died. And then another dear old friend in Washington state told me she was dying of cancer. I planned to visit her after I got back from Springwater, where I was scheduled to lead a five-day retreat over Easter, but when I returned to Oregon, it was too late. She was gone.

I had a wonderful time at Springwater, but I had severe rectal bleeding the whole two weeks I was there. I'd had severe rectal bleeding once before, while living in Chicago, and I'd been through numerous colonoscopies in Chicago, having polyps removed every time. But my last colonoscopy, which was done in Ashland soon after I moved here, had been totally clean, and I had been told I didn't need another for ten years. What a relief that had been!

When I got back to Ashland, the rectal bleeding stopped, but because it had been pretty severe and had lasted several weeks, I went to my primary care doctor just to have it checked out. She wasn't available, but her PA did a rectal exam and said I had a hemorrhoid. She was very adamant that I should have a colonoscopy right away. So I made an appointment with my gastroenterologist. He didn't do his own rectal exam, and he thought the bleeding was probably just "travel stress," since it had stopped when I got home. He didn't think we needed to do a colonoscopy. As I recall, he did have me do one of those mail-in-your-poop tests, and it showed no abnormal amount of blood. According to the American Cancer Society, these mail-in tests "are recommended for people who have an average risk for colorectal cancer: no personal history of pre-cancerous polyps, no colorectal cancer that runs in the family, or no other risk factors." I had all of those things, and travel stress made no sense to me, since bleeding hadn't happened on any previous trip, and this trip didn't feel particularly stressful. But I was delighted not to have another colonoscopy. The prep he had given me for my last one had induced not only explosive pooping all night but also explosive vomiting simultaneously. It had been one of the worst nights of my life, and I was in no hurry to repeat it. And so, I didn't protest.

Meanwhile, the whole state of Oregon was on fire again. The smoke was really getting to me. Being indoors all the time, windows closed, no walks. Looking out at this ever-present reminder of the slow death that is happening from climate change. My eyes burn. I cough a lot.

I had a nightmare, my first in ages. I was in some empty Kafkaesque city, trying to find my way somewhere, and I was totally lost. I'd also lost the address of where I'd come from, which must have been where I was staying, and I didn't know how to get back there. I had no map and no idea where I was or how to get home or where I was going. Sounds like life. In the dream, I was filled with anxiety and panic. I woke up in a complete panic. A friend and fellow satsang teacher emailed me that morning to say that she dreamed last night that the two of us were leading a retreat together. So at the same time I was totally lost in an anonymous city, riddled with anxiety, I was simultaneously on retreat with a friend, calmly teaching the dharma.

Autumn 2016

I got a call out of the blue one night in mid-September from my land-lady telling me I had to move out by mid-November. This was a total shock. I had been repeatedly told that I had this place forever if I wanted it, that she would never want my apartment. But now she does. I'm scheduled to be out of town speaking at the SAND (Science and Nonduality) Conference and visiting friends for almost all of October, so the timing is terrible; and she is unwilling or unable to be more flexible about it. I was in complete shock but awoke the next morning with a sense of excitement about new beginnings, seeing it perhaps as a friendly shove from the universe toward a new future.

As I began to look for places, I realized how much rents had gone up. It was worrisome. But just before leaving for California, to my enormous relief, I found a great place. I would go down to California, cut my trip short, and then move in when I returned.

Meanwhile, as a backdrop to this move, there was the presidential election, with Donald Trump running against Hillary Clinton. My father would be appalled by what has become of his beloved Republican Party. First, they jumped in bed with the fundamentalist Christian right, which was bad enough, but now they had united behind a sleazy conman who has built his whole campaign on barefaced lies and racist demagoguery. Everyone assumes Hillary will win, but I don't underestimate Trump or the level of misinformation and unrecognized racism and sexism in this country that might elect him, not to mention the fact that half the country doesn't even bother to vote, either because they think it doesn't matter or because it has been made as difficult as possible to do in many states—you must often stand in long lines, sometimes in rain or snow, for hours and hours, often at out-of-the-way polling places, all of which is hard on anyone and impossible for many. Furthermore, Hillary is unpopular with many people on the left as well as on the right, and many people on both ends of the political spectrum have grown tired of business as usual and want something more radical and authentic—and Trump masterfully played on this desire and on the frustrations many Americans were feeling.

Many people are hurting in America, and that creates fertile ground for demagoguery. Trump's rallies are frightening, often violent affairs that portend the very real danger of America descending into fascism or civil war.

But in happier news, after more than a century-long losing streak, my beloved Chicago Cubs won the 2016 baseball World Series. I was on my feet in front of the TV during the entire last game waving my arms, yelling and cheering them on. Dorothy would be so thrilled. She used to take me to Cubs games when I was growing up.

I only hope the election turns out as well as the World Series. But, of course, like a ball game, not everyone is rooting for the same team.

215

Descent into Darkness

I returned bone-tired from the trip to California and the long drive home. And in the midst of packing up my apartment, exhausted and surrounded by packing boxes and the total chaos of an impending move, I witnessed with stunned horror the election of Donald Trump. We now have a president backed by the alt-right and the KKK in the White House, with both houses of Congress and over half the governorships in the country in Republican control, and we'll soon have an even more conservative-leaning Supreme Court, almost certainly for the rest of my life, not to mention lifetime appointments of extreme right-wing federal judges across the country who will decide cases involving environmental protections, voting rights, corporate power, affirmative action, women's reproductive rights, marriage equality, LGBTQI civil rights, immigration, physician-assisted dying, gun control, capital punishment, unions—decisions that will affect everyone in this country for decades to come. Trump's campaign slogan, "Make America Great Again," was seen by many as a thinly-disguised dog-whistle for "Make America White Again." I felt sick.

I grew up in a world like the one Trump is promising to take us back to. We had Jim Crow laws, virtually all important jobs were held by men, being gay was illegal, abortion was illegal, white men ruled the day, and the earth was mindlessly trashed. I lived through what that was like. It's not abstract to me. I have vivid and horrible memories of what women went through, what Blacks and gay people endured. With this man in the White House, I wondered what was ahead for the country, for the whole world, for all living beings.

Toni Packer, who grew up half-Jewish in Nazi Germany, once gathered the whole staff at Springwater together to watch a documentary about Rush Limbaugh. It was early in his career, when this kind of extreme right-wing media was just beginning to emerge, and Toni said Rush reminded her very strongly of the early Nazi rhetoric in Germany, and she was obviously deeply concerned. Thankfully, she didn't live to see Trump elected and white supremacists marching openly in the streets, the president himself egging them on. You think it can't happen here, but that's exactly what they thought in Germany.

As Hitler rose to power in Germany, many German Jews said it wasn't going to be as terrible as others were worried it might be. But the worriers turned out to be right. They were the ones who escaped. And now, many Americans wonder, is this country headed in a similar direction, or is it not really that bad? And of course, there is no way to know.

Donald Trump is certainly not the first racist, sexist, liar to occupy the White House, but never before has it been this unapologetically overt, nor has it ever been this unhinged and in-your-face every day on Twitter. We've definitely hit a new and previously unimaginable bottom.

But one thing I've learned from growing older is that we take several steps forward, and then we go backwards. We lean one way, and then the other. And just as the light and dark interpenetrate each other in the Yin/Yang symbol, so Obama inadvertently ignited a resurgence of white supremacy; and Trump would soon inadvertently ignite a new wave of progressives. And who knows, maybe this dark time ahead will be the bottom we need to hit in order for things to take a turn in a genuinely new direction.

I wasn't walking around in a state of suicidal despair over the election, but I did feel a deep sorrow and a heavy heart. I could feel the pain that was coming. In short, November 2016 was a rough month, for me and for much of the world. But it was also an exciting new beginning for me in a wonderful new home.

Eventually, as I settled into my new home, I felt myself release the pain of the election. Since my move, I had no cable TV, and I was enjoying that immensely. I still followed the news online, so I was not tuned out, but I was not obsessively submerged in it for hours every night as I had been at my previous place. It's a relief to be without it. As citizens in a democracy, or what passes for one, we have a responsibility to stay informed. But we also have to be careful not to get swept up in the negativity storm of cable news and social media. Being overwhelmed by fear, despair and anger isn't really helpful at all.

As the months went by, I noticed, to my surprise, that I rarely got upset by the news, as horrible as it often was—environmental protections being revoked, toddlers separated from their mothers at the border and locked in cages, women's and LGBTQI rights being stripped away, seemingly endless mass shootings, white supremacists emboldened. Occasionally in all this madness, something still triggered me. But mostly, I was watching it all with a kind of equanimity.

Winter gradually moved toward spring. There is truly nothing more magnificent than listening to the sounds of rain. Plopping, tapping, splashing, gurgling—all these exquisitely beautiful sounds filling the silent darkness of a spring night, nurturing the buds that are unfurling, bathing the blossoming trees. The next morning, opening the window shade, a herd of deer are grazing on the wet emerald green grass across the street. A single bird is flying through the milk-white sky. Fog is draping the green mountains. There is the mournful cry of a dove, the ecstatic chirping of frogs, a rainbow arching across the sky.

The Most Beautiful Silence Never Heard

I was on YouTube one night that spring searching for a reading by Charles Bukowski of his apocalyptic poem, *"Dinosauria, we,"* a poem that chronicles the collapse of our dehumanizing civilization, ending in a strangely beautiful affirmation of life: *"there will be the most beautiful silence never heard... the sun still hidden there, awaiting the next chapter."* While searching for this reading, YouTube suggested I might like a satsang with Mooji that was being broadcast live from India at that very moment. Instantly, I clicked on it. I'd met Mooji once in Chicago years ago at a small gathering and had been deeply moved by him.

This turned out to be a whole series of satsangs in India, and I found myself watching and listening to all of them that spring. Once again, hearing Mooji opened up a profound emptiness—everything fell away. He points so simply and clearly to the unseeable seeing that is subtler than space, subtler even than the sense of impersonal presence. He compares that impersonal presence, the knowingness that I

Am, to the fragrance of a flower—formless, but still phenomenal. The flower itself is the Absolute, the unfindable Self, most intimate and all-inclusive—what I call Here-Now or groundlessness.

In addition to the satsangs, there were these wonderfully passionate and exuberant bhajans that I loved, love songs to God, and I sang along and danced in my living room. The absolute emptiness that Mooji evoked was full of love, which poured out as devotion—not necessarily or primarily guru-devotion, but devotion to the heart, to what is—dissolving into this mystery in ever-deeper, subtler ways, not in order to get somewhere or attain something, but simply because it is the nature of love to dive ever-deeper into itself, to pour itself out in song and dance, to die to everything and be what remains.

As I watched these live satsangs from India that spring, singing and dancing with the bhajans, my heart opened. I was taken to a deep and beautiful place. The world might be descending into darkness, but I was realizing once again what is untouched by darkness.

My Mystery Illness

That summer I had a strange illness that went on for weeks. I hadn't been that sick in many years. My stool was coming out pencil-thin. I had an anal discharge along with headache, nausea, fevers and gut pain. There were even strange brown stains showing up occasionally on my urinary leakage pads, at the front end, not the rear. It went on for weeks.

At the urging of a friend, I did finally go to my new primary care doctor, a bright young woman who had recently taken over the practice from the doctor I'd been with since I moved to Ashland. My new doctor did a rectal exam, and I was told once again that I had a hemorrhoid. She thought I probably had some viral gastroenteritis that was going around. When I mentioned the brown stains, she looked mystified but seemed unconcerned. Eventually, after endless meals of oatmeal, rice, apple sauce, bananas and toast, the fever, headache and nausea subsided and, although my intestines were still not functioning in any normal way, I figured I was on the mend.

The whole time I was sick, it felt like being stopped in my tracks at a moment when I needed to stop. There is something oddly refreshing and grounding about being unable to function. It returns one to the essential. And it takes one to those liminal places. In my dreams one night, I was back at my childhood home outside Chicago with my mother and Lydia. It was winter, the ground covered in snow, and Lydia and I were on our way to the theater in Oregon.

In August, we had a solar eclipse. I watched from my back deck. I loved how the air grew cooler and cooler. I was amazed at how much light that tiny, thin sliver of sun that was left at the end actually cast. I guess in Carbondale, Illinois, the best viewing spot, the sky went black, and they could see the stars, but not here. Still, it was beautiful.

Toxic smoke from wildfires filled the valley here for much of the summer, and once again, I was trapped indoors because the air was hazardous to breathe. Just when it finally cleared, I was due to go down to the Bay Area for the SAND (Science and Nonduality) Conference. Huge wildfires were by then burning in California. So in October, I headed down the interstate to California, driving through smoke the entire way. The Bay Area was filled with smoke. Several people I knew there lost their homes, many others were evacuated. They had huge wildfires in Europe as well. Mooji's place in Portugal burned. The world was literally on fire.

I was unusually fatigued during the conference, my stool continued to be pencil-thin, I had persistent gut pain so, when I got back to Ashland, I decided that perhaps I better see my gastroenterologist. He was booked up for over a month, but I made an appointment for mid-December.

My Descent into the Bowels of the Human Experience

A student of the way asked Yunmen, "What is Buddha?"
    Yunmen replied, "Dried shit-stick." [in modern vernacular, used toilet paper]

It had been getting harder and harder to insert the thin estrogen applicator into my vagina twice a week, as I was supposed to do, and one night in November, it wouldn't go in at all. It seemed to be hitting an obstruction. And there was blood on it. Those brown stains began showing up again on my leakage pads, and it was definitely coming from my vagina or my urethra, not my rectum. It looked like a poop stain, not a blood stain. I knew something was very wrong. I wondered if that hemorrhoid had invaded my vagina, if there was a fistula. I called my urogynecologist. Hearing my symptoms, she got me in that same day and, after examining me, got me in to see my gastroenterologist the following morning.

I'd had gut problems and frequent colon polyps ever since menopause. I'd had those two weeks of severe rectal bleeding a year earlier. I had a family history of colon cancer. I'd had cervical cancer in my twenties and more recently, I'd been treated for lichen sclerosus, both of which put me at higher risk for anal and throat cancer, as they are all linked to HPV, the human papillomavirus, but that I discovered much later, on the internet. Even when my urogynecologist assured me that my gastroenterologist would be fitting me in the very next morning, I was still blissfully thinking it was a hemorrhoid—after all, that's what I'd been told.

The next morning, my gastroenterologist did a rectal exam, and when I sat up, he put his hand on my shoulder and said, "It's a malignant tumor. It's cancer. I'm sorry."

My first question was, "Will I have an ostomy?" And he replied, as if working his way through the stages of denial, "Maybe... probably...yes, you will."

He did a colonoscopy and biopsy the very next day. After that, an MRI, a PET scan, a CT scan and several more rectal and vaginal exams followed, and I was officially diagnosed in mid-November with a stage three anal cancer. The tumor had spread up my rectum and invaded my vagina. It's possible that the rectal bleeding I'd had the previous year *was* actually a hemorrhoid, that the tumor came later. We'll never know. But I'm thoroughly convinced that by the summer of 2017, the cancer was there and had already started to invade my vagina.

In any case, whatever was or wasn't there before, it was definitely cancer now. I had cancer in all the places one is not supposed to mention out loud or in public. And thus began what I came to call my descent from the transcendent down into the bowels of the human experience. It wasn't about *denying* the transcendent; it was about finding it right in the very heart of what *seems* to be its polar opposite.

It has never been my desire to live too long and end up incapacitated in a nursing home. So I wondered, at age sixty-nine, if I should perhaps take the exit door that the universe was offering to me while I still had my wits about me. I asked the doctor what would happen if I did nothing, and he told me that I would probably be dead within weeks from a bowel blockage. He also told me this was not a pleasant way to die—it's very painful and you vomit up poop.

I didn't even need to think about it. I didn't want to be dead in a few weeks—I had to finish this book, after all—and so, I agreed to the treatment plan. In early December, I would have a colostomy followed by radiation and chemotherapy and, because my bowel was so close to being completely obstructed, this was all moving very fast. The radiation would probably go for six weeks, five days a week. I'd have two rounds of chemo simultaneously. The side effects sounded challenging, but others had gotten through it, so I assumed I would too. The surgery would allow my bowel to empty—into an ostomy bag—thus keeping me alive. The radiation would hopefully eradicate the tumor. And the chemo, as I understood it, would help with that and also hopefully prevent further spread.

Having cancer turns out to be a full-time job. I don't think I've ever had so many appointments and procedures in one week in my entire life, and I now seem to have a multitude of doctors overseeing my case. Initially, I was doing quite well, sailing along quite calmly, seemingly unafraid and in good spirits, but then when I spoke to the surgeon and the wound-ostomy nurse, who sent me home with sample ostomy bags and DVDs about ostomies to watch, I had a brief dip into the darkness.

The surgery, a laparoscopic colostomy, will bring my colon out of my abdominal wall where it will protrude and empty into an ostomy bag. The bag is stuck onto the belly with adhesive backing and must be emptied into the toilet when it fills up with poop. Every third or fourth day, the bag is removed and replaced with a fresh one after the area around the stoma—the end of the intestine that sticks out—is cleaned up. All of this appears to involve a lot of up-and-close encounters with poop, and managing it with one hand looks like it will be challenging; but the doctors and the wound-ostomy nurses all assure me that I will find my way. A friend told me that they may even be able to reconnect my bowel in the future, but as my doctors have explained, there are many uncertainties and other less cheerful outcomes also possible. But they do expect me to live.

Local friends have been amazing, and old friends from far away, and people I don't even know. The wife of a man I've never even met in person knitted colorful caps and mailed them to me for when my hair fell out. On Facebook, I got wonderful messages of support. I received so much love that it was mind-blowing, heart-opening, and totally transforming.

This kind of diagnosis really does bring you right into the present moment. Thoughts of elsewhere and elsewhen vanish, and everything seems amazingly precious and beautiful—the mulchy smells of wet leaves on the ground, the last colored leaves blowing off the now mostly bare trees—every moment of life.

In this pre-surgery, pre-treatment phase, I feel a bit like I'm on a roller coaster that is climbing higher and higher, up, up and up. I know that soon it will crest and begin it's long, terrifying downward plunge.

Or at least, it sounds terrifying, especially the side effects from the radiation that have been described to me. My private parts will literally be burned. I'm told there will be intense pain and also itching in my anus and vagina, that the outer surfaces down there will blister and that the pain can be really bad. I may lose the ability to pee and need to be catheterized, hopefully just temporarily. I'll have diarrhea and fatigue and, if the radiation messes up my urinary tract, I might end up with a bag for urine as well as one for poop.

I feel like I'm about to make a long dark descent into hell. But so far, everything seems almost normal, and part of me thinks it's all a dream. I'm in functioning mode most of the time, getting to appointments, making preparations, getting things done—one foot in front of the other—busy, busy, busy. But when the action stops, I feel the heaviness and terror. I'm a wimp when it comes to pain, but my surgeon tells me I'm tough and I'll be fine. I hope so.

I'm not afraid of dying. It sounds quite relaxing. But I *am* afraid, *if I think about it,* of the things that come before death—pain, disability, dementia, and so on. When people say, "You are not your body or your mind," I want to say, "Yes, I am. That isn't *all* I am, but yes, I am very much this body, this mind, this present experiencing, this particular wave." There's no denying that. Spirituality that focuses on trying to identify *exclusively* as pure consciousness, and that insists we are *not* the body, has never worked well for me. So, more and more, as I embark on this journey into the bowels of the human experience, the spirituality that interests and attracts me is not about transcending all of this by detaching from it, but rather, leaning into it and being just this moment, exactly as it is.

The outpouring of love and support I'm receiving is changing me. You don't really know how much people love and care about you until something like this happens. It's very moving. For this hermit recluse, the outpouring of friends calling and dropping by is sometimes a bit overwhelming—I'm so tired from everything that I've been through in the past three weeks that I can barely stay awake sometimes—but it has been immensely moving and heart-opening.

The PET scan showed a small spot on my thyroid and something on my lung, both of which could have other explanations, and my medical team doesn't seem terribly concerned about them. But it also showed suspicious lymph activity in the pelvis and abdomen—two spots lower, nearer the tumor, one higher up—and that is concerning because the lymphatic system can spread cancer. So they'll be zapping that with the radiation as well.

If the radiation and chemo don't do the job, I'll need a bigger surgery that will remove my anus, rectum, vagina, uterus, and possibly urethra. I will end up with a permanent ostomy bag and a second bag for urine. This would be a major abdominal surgery requiring several weeks in a nursing facility afterwards and a long recovery period. Faced with that, I might very well elect to let the cancer take me. But hopefully, the treatment they have planned will work.

I am endeavoring in this book to show the beauty of aging and dying, *including* the gritty details that are so often air-brushed out of the picture, and to do the latter not in a way that invites despair or horror, but in a way that finds the beauty in how it actually is. I'm taking a similar approach to writing about this cancer. I'm not mincing words, and some may find it too intimate, too personal, too graphic, or too unmentionable, but I am trusting that it will speak to some. After all, we must all eat and poop, one way or another, however enlightened we may be. And from my perspective, this human life with all its twists and turns is actually a gift, not a giant mistake.

The Downward Plunge Begins

The night before the surgery, and again that morning, I shower with special Hibiclens soap to disinfect my skin. My friend Ann drives me to the hospital in the morning and insists on staying with me in the pre-op room, where I am instructed to wipe my whole body with these special disinfectant wipes. Ann does my back for me. I am nude. This is a very intimate moment, the first of several. And this is the last time I will see my belly without a stoma protruding from it. They insert the line in my hand for the anesthesia and begin a saline drip. Finally, I am taken to another room where Ann is not allowed to follow, where I am given a shot in my spine by the anesthesiologist to help with the post-op pain, and then I am wheeled into the OR. They start the anesthesia, and I feel consciousness slipping away.

I have no memory of the recovery room where my surgeon tells me he talked to me—"No one ever remembers these visits," he says later—or how I got from there to my hospital room. My first memory is a nurse in my hospital room asking me if I'd like a popsicle.

I was in the hospital for four days. The surgery also involved installing a port for the chemotherapy under the skin on my upper chest, just below my collarbone, with a tube that goes directly into a vein in my neck. This they will use to administer the chemo drugs and also give me hydration at several points. The port installation and the colostomy both went well.

I had amazingly wonderful care in the hospital. I had a private room—apparently most of their rooms are private—and the staff was beyond excellent. I joked that being in the hospital is a little bit like being at a luxury spa—they bring you heated blankets if you feel cold, they come whenever you push a button, they serve you your meals in bed, they do all your housework for you. They even bathe you if you need a bath. Of course, there's the vampire, aka the phlebotomist, who comes faithfully every morning between four and five a.m. to draw your blood, not to mention the occasional things that are not so much fun, such as being catheterized at midnight for a long time when you can't pee. So it's a bit of an odd spa, but still, on the whole, not a bad place to spend four nights. I felt surrounded in love and very well cared for.

On my way out the door to the hospital, at the last second, I had spontaneously grabbed *My Grandfather's Blessings* by Rachel Naomi Remen off my bookshelves to take with me. I read that book aloud to my mother the last year she was alive, some thirteen years ago, and we both wept over the beautiful stories drawn from Dr. Remen's life and her practice with chronically ill and dying patients. I hadn't looked at it since then. It turned out to be the perfect book to read. On top of all the other ways it was perfect, in one sentence, she mentions having an ostomy herself, which I had not remembered.

The nurses are so calm, even under so much pressure, with multiple demands coming at them at once. One night toward the end of my stay in the hospital, I decided to go off all my pain meds, and that night I didn't take any. I woke up in the middle of the night in pain, unable to move. I pushed the nurse call button. A wonderful male nurse came to my room. I told him I was stuck. He listened. He didn't rush in to help me up. Instead, he calmly guided me with his voice. "I want you to bring your left leg up toward your body…" and so on, and next thing I knew, I was sitting up on the edge of the bed, ready to get up. "I can do it!" I said, delighted and relieved.

One of the nurses who attended me was born in the Philippines, and one afternoon we had a long conversation about many things. I told her I feared the pain that would come with the radiation. She told me the way through pain is to keep your focus on Jesus. "That's where Peter went wrong," she told me, "on the sea, when he was walking on the water, he took his eyes off Jesus and then he began to sink. You have to keep your attention on Jesus." I remembered that in the story, Peter had been distracted by the ferocity of the wind and had become afraid and filled with doubt and had lost faith. In my mind, I silently translated "Jesus" into my own language and understanding as Presence, Awareness, Here-Now, God—and perhaps "the wind" is the ever-changing play of thoughts, emotions, circumstances, and also what a friend of mine calls the "doubt app"—that doubting mind that feels separate from life and therefore endangered, the mind that loses faith—not faith in some external thing or some belief system (some golden chain), but faith in what is actually trustworthy—that open, spacious unconditioned aware presence Here-Now. And so I told her I agreed, that was the key, staying focused on Jesus, although not always easy. She nodded. "Not always easy, but that is the way."

In the hospital, they rang soft, gentle little tinkling bells whenever a new baby was born. I heard those bells at least once while I was there. This Living Reality is endlessly recycling and evolving, dying and being born, like the waves on the ocean, distinct and yet inseparable, moving together, intermingling, never the same from one instant to the next and yet ever-present as the ocean itself. Whether we call that shoreless ocean consciousness, matter, energy, unicity, or no name at all, it flows on, ever-changing and yet always Here-Now. In this unbroken wholeness, there is no inside or outside, no self or other-than-self. And yet, each wave, each person, each newborn, each snowflake, each moment is utterly unique and beautiful and precious and unrepeatable and perfectly formed, just as it is.

Friends have been wonderful—getting me to and from the hospital, filling my refrigerator with food, making sure I'm comfortable, and even offering to spend the night my first night home. But I was 100% sure I was going to be fine on my own, and I was. It was heavenly to sleep in my own super-comfortable bed, and to be back in my own home. I cleaned my CPAP hoses the next morning, cooked my breakfast, did a load of laundry, and then took a brief rest in my bliss chair.

No poop came out of my stoma the whole time I was in the hospital, so I never got to try emptying the bag one-handed when the ostomy nurses were there to help or advise me. That was a bit worrisome, but I will have home health nurses coming out once or twice a week for a while, and I'm told they have someone on-call 24/7, someone I can call if I get in trouble—although as I soon learned, that was only one nurse for the whole county.

Cancer is proving to be a huge awakening of gratitude and love and appreciation for my many blessings, including friends, and this morning, the first snow. I feel surrounded by love. I'm doing very well emotionally and have been in good spirits throughout.

The ultrasound they did the week before surgery did show nodes on both sides of my thyroid, one big enough to warrant a needle biopsy, which I had the week after my surgery. My stoma finally started putting out actual poop for the first time just as I was leaving the house early that morning for my thyroid biopsy—five needles into the neck—followed by a visit to my surgeon for post-op check-up, and then to a different hospital for an echocardiogram to certify that my heart is strong enough for chemo. Meanwhile, my bag is very slowly filling up, little bits at a time, so when I get home, it seems full and I try emptying it, but find I can't. The poop is sticky, like peanut butter, and doesn't come out easily. Soon I've got poop on myself. I've stripped down to no clothes to at least keep poop off my clothes.

I'm sitting on the toilet crying. I call home health. They call back an hour later to tell me no one is available, the one nurse is elsewhere dealing with more urgent and life-threatening situations. I call my friend Ann, a breast cancer survivor herself. Heroically, she gets out of her bath and comes over and helps me. I cleaned up my mother's poop, but that was my mother. I hadn't wanted any of my friends to be doing this for me. But Ann is here, amazingly calm and undisturbed by the mess or the smells. Dignity, in the classic sense, is gradually stripped away. But luckily, we know a deeper dignity. Ann knows the ropes because her husband had colon cancer and an ostomy, and then died of sepsis during the treatment—which points to the ever-present danger of infection, especially during chemo and radiation, when your immune system is no longer fully functional. I picture myself with open sores, covered in poop, trying not to get an infection.

Together, we change my bag, since emptying it is not working. Ann leaves. I clean up the bathroom, make an omelet and toast, eat dinner, watch an episode of *The Crown*, and my bag is filling up again already. I've been constipated since the surgery from the narcotics, so nothing but little drips of mucous had been getting through, but now after three days of Miralax, which they put me on, the dam has broken and everything from the last eight or nine days is pouring out nonstop, a veritable flood of poop. I may be up on the toilet much of tonight covered in poop, but I feel calm again and able to handle it.

I rose early the next morning to go with my friend Judith to the "chemo educational" in Medford about what to expect during chemo, and also to have a blood draw. They explain that I'll have two rounds of chemo, each of which will include an on-site infusion for about an hour, and then a fanny pack that I'll wear for four days that will continuously infuse the drug into my port. They gave me a little HAZMAT kit in case of a chemo spill, and told me that anyone coming into contact with my body fluids should wear double gloves. I'm told that the chemo can cause sores on hands and feet, plus mouth and throat sores, loss of appetite, nausea, fatigue, and many other dreadful but less common things. It could damage my heart or lungs. With both the chemo and radiation, the effects are cumulative, so I may be feeling okay for the first few days or even weeks, but gradually, it will get worse and worse, and the side effects will linger after the treatment ends for at least several more weeks. Some of the effects will continue to unfold for years to come.

After the session ends, I'm picturing myself trying to sleep with an ostomy bag, a fanny pack with tubing going into my port, a CPAP mask and hose, and the lingering abdominal pains of the surgery. All I can do is laugh at the thought of this.

My chemo oncologist, feels I will probably "sail through" the first chemo session, but that the second will be the hard one. I've been told that the side effects of the radiation are cumulative, so those will be getting progressively worse over the six weeks of treatment, and by then I will be quite worn down. The days ahead are filled with more appointments. It is unending and relentless.

Cancer is a stripping process, a journey through the flames, burning away all those illusions of control and all the ways we so often—falsely—measure dignity as being independent and needing nothing—finding ourselves instead naked on the toilet, covered in poop, calling a friend for help. Some might say humiliating, but I would say it's more a growth in humility, love and trust in life. I am finding it heart-opening and life-changing.

I'm getting used to being covered in poop and having poop everywhere. To empty the bag, I strip down naked—to avoid soiling clothing—and then try to get as much poop as possible into the toilet and as little as possible on me, the floor, and so on. Changing the bag is more challenging, especially since I have a grapefruit sized hernia where the stoma came through the muscle, but I did it all by myself for the first time this morning after it started leaking. Eventually, I discover that by reclining in bed, the hernia flattens out, and I can get a new bag on much more successfully. And a wonderful home health nurse who came out one day figured out that by sitting on a folding chair in front of the toilet and pouring a small amount of water into the bag, I can empty it very easily into the toilet.

I'm having some truly remarkable moments down in the shit and piss and grittiness of life, such as my experience with this wonderful home health nurse. I was totally naked on the toilet, he was kneeling in front of me, at one point poop was spilling between us onto the floor, he was cleaning it up. And while all that might sound horrible, it was strangely beautiful, so much human kindness, all of us in this together.

I do not regret that this is happening, and in some way I cannot explain, it seems entirely on course and a perfect way to spend the winter of my seventieth year on planet Earth, exploring this scary place and finding the way through it, and also taking in the immensity of love and support, from friends and from medical people, who are all quite wonderful.

The doctors have been very honest with me. Chemo could cause another cancer some years down the road. The radiation could permanently wreck my bladder and my urinary tract. But on the other hand, I could be cancer-free in a few months with none of these complications, maybe even with my bowel reconnected again, with five or ten good years—maybe more—ahead. So I took the gamble. I didn't even have to think about it. The way forward was just clear as clear could be. A doctor friend says she had a patient with this same cancer who stopped the radiation midway along—the woman couldn't take the pain and decided death was preferable. So again, we never know. But right now, I'm choosing life—or my best shot at it.

I've had physical pain in my life, severe at times, but not chronic, and this pain from the radiation will be largely in my anus and vagina, vulnerable private places where I have old traumas. I've been catheterized several times already and might lose urinary function for a while (or forever) during the treatment. Interestingly enough, everything I feared most about old age and the nursing home is happening now. It's like I'm facing my worst fears. I'm terrified, but also calm, and in a strange way, interested and curious and maybe I can even say excited by the challenge.

Tomorrow morning, bright and early, I will have my first radiation treatment followed immediately by my first chemotherapy treatment. Meanwhile, I'm having a deliciously quiet and solitary Christmas Day today—no appointments, no procedures, no holiday celebrations—just a delightfully quiet day by myself. What a blessing. Tomorrow the rollercoaster ride starts again, full-tilt.

Chemotherapy and Radiation

It's an adventure, trying to manage an ostomy with one hand. And now they've added a fanny pack and some new tubes into the picture just to up the complexity a bit. So far, I'm feeling fine. They seem to have made advances both in the targeting of chemo and in the palliative aspects of making it all more bearable. For example, they infused me with an anti-nausea drug before administering the chemo, a drug which they said should keep nausea at bay for two or three days. And I've been given an arsenal of drugs, salves and sprays to help reduce all the anticipated side effects. The doctors, nurses, PAs, technicians and staff in general all continue to be beyond wonderful in their care of me.

One of the gifts of apparent limitation in any form, as I've discovered before in other situations, such as losing my right hand early in life, is a waking up to the immensity of freedom right here, in exactly this moment, just as it is. One morning during my cancer treatment, for example, I had plans—things I wanted to do. Instead, I had diarrhea, a side effect of the radiation. I had to keep emptying my ostomy bag, again and again. This is a somewhat involved operation, especially doing it with one hand. It's messy and takes time. As this kept happening, there was a brief second of resistance—"This isn't the morning I had in mind, I don't want this." Then something shifted, and there was the realization, this *is* my morning, this *is* what's happening. And suddenly it was no longer a limitation, a disappointment, a drag, or an unpleasant smelly task. It was wide open, interesting, perfectly okay, every bit as good as a beach in Hawaii or a trip to the Grand Canyon. Yes, I really mean that.

Would I have wanted an ostomy? No way. Would I have wanted to go through chemotherapy and radiation? No way. And yet, all of this has had an enjoyable side that I could never have imagined, such as my encounters with the medical people and other patients, some of which have been so deep and intimate and wonderful, and I'm grateful for all of it. As someone once replied when asked how it was being sick, "It was marvelous!" I concur.

In the same way that I wouldn't have wanted to get cancer, I don't want a nuclear war, another genocide, climate change or a racist-sexist president; but I know intuitively that everything that happens cannot be otherwise in this moment than exactly how it is. I know that the light and the dark go together like yin and yang, and that somehow, we need the dark to reveal the light. I know that there is something that will still be here even if the whole universe blows up, and that nothing real ever dies.

I was surprised after my diagnosis to discover how much I want to be alive. I was returned, more vividly than ever, to the present moment. The astonishing radiance and beauty of every sight, sound and texture is so obvious, whether it is an exquisite flower or a crumpled napkin on the table. I'm drinking it all in so deeply. And I am discovering something about love and community and the interconnection of all beings and how important it is to show up for each other. Yes, life is a fragile affair. And yet, something survives all the blows and carries on, one way or another.

I discover I have a huge community here in Ashland, and not just here, but everywhere—people who love me and want me to be alive, people doing amazing things for me, a generosity that is beyond belief. It is changing me. And I'm letting it in.

I don't have a sense of *fighting* cancer. I'd say, it's more like *welcoming*—welcoming the pain, the helplessness, the terror, the vulnerability, the loss—welcoming the (inescapable) parts of our human life that we have so long been told are shameful—poop, pee, aging genitalia, bags full of shit—welcoming this nakedness and human need—and yes, welcoming the love, letting it in, welcoming the whole of this. That's what it feels like. Welcoming. And, of course, sometimes, not welcoming. But then remembering, *this too* can be welcomed.

It's the dead of winter, but when I took out the trash this morning, it was 63° F here in Ashland. We've had no measurable snowfall; even the tops of many surrounding mountains are bare of snow. Climate change.

I have finished round one of chemo. We're having only a four-day week this week at radiation because of New Year's, which is a blessing! I'm almost one-third through the six-week treatment schedule. The side effects are definitely increasing, blistering open sores on my hand and the end of my arm are currently the worst, making it hard to do the simplest tasks like raising and lowering the blinds, opening a jar or pulling up my pants. I have mouth sores as well, which makes eating and drinking painful. I have a touch of neuropathy in my feet and my typing finger. These are all typical side effects of the chemo protocol I'm on. And I have rectal-vaginal-anal pain from the radiation, but nothing off the charts yet. I have some fatigue, but I'm still functioning quite well, usually driving myself to radiation. And I'm becoming more comfortable and proficient with the ostomy, although still nowhere near the level I'd need to consider traveling or taking a day trip away from home. I've had almost no nausea, and when I do, the drugs knock it right out. My hair is gone, which is a blessing. I've always wanted to shave my head, but never have. So I guess if you don't do something you want to do, sometimes the universe does it for you.

Friends here and elsewhere continue to move me with their generosity and kindness. Friends here drive me when I can't, shop and cook and wash my dishes when needed, give me foot massages, bring me soup and bone broth. I feel very blessed.

But then my white count fell into the danger level, my blood pressure dropped, and they decided I have something called neutropenia that I keep accidentally calling necrophilia—which, fortunately, I do not have. What it means is that I am highly susceptible to infections. I was given two shots, a day apart, to boost my bone marrow and was told to stay out of circulation.

Of course, the flu is rampant now, the worst flu season ever recorded they say on the News, with hospitals running out of beds, and those who don't have the flu seem to have colds or bronchitis or pneumonia. So it is the worst time of year to be neutropenic.

I am told to stay out of public places, other than those I go to for treatment, wear a mask if I'm anywhere with people, avoid contact with anyone who is sick or anyone who has been strongly exposed to anyone sick, avoid foods that are more likely to contain infection-causing organisms, a list that includes berries, tempeh, soft-boiled eggs, raw nuts, uncooked oats, sprouts, miso, blue cheese, and much more. I must be careful what I touch and wash frequently which, with my hand and stump covered in open sores and while handling poop, is challenging. I must monitor myself for fever, get extra rest.

I spiked a fever one night past the one where they tell you to call in immediately, and I was sent by the on-call oncologist to the ER. It was a rainy night, and the place was filled with adults and children with flu. They had only one doc on duty and no PAs. They gave me the kind of mask that protects people from my germs rather than the one that protects me, and told me to sit in a crowded waiting room full of people with flu. That seemed like incredibly bad advice, so I went and sat at the end of the hallway. My friend Judith had shown up, and she sat with me.

Two hours later, I was still waiting to be seen and more and more sick people kept arriving, and finally they came to re-check my temperature. It had gone down into normal range, so I called the on-call oncologist, asked if I could go home, and he said yes.

Next time I spiked a fever, I just waited ten minutes, took my temperature again, waited another ten minutes, then another and by then, thankfully, it had gone down. I figured if it stayed over the danger mark for thirty minutes, I'd call, but otherwise, I'd just stay put and not expose myself to the flu again.

My chemo oncologist had to cut the dose in half on my second round of chemo because of the neutropenia—his belief that I would sail through the first round had not panned out—and that means I'm a bit more vulnerable to metastases down the road and whatever else the chemo is designed to ward off.

I enjoy my daily visits to the cancer centers, the contact with younger people and people not in my usual circles. It is refreshing. And there are so many patients there, all dealing with cancers. I am not alone.

It's hard to believe it has been only a month since I had surgery. It feels like years have gone by since that day when I was wheeled into the OR. And it's been less than two months since I was diagnosed. My home health nurse reminded me how much I've accomplished in that short time—I can empty and change my ostomy bags by myself and don't really need home health anymore. I'll be cut loose very soon. Although I do get tired sometimes, my energy is surprisingly good, at least much of the time. Last night, with a new ointment for those lower regions that burn and itch and keep me awake, and with a dose of CBD tincture, I slept like a baby, and a CBD salve has worked miracles on my hand blisters. The pain has not gotten unbearable—and, as we know, even that always does turn out to be bearable—and so, while definitely not fun, it's not as bad as I had expected, at least not so far. All in all, I'm doing quite well.

I learned today that my thyroid biopsy was inconclusive, probably not malignant, but might be. No one seems very concerned, but they will monitor it.

My radiation oncologist said the tumor has shrunk a lot. He seemed very, very pleased. Also, my white count, while still not up where they'd like it, is now out of the danger level, no longer neutropenic, so I'm free to go about unmasked, cautiously, but significantly less restricted.

The side effects are getting worse though, especially the diarrhea and fatigue. I've had pretty great energy until the last few days, and then, crash—I'm wiped out most of the time now, taking long naps. And the burning pain and intense itching in my private parts have both increased dramatically.

I feel a little bit like the Olympic runner Carl Lewis—I'm relaxing and going faster, with no concern about how I'm doing or where I'm headed. Something else is running this show, not "me." Which reminds me of a favorite quote from Wayne Liquorman. He notes that, paradoxically, when the false sense of individual authorship dissolves, when we recognize our personal powerlessness, suddenly a new kind of power flows in, an impersonal power: "Once we know ourselves to be Ocean in the form of wave, we become free to be ourselves in a way we never dreamed possible. It is as if we had spent our life driving with the emergency brake on and suddenly it is off." Awakening doesn't mean that we dissolve into formless mush, devoid of personality or individuality or ability to act. Instead, we become evermore fully, freely and authentically this utterly unique waving of the Great Ocean that we are.

So, on this winter morning, I bow in deep gratitude to this mysterious malignant tumor, this literal pain in the butt, that has served me so well.

My blood work today showed I am neutropenic again, worse than before. I'm getting three of the shots they give you for that, plus I'm being put on some super strong antibiotics and antifungals. I'm back to staying out of public places, wearing my mask when I must go out, and being super-careful about infection or exposure to sick people. My friend Judith is picking up my prescriptions at Walmart as I type. My radiation oncologist gave me two days off from radiation to help my body regroup.

The drugs seem to have worked. My white count has improved. Both oncologists feel that, all things considered, I'm tolerating the treatment very well.

I've lost quite a bit of weight. I was a bit overweight since menopause, so that's a good thing and, oddly enough, I think my digestive system is actually working better.

The End Is in Sight

My radiation oncologist ended my radiation treatments a week earlier than he had originally planned. They play a "graduation medley" during your final treatment as the machine whirls around you: "Hit the Road, Jack," "Happy Trails to You," "So Long, Farewell" from *The Sound of Music*, and finally, the good old graduation march. It was a bittersweet goodbye because I've grown to love the radiation technicians who administered my treatments. We joked and laughed a lot and got into some deep territory during these sessions. I saw them every day, five days a week. One of them told me his mother has an ostomy and his daughter has one arm. I've bonded quite deeply with these people, and also with a number of the patients I've met over time in the waiting room. I'll miss all of them, but I won't miss radiation!

The less happy news is that the last week and a half has been quite rough, and it isn't over yet and may persist for weeks. The mouth sores caused by the chemo have spread down into my throat and esophagus, making eating and drinking challenging. That has led to dehydration, so they are hydrating me through my port. The second round of chemo also brought on another case of hand and foot sores.

237

But the radiation is the worst. It's like having the most severe sunburn you can imagine on your genitals, anal area and fanny, open sores, making it very painful to sit down, pee or wash myself there. And mucous is now leaking uncontrollably out of my anus, which is still connected to a flap in the ostomy for drainage, soiling one pair of pants and bed sheets after another, so I'm wearing gigantic pads and sitting and sleeping on pads. I've also had a lot of fatigue in these last weeks. Hopefully all this will be gone in a few weeks, a month at most.

I'll still have plenty of doctor appointments ahead of me—weekly blood draws for two more weeks, follow-up meetings with both my oncologists and my surgeon, a visit to the urogynecologist who is handling the vaginal part of all this, an endocrinologist who will be monitoring my thyroid, and then down the road, in a few months, more scans to see if the treatment worked and if I am indeed cancer-free. And maybe, *maybe* there will be a possible reconnection of my bowel at some point, undoing the ostomy and reconnecting my intestine to my rectum and anus, just like it was before all this happened. But that may or may not be possible or advisable.

There is always a risk with a reconnection of having poor bowel control or even no bowel control. Having gone through that nightmare with my mother in her final years, I'd rather have an ostomy than that. But hopefully, with an end to chemo and radiation, my bowels can at least stabilize in some kind of normal pattern instead of constant diarrhea and bag-emptying at all hours of the day and night.

It is snowing and graupeling here today. Graupel is a word I'd never heard before moving to Oregon. It's neither hail nor snow, but tiny balls of snow encased in ice. After weeks of premature spring, suddenly winter has decided to arrive.

I woke up one night to the realization that I was totally covered in diarrhea. It had over-filled the bag and popped one side of it off my belly. This was the third time this has happened, but this was by far the worst. I was sleeping in nothing but a pullover jersey, and it was full of diarrhea. The only way to get it off was to pull it over my head. Thank God, because of my anal discharge, I am sleeping on large protective pads, and thank God I don't have carpeting, just flooring that is easy to clean up. Dripping poop, with poop in my hair, I made it into the bathroom, detached and threw away the ostomy bag, got into the shower bagless, washed the poop off, prepped and put on a new bag, cleaned the bedroom and bathroom, took out the trash, pausing to revel in the orange sunrise light on the mountaintops and the cold bracing fresh morning air, washed my bedding, and called the ostomy nurses. They got me in that afternoon.

I handled the situation calmly, without freaking out, which feels good; but the fact that this keeps happening—three times in a row now—is definitely not reassuring in terms of a return to public life or travel.

Seems I may have an infection, so the ostomy nurse got me an appointment with my surgeon tomorrow. Meanwhile, I've gone on the BRAT diet (bananas, white rice, apple sauce, toast and oatmeal) to hopefully—along with Imodium—stop the diarrhea. But the Imodium then triggers impacted stool, which results in severe and painful abdominal cramps, so it is an ongoing dance between Miralax and Imodium.

My surgeon says everything is fine, I was just cutting the bag hole too small and blocking off the mucous drainage opening in my stoma. You have to prepare the ostomy bags by cutting holes in them in the size and shape of your stoma, which is another challenging part of having an ostomy, especially when your stoma is an irregular shape as mine is.

I've joked that the Tibetans send monks into the graveyard to contemplate death and impermanence and that I have been given the even more advanced practice of contemplating poop in great detail and seeing the end of my intestine sticking out my belly. A very advanced practice indeed, often involving immersion in poop.

But happily, the side effects are diminishing now every day, especially the radiation burns on my butt and genitals, which are finally healing up and subsiding. I'm enjoying not having medical appointments every day.

All in all, I feel very lucky. I met so many folks at the cancer center who have been dealing with one cancer after another and who will be on chemotherapy for the rest of their lives. I had a relatively short course with a good prognosis. My spirits have been good throughout, and I've received wonderful support from friends.

I'm slowly cleaning out the things from my apartment that I no longer need—the medications, ointments, various mouth washes, bottles of pills, hand sanitizers, face masks, the thermometer I used many times daily when I was neutropenic, the cards in my wallet identifying me as a chemotherapy patient. Friends have gradually stopped their daily visits and check-in calls. I have weeks until my next medical appointment. My days feel amazingly open and free. I'm resuming meetings, private and public, in March.

Now the whole thing is kind of like a dream—the diagnosis, the surgery, the treatments, the side effects, the friends who supported me and came to my aid in so many ways—it's all like a dream. And now, here I am, sort of back to normal, but in some ways deeply changed, inwardly and outwardly.

There is still a slight discomfort when I sit down, but all the open sores from the radiation burns are healed, the scabs are gone. It is no longer painful to pee or wash myself there, and the discomfort in sitting is very slight now. I've gone back to the gym and feel like a normal person again, not a cancer patient.

I'm happy to report that I've lost over thirty pounds. I'm back to what I weighed before menopause bulked me up. And my hair is growing back.

Post-treatment Limbo

I'll be having a sigmoidoscopy and anal exam under anesthesia in May, and then a PET scan in June to determine if the tumor and the cancer are gone, if the treatment worked. Waiting for that is a bit like being in limbo.

It's kind of odd being back to "normal" again. Once again, I'm a reclusive hermit. And in a strange way, I found the period of several months after my treatment ended and before the exams and tests provided results to be more difficult emotionally than the treatment itself, which surprised me, but I've learned it's not uncommon.

During the treatment, I was totally in gear and focused on getting to my appointments, dealing with side effects, and so on. And I suppose I was still in shock in some way, absorbing the diagnosis, the surgery, my new life situation. Friends were being immensely supportive—people were dropping by every day, helping me out, emailing encouragement from afar, sending cards and gifts. I was driving to Medford every day for radiation, there were wonderful connections with doctors, nurses, technicians and other patients I saw there. In a funny way, painful as it all was, it was a bit like being at a party where I was the guest of honor. And with the chemo, they give you steroids, so I actually had great energy through much of the treatment. My mood was generally exceptionally good. It truly did feel like an enlivening, awakening journey.

Then the music stopped, the "party" ended, the guests all went home, and I was alone with the wreckage and the silence, back to "normal" life, except it wasn't quite normal.

Of course, friends still call and come by, just not as often, and of course it's a relief to be done with the painful parts of the treatment. I'm a solitary person by nature who doesn't really want visitors popping in every day and calling me constantly so, as with the ending of an actual party that one is hosting, it's both a relief and a certain feeling of emptiness when it ends. I'm sure this might be different in many ways for people who live with family and/or work an outside job with lots of daily human interaction.

Anyway, now I'm in limbo, not knowing if I'm cancer-free or, if I'm not, what lies ahead. I'm being with all this pretty well, not obsessing over it, not filled with fear, but there's a cloud of uncertainty in the background. And I've been tired. The steroids have definitely worn off. Apparently, there's an actual phenomenon that has been identified in the medical world, something like PTSD that happens in the aftermath of serious medical treatment.

The burns in my private parts have all healed and I'm no longer in any pain. I have learned, however, that radiation can affect and cause changes in the tissue and muscles for years to come.

241

CHAPTER SIXTEEN: Devotion

My Own Private Tropical Fish Tank

I was examined by the urogynecologist who first found this tumor. She said my vagina looks good, with no sign of the fistula, the hole where the tumor invaded from rectum to vagina. I saw both my oncologists and learned that I'll have sigmoidoscopies every six months for several years. And then I saw my surgeon, and that was sobering.

I had been cruising along on the optimistic idea that the treatment was going to work, the cancer would be gone, my bowel would eventually be reconnected, the ostomy would be gone, and all this would be behind me. I think they call it denial.

My surgeon told me that if the tumor is still there, they might consider a surgery to remove it. That would be the major abdominal surgery, and he said that from what he understands about my healthcare wishes, and I think he gets me quite well, I would probably elect not to have it because it's a long recovery and reduction of quality of life. I think he said I'd probably have six months to a year to live if the cancer recurred and I did nothing.

As for the possible reconnection of my bowel, he feels that, in my case, this would be a mistake. The tissue in my anus and rectum is already damaged from radiation, and the negative after-effects of radiation can continue to develop over years. Even if I had perfect bowel control when my intestine was reconnected, it could all be different a few years later. Not to mention the effects of aging, such as what happened to Mom, who lost bowel control in her last years. If that were to happen, if I had poor bowel control or no control at all, re-doing an ostomy is apparently very difficult. They can't put it in the same place on your belly where they put it before, which means it would be in a much more inconvenient location, perhaps utterly impossible to manage with one hand, and the risk of additional hernia increases.

Hearing all this was sobering. It ended my fantasy of the ostomy going away. I realized I would not want to take the risk of trying a reconnection, even if I looked like an ideal candidate for it, which I'm not. I'd rather have an ostomy than no bowel control.

I didn't sleep well that night.

I am supposed to be a presenter again at the SAND (Science and Nonduality) Conference in October in San Jose, but I can't really picture how traveling would work well with this ostomy bag. Of course, many people with ostomies travel the world, but my situation is a bit different, managing it one-handed; and I imagine everyone's situation is different in terms of bowel function, digestion, what types of ostomy bags fit well and which ones don't, and other factors as well.

Pooping in a bag is really not so bad. When I first saw my stoma in the hospital, I was admittedly rather repulsed, but I've grown fond of it. Once I got past the initial repulsion, I have found it rather marvelous to have the end of my intestine protruding out my belly. It's pink and slimy, and it undulates, expanding and contracting, shrinking and extending, and poop slides out of it into the bag in amazing varieties from liquid to solid. I often say it's a bit like having my own little tropical fish tank—like they have in waiting rooms as eye candy. Sometimes, in a solitary moment, I enjoy just peeking inside my pants and watching my stoma as it undulates. It's almost as good as Netflix, although I'm grateful to have that as well. Perhaps when I get older and more senile, I will begin watching my fish tank while out in public, unaware that I am transgressing social norms. This is something to look forward to. In addition to watching it, I talk to it. I even sing to it sometimes. Again, this may happen more publicly as senility increases and my remaining inhibitions fall away. I feel an exciting old age awaits me.

My radiation oncologist has given me a vaginal dilation kit to keep my vagina from closing down as an after-effect of the radiation. This is important so that my urinary system will continue to function. It looks like a collection of dildos of varying sizes with lubricant, and I am supposed to insert them for twenty minutes three times a week. Life is exciting in our sunset years, is it not?

My interest in sex and romance is now zero, and I find that a huge relief. Sex and romance took up a lot of time and energy back when all that was one of The Most Important Things in Life that I couldn't imagine living without. As I told my surgeon when he once mentioned the possibility that they might need to remove my vagina, "I wouldn't miss it. I'm not using it, and the care and management of the aging vagina is something I could happily live without."

If you'd told me when I was twenty that any of this would happen, I'd have been horrified, but now it is just ordinary life. Emptying the poop bag, dilating the vagina, singing to my stoma, enjoying my private fish tank.

Shining One Corner of the World

After retirement, people who felt like they were useful and productive members of society often feel that now they are useless, doing nothing important. Some sense of purpose or meaning seems to be missing. The prevailing advice to seniors is to stay busy—volunteer, take classes, be as active as you can be. But I would suggest at least considering the opposite possibility. Consider doing less. Consider relaxing. Consider spending time enjoying simply being alive. Watch the clouds, listen to the rain, taste the coffee, smell the roses. Of course, if you're drawn to being busy, by all means go for it. But don't assume the prevailing advice is necessarily worth following.

Maybe the one thing all of us can do to save the world is to simply take care of what's in front of us. In one of his talks, Suzuki Roshi said our job is "to shine one corner of the world—just one corner. If you shine one corner, then people around you will feel better." And it's true, isn't it? When we walk down the street and see a beautiful garden or a beautifully maintained house, it impacts us—just as it impacts us when the checkout clerk smiles at us or a passerby wishes us a good day.

Even something no one else will see, for example, the care and maintenance of my ostomy bag, impacts the whole universe. As Thich Nhat Hanh so beautifully explains, every apparent form contains the whole universe, which is the Buddhist teaching of emptiness, interdependence or interbeing. A piece of paper contains the trees, the sun, the rain, the lumberjack, the cows he ate, and so on—the whole universe. Each of us contains the stars, the oceans, all of our ancestors, and the whole universe. How we care for each small thing and each small moment is how we care for everything.

In Zen, they say things like, sweeping the floor is sweeping your mind. Cleaning the bathroom is seen as a spiritual practice every bit as important as sitting zazen, chanting, or reading the scriptures. Zen practice prepared me well for life with an ostomy. And truly, squeezing out poop, changing the bag, dealing with spills is no less sacred than bowing in front of the Buddha or sitting in darshan with Ramana Maharshi. Perhaps it is even one small way of saving the world. And, of course, ultimately, the world won't be saved any more than any of us will be saved from death and all the little deaths that life offers so abundantly along the way.

Maybe our challenge is to see only God everywhere, to find the beauty even in the darkness, to shine one corner of the world to the best of our ability, to *be* the freedom and the love and the joy that we seek.

Cancer Free

I had my long-awaited post-treatment sigmoidoscopy and exam under anesthesia by my surgeon, and I got the best possible news: no sign of tumor, no areas of concern requiring biopsies, everything looking good in there. Then I cleared the PET scan, which also showed the cancer gone, no areas of concern. Huge relief! I can truly say I'm cancer-free.

I'll be having biannual sigmoidoscopies and vaginal exams to make sure the tumor is not recurring, periodic blood tests, periodic ultrasounds to monitor the thyroid nodes that keep lighting up on my PET scans, and they want me to have annual CT scans to monitor a small spot on my lung that has lit up on both PET scans and to make sure the cancer isn't showing up anyplace else. I'm realizing that the cancer train doesn't exactly stop, or at least, not for a while.

My aunt who had an ostomy for colon cancer lived to be

ninety-nine. I don't want to live that long and be incapacitated, in constant pain and unable to take care of myself, as she was. But I'm not ready to sign off yet.

I don't think we ever know what we'll do until we're in a situation. But I wonder how many cancer screenings I'll agree to going forward. Once again, I'm struck by the paradoxes of this liminal age, on the cusp of truly old age, but not quite there yet, still basically mentally and physically okay. Yes, joints are stiffer, there's arthritis here and there, the bones are thinning, I have an ostomy and a CPAP machine. But I'm still able to live independently, still have good energy most of the time, still feel happy to be alive. At what point, do you stop trying to survive?

Southern Oregon is on fire again. We have fires burning all around us. My car is coated in ash, the air is toxic and smoky for over a month. We are told to stay indoors as much as possible and keep windows closed. I'm a bit stir-crazy, but at least I have the gym for some exercise. It's been very hot as well, triple-digits and high nineties, Fahrenheit. Last summer it was over a month of toxic air. This is the new normal apparently. Fire season begins earlier, lasts longer, and is more severe every year. I imagine we'll get some good years here and there, and indeed, the following summer will turn out to be almost entirely smoke-free, but the trend is getting worse, not better.

I finally cancelled my trip in October to California and my annual presentation at the SAND Conference. The ostomy is still presenting too many challenges to make travel feel doable. I don't know if this will change in time—it might or might not. The good thing is, I'll be here in Ashland for October, which is one of my favorite months here. We get fabulous autumn colors, like New England, and I have often missed most of it by being down in California then.

Autumn into Winter

I saw my oncologist's nurse practitioner today for a routine visit and learned that less than half the people who have the cancer I had, at the stage it was at, live more than five years. Maybe I'll be one of the forty-five percent who survive beyond that, but it was sobering. I could feel tears in my eyes, feeling how much I love being alive, how precious it is, even though I don't fear death.

I popped a crown off my back tooth on Thanksgiving morning. My dentist glued it on again the following week. Meanwhile, Paradise, California burned to the ground in the most destructive wildfire in California history.

My one-year sigmoidoscopy showed no sign of recurrence and nothing that needed biopsy. Ann and I went out to dinner to celebrate, followed by very decadent chocolate cake.

My blood work, which they've been doing monthly, is all good as far as tumor markers and everything else, except for my white count, which has been low. I've been mildly neutropenic again, but on the last test, it had finally gone up slightly. Hopefully, it's just an after-effect of the radiation to the pelvis and will bounce back.

The ostomy feels quite normal now and managing it has become easier and easier. It does limit my life in some ways, including so far making it impossible to travel, but I'm okay with those limitations.

There *are* different kinds of ostomy bags including disposable ones that you throw away rather than emptying when they fill up, which might allow me to travel with ease. I haven't yet found one of those that works well for me, but I haven't dedicated enormous time and energy to that project either. If I were younger and at a different stage of life, I would probably be much more concerned about trying to find a way to travel again. But at this stage of life, I'm quite content to be where I am.

And then I get word that one of my Bay Area friends just died of a heart attack. It was sudden and unexpected. She was out having dinner with friends before going to the theater, and zap. She was gone in an instant. One more down.

The True Home

I'm at peace with the reality that I probably won't ever travel again. In some ways, it is a blessing. All my life, I've moved from place to place, never feeling that any place was quite right.

But I have realized finally that the only true Home is Here-Now—this timeless, placeless immediacy or presence where we always already are, and which we can never really leave because it is what we are and all there is. And somehow, it feels oddly appropriate that, after this long life of playing musical chairs, the music has finally stopped, and this small city in rural Oregon is where I am. Grounded at last, right here, right now, finding the Holy Reality in this very moment and not seeking it elsewhere. I've gotten more interested in the actuality of whatever presents itself in the moment than in those glossy travel brochures in the mind that promise a better somewhere.

A Close Call

In early December, I developed some back, hip, groin, and leg pain. I mentioned it to my oncologist on a routine visit. He had told me to report any such pain, as I am apparently at risk for bone cancer. He said we'd wait until Christmas and, if I still had it then, I should let him know. By Christmas, it hadn't gone away, and the pain was fairly intense. So he scheduled me for a nuclear bone scan, which looks for bone cancer. I was feeling quite confident this was arthritis and not bone cancer, but my oncologist wanted the scan.

Meanwhile, in other bodily realms, my dentist has glued my crown back on for the second time, after it popped out first on Thanksgiving morning and then, after he re-glued, again on Christmas morning. But, aside from these minor crumblings, I seem to be in good health, and my spirits have been good.

I have to get up very early the morning of the scan to allow time for stretching, shower, ostomy bag change, meditation, breakfast, and then the morning ostomy extravaganza—pooping and emptying several times—all before I leave in mid-morning for my scan, which is in two parts and will take until late afternoon.

I have an appointment to see one of my oncologist's PAs later in the week to get the results which, they told me, they never give out over the phone. But by mistake, the results came to my online

MyChart, because it's a different system, and it was an automated send. So, on the night of the super blood wolf moon, which is a rare, large, full moon with total eclipse, invisible here because of clouds and rain, I saw the report.

Doesn't sound good: "Findings suggest metastatic disease." I start googling, deciphering the medical terminology, trying to get some idea what this means. Bone cancer sounds like the cancer you definitely don't want to have. I will learn much more about what this means and what my options are when I see the oncologist's PA. Probably I will be embarking on another medical whirlwind, and I don't know if I will come out of this one alive. From what I've learned on Google, and from talking to a friend who is a doctor and reading her the report, a quick death might be the best outcome, but it doesn't sound like the most likely. However, I'm trying not to jump to conclusions until I hear from the oncology PA.

At the oncology appointment, the PA told me my cancer has metastasized to my bones, that they now consider it incurable. All they can do now is try to slow it down and provide palliative measures. I probably can't have any more radiation, except possibly palliative radiation, which is different, so the only option for slowing it down will probably be chemo. They will follow my lead about how much treatment I do or don't want. Meanwhile, they've ordered a CT scan to get a better look and see if it has spread to organs and/or lymph.

Another week. A CT scan. And then I go to the appointment with my oncologist to get the CT results. I'm imagining I may very well be told it has spread to my organs and that I have only months to live. But, surprise! No sign of cancer anywhere else, and the radiologists interpreting the CT scan, including one who specializes in bone, think it's not cancer after all. The fractures in my back and pelvis appear to be healing, which would not be the case with cancer. Now they think it is more likely a mix of "insufficiency fractures, weak bones, spinal deterioration and arthritis."

In the space of an hour, I went from being totally sure it was incurable cancer to being fairly sure it's not. Given my history, they can't totally rule out the possibility that it could be cancer, but that now looks very unlikely. They'll do a repeat CT in six weeks to check again. As a friend of mine later said, "Who would have thought that a diagnosis of fractures, weak bones, spinal degeneration, and arthritis would be good news? But indeed it is!" I could literally feel my intestines unwinding on the drive home from the oncologist. They had apparently clenched up more than I had realized.

Meanwhile, the crown that popped off my tooth first on Thanksgiving, then again on Christmas, popped off again and this time I swallowed it, so I've been literally combing through my poop ever since then, so far to no avail. This is definitely a new level in my journey down into the bowels of the human experience. But finally, after many days, I stop searching because my dentist decides that extraction is the best solution given all the variables of my situation. I make an appointment with an oral surgeon to have that done.

I had been in good spirits through this whole drama, putting one foot in front of the next, and suddenly I was hit with massive exhaustion. Apparently this close call with the grim reaper and the thought of more chemotherapy took more of a toll on me than I realized. I'm realizing now that this kind of rollercoaster ride comes with the territory of cancer recovery, at least for the foreseeable future. Plus, chronic back pain is exhausting.

Some days we don't know how we can go on. A heaviness comes. I've had and continue to have a very blessed life—so many blessings and such small hardships in the larger scheme of things, when I think of what some people endure and have endured. But still, the heaviness comes at times. This morning, I had a leaking ostomy bag for the fifth time in less than a month. Poop landing on the floor. My back pain had been much worse again. I've had serious fatigue. And this morning, there was a great heaviness, a feeling of being worn down, of not knowing how I can go on.

And then there was a remembering of the simplicity of being still, being present, simply *being*. I felt the heart open, and suddenly all was well. The pain was still there. But everything had shifted. This is the miracle of the crucifixion turning into the resurrection, the alchemy of genuine transformation, the possibility of being liberated on the spot.

The repeat CT confirmed that the fractures in my back were healing, further validating the conclusion that it isn't cancer. I had months of physical therapy. The pain improved, got worse, then improved again. It migrated from one spot to another. Finally, in August, after nine months, it was gone. But those eight months gave me great compassion for people who live with chronic back pain. Now I just have the normal mild occasional passing backaches that seem to be a feature of the aging body.

Meeting the Darkness

We need not fear the passing of the world. Do we regret a dream, a day? They pass to re-emerge—each one a wave upon the shore. Regret marks the limit of our sense of life, our fear of the beyond.

—John Butler

In the private meetings I hold, many people express grave concerns and deep fears these days over both escalating climate change and America potentially descending into fascism.

It has occurred to me how much more vulnerable I am with an ostomy to any kind of collapse. I am much more dependent now on the fragile systems that we take for granted, the systems that any natural disaster, civil war or cyber-attack could so easily topple. For example, it is predicted that the Cascadia earthquake will be the worst natural disaster in US history when it occurs. The tectonic plate subduction zone runs up the ocean floor along the Pacific Northwest. I'm told that Oregon is expected to take the brunt of it, and the predictions for this area in southern Oregon, inland from the coast, are that we will be completely cut off from the outside world, possibly without electricity or running water for several weeks. Rescue operations will likely have to focus on the coastal areas, which will be hardest hit. What will I do if I can't get my ostomy bags and other supplies, which are shipped here from elsewhere? Without my bags, poop will simply pour out my belly uncontrollably. And imagine dealing with a bag leak in the middle of the night and being covered in diarrhea without electricity or running water. Without being able to wash and clean the area properly, I'll be at high risk of infection.

Of course, all of this is *thinking* and *imagining*, and if any of it *actually* happens, it won't be the way I imagine it now. One way or another, even if I die of sepsis, covered in poop, moaning in pain, I will be okay. All will be well in the deeper sense. So I don't dwell on these scary "what if'" scenarios, but they *have* occurred to me. Wildfire and earthquakes are always a possibility in southern Oregon, and being prepared for these disasters is something people here take seriously. Obsessively thinking and worrying about such things is useless suffering, but giving them intelligent thought and preparation is common sense. I have a flashlight, a hard hat and a pair of shoes by my bed, for example, in case the earthquake leaves us in the dark with falling debris, walking through broken glass. I have bottles of water and some canned goods on hand. And now, I have a box of already-cut ostomy bags and supplies packed in the closet ready to grab if needed.

Our ability to think about what might happen and prepare for it has gotten us to the moon and to the top of the food chain. Imagination and thinking are great powers, beautiful powers. But they can also bring us great suffering. As Mark Twain famously said, I've been through some terrible things in my life, and some of them actually happened.

It's helpful to share our concerns, to share information and to stay informed. And it's important to speak out against injustice and harm. In times of darkness, community is important. At the same time, it's important not to get caught up in recycling despair, spreading fear and stories of doom. It's a balancing act between not turning away and not becoming hypnotized by negativity.

After all, nothing is set in stone. This whole manifestation is not as solid as it appears. It's worth remembering how powerful each of us is, not just in our overt actions, but in our imagination, our thinking, the moods we transmit and share, the things we do and don't do. In a very real sense, consciousness is *creating* the world, not showing us some objectively existing "outside" reality. The biologist Rupert Sheldrake once proposed that most of the so-called "laws of nature" are more like habits, which suggests that maybe everything is far more malleable than we think. And if everything *is* made of pure consciousness, as even many scientists are now beginning to think, who knows what might be possible? One way or another, maybe there *will* be a huge shift in consciousness and real action globally on a level that so far has not happened. Maybe a solution will show up that no one can yet imagine. Or maybe our species will not survive.

Humans didn't do this deliberately. We simply followed our nature—seeking comfort, avoiding pain, exploring new places, inventing tools, inventing bigger and better tools to make our lives more comfortable and enhance our chances for survival. We invented deadly pesticides to make life more comfortable, not to poison the planet. We built up industries for the same reason, not to pollute the earth or bring about our own extinction. And yet, that's where it has taken us. And who is to say this is unnatural or tragic?

Maybe from a larger perspective, it's all in perfect balance, including the possible demise of the human species and even all organic life on this planet. After all, these profit-seeking, gas-guzzling, meat-eating, baby-producing, jet-traveling, tree-felling, plastic-using sapiens who seem to be mindlessly overrunning the earth are themselves an expression of the natural world, a movement of the universe. *Everything* is an appearance in consciousness, all of it empty of enduring form or substance, very much like a dream. Everything passes. No-thing remains.

One way or another, with or without climate change, all humans will eventually die. The planet will die. The sun will eventually explode. No form survives. And that's not bad news. That's what makes life so alive, so dynamic. Knowing this doesn't eliminate heartbreak and grief or the experience of loss, but it puts it all in a different light.

As I realize more and more deeply, the greatest gift we can offer to ourselves and the world is to be awake and rooted in love. That doesn't mean ignoring the darkness or always being in a good mood, but it means seeing the light and the beauty that is here even in the darkness, and not wallowing obsessively and pointlessly in negative spin. It means being vulnerable and undefended, allowing the heart to open, again and again, relinquishing our certainty about what is right. It means giving up the control we've never really had, dying to the past. From love, from presence, intelligent action arises—whether it is the environmental activism of a Greta Thunberg, the silent contribution of someone like Ramana Maharshi, or those musicians making beautiful music on the deck of the Titanic as it sank.

It's always worth noticing what we are *actually* devoting our time and energy to, where we are putting our attention, whether it is on scary thoughts, social media, people we dislike, or the unconditional love that permeates it all. When we open to love, when we devote ourselves to presence, when we're awake Here-Now, we know in our hearts that all is well, no matter what seems to happen in the movie of waking life.

True Devotion

Open the Eyes of Your Heart, Look, Everywhere Is God.

—Mooji

Devotion is a word I like a lot. It has a warmth to it, a heart quality. Devotion is a kind of curiosity, attention, exploration and wonderment, like a lover exploring the beloved, or a child discovering the miracle of every ordinary thing. Devotion sees only the Beloved everywhere.

Some people think devotion means being at the feet of some guru, but it's equally possible to be devoted to the sounds of rain, the taste of tea, the aroma of coffee, the sensations throughout the body, the ways the afternoon light dances on the wall, the listening presence, the silence, the stillness beholding and permeating it all. Devotion is awake to both the beauty and the brokenness of life. It finds the extraordinary in the ordinary, the perfection in the imperfection, the miraculous in the everyday. Devotion is unconditional love and gratitude for everything. It can only manifest in duality, in the great paradox of lover and beloved—not one, not two—the melting away of all separation in love, the wholeness that transcends and includes the seemingly opposite polarities. Devotion is at once intimate and transcendent, bringing earth and heaven together in the heart. Devotion is another word for meditation, prayer, yoga, or the pathless path of awakening Here-Now. And it's a wonderful question to live with: what are we devoting ourselves to in this moment right now?

What Is This? What Matters?

If something seems complicated, beware. Truth is very, very simple.

—John Butler

I don't actually know how it all goes together—heaven and earth, spirituality and politics, consciousness and the material world. What's real? What matters? These are questions to meditate upon, to live with. They are ultimately unanswerable, except in whatever way each of our lives answers them. Clearly, it's not all neatly resolvable. Life is messy and mysterious and no one really knows exactly what is going on here, even as we know it intimately in another sense.

Most of us are taught that we're born into a world made of matter, that our brains somehow produce consciousness, and that through our senses, consciousness perceives an actual outside world. Scientists now tell us that the brain doesn't actually *show* us an outside world, but in many ways—and maybe in every way—*creates* it. Consciousness finds or creates patterns, divides and freezes an ever-changing subatomic dance of energy into apparent forms that appear solid and separate, and creates the illusion of a self with agency and control pulling the levers. Dogs, ants, bats and other creatures see a different "outside world" from the one we see and, even among humans, we don't all see exactly the same world. As Mooji says, there is one Earth but billions of worlds. And as Buddhism would point out, even "the earth" is not one thing that stays the same.

In fact, I have no way of knowing what you mean by "red," "orgasm," "fear," "the taste of coffee," or anything else. I simply infer that it is more or less the same thing I mean. And actually, I have no way of knowing that "you" even exist as anything other than a character in a dream I am dreaming.

Any dreamer I can imagine, such as a brain in a skull, an activity of a nervous system, a computer simulation in the matrix, or even some conceptual image of "Consciousness" or "God," is itself witnessed by a seeing that cannot be objectified or seen.

All we ever *actually* have is present experiencing, which boils down to the undeniable knowingness of being here now, present and aware, and the undeniable fact of this ever-changing appearance— sensations, thoughts, feelings, perceptions—not those words or concepts, but the naked actuality to which they point. And that naked actuality is an inconceivable, immediate happening that can never actually be grasped or contained by *any* concept or formula.

We can never know with certainty that anything exists outside of present experiencing. We can *believe* or *imagine* or *think* that something is "out there," outside of present experiencing, but that belief, that thought, that imagining is nothing but present experiencing. Of course, the very notion of anything being "outside" or "inside" anything else presumes the existence of separate objects; and the more closely we look at reality, the more all such apparently separate objects turn out not to be separate, independent or definable at all. In actual direct experience, we can't find any place where what we call "consciousness" ends and what we call "the content of consciousness" begins, or for that matter, where "I" end and "you" begin.

The thinking mind loves to divide reality up into pieces and then tie itself into knots trying to figure out which piece comes first and which causes which. Which comes first, we wonder, the brain or consciousness, mind or matter, the chicken or the egg? Is consciousness occurring in the tissues of the brain, or are the tissues of the brain an appearance in consciousness? We get into Great Muddles over such questions. *But what are we actually talking about?* The more closely we examine "tissues," "brains" or "consciousness," the more indeterminate, unknowable and unresolvable they all seem to become. It all slips through our fingers like water or smoke. These words are sounds we make, sophisticated animal grunts, black squiggles on a page, referring to no actual *thing* that can ever be found or pinned down—but

257

we *think* we know what we're talking about. Any form that seems to exist, if we look closely at it, either with science or careful open attention, turns out to be nothing solid or persisting or independent from everything it supposedly is not. There is no chicken without an egg, and no egg without a chicken—in fact, there is no egg and no chicken. Which isn't to say there is nothing, but *whatever-this-is,* it is simply not resolvable into such apparent "things" as eggs, chickens, consciousness and tissues.

It does *seem,* in the movie of waking life (present experiencing), that there is an undeniable relationship between "the brain" and "consciousness." If you sustain a head injury, or if a neurosurgeon probes different spots on the brain, your conscious experience changes or disappears. By probing a certain spot on the brain, they can even induce an out-of-body experience where you will seem to be looking down on the operating table from above. Or at least, *so it appears in the movie of waking life,* i.e., in present experiencing or consciousness. Because all these experiments are *themselves* appearances in consciousness, as are measurements of brain activity and the experiences of having or performing brain surgery. In fact, no brain has ever appeared outside of consciousness—i.e., outside present experiencing. Any brain you— or any scientist or surgeon—has ever seen, read about, operated on, or touched was an experience in consciousness. If we cut open the brain, we won't find the room you're sitting in or the book you're holding or the sounds you're hearing at this moment. So where exactly is all that happening? Stimulating a part of the brain may trigger certain sensory experiences, but where do these experiences actually occur?

Here-Now—present-ness, immediacy, aware presence, consciousness—is the common factor in every different experience. But what exactly *is* that? "It" can't be grasped because "it" is more like the *it-less-ness* of everything. Here-Now is not an object that can be defined, measured, photographed, held in your hand, pointed to, or pinned down. And yet, there is nothing you can point to and nowhere you can go that is not Here-Now.

Having spent considerable time listening deeply and feeling into the nature of Here-Now, it seems clear that whatever is going on here is far subtler and more elusive than any of our stories about it or our usual clunky ideas, even our most refined scientific or spiritual ideas. And as science continues to explore matter, what seems solid on the surface is discovered to be less and less solid in reality and more and more dependent on the observing consciousness. And the more I explore my own conscious experience directly, the same thing happens. The living actuality seems to reveal itself as less and less concrete or locatable, and more and more an evaporating appearance that vanishes as soon as it arrives.

The more closely one examines the living reality, the more one sees that one's life story, family history, world history, the current political scene, and the whole movie of waking life is not objectively "real" in the way we think it is. Do the events in a dream really happen? Nonetheless, there is *something* that *is* real in every experience and every memory, just as there is something real in a dream, a mirage, or an optical illusion. That reality, it seems to me, is the *presence* of it, the awaring presence that is at once being and beholding it—consciousness itself. And yet, we can't exactly get hold of what that even *is*.

More and more, it seems to me that so-called awakening is nothing more or less than simply noticing—again and again, as it happens—how this fluid and ungraspable actuality has seemingly solidified into something coherent and understandable. To wake up is to *see* this illusory solidification and reification for what it is. Of course, that solidification and reification is itself part of the dance, part of how the universe is moving. We can't eliminate it or function without it. But it can be held more lightly and allowed to dissolve.

Reality seems to have multiple holographic or fractal perspectives or viewpoints from which it can be seen. There are billions of different movies playing simultaneously in unicity. And we can look at this living reality—or more accurately, it can look at itself—in so many different ways. It can be seen and experienced as formless consciousness, as energy, as sensations, as an apparently coherent world of people, families and governments, as a multitude of narratives, stories, maps and mythologies—and it's *all* included in *what is*.

At one level, we have moral discernment, ethical considerations, social and political relationships of varying kinds, human feelings, family ties, marriage vows, history, future goals, presidential elections, and so on. We care about climate change, whether we will have enough money for our retirement, what we're going to eat for dinner. At another level, all of this is some inconceivable and impersonal movement of energy without meaning or purpose, neither good nor bad. And *all* these levels or perspectives are real. Absolute truth doesn't negate conventional truth, just as quantum mechanics doesn't negate Newtonian physics at the level of ordinary life. We can have beautiful experiences of transcendence, but we still have to pay the rent or the mortgage, buy groceries, deal with the overflowing toilet, and respond in one way or another to the latest family crisis or world situation. And no matter how strongly we might *believe* that consciousness is all there is, and that the world we see is nothing more substantial than a dream, most of us won't test it out by jumping off a tall building to see if we can fly. In some way, the laws—or habit patterns—discovered by physics and biology are not to be dismissed or ignored.

Universes come and go. Zoom in close enough, down to the subatomic level, or zoom back far enough to the distant reaches of outer space, and nothing that happens in this human drama seems all that consequential or even meaningful anymore. In fact, it's not even *here* anymore in any recognizable way. And yet, at the same time, there is the phenomenon of quantum entanglement and the way that one particle is instantly in touch with its partner even at vast distances. Nothing matters, in one sense, and everything matters in another. We can't dismiss or ignore either side, relative or absolute, fleshy or transcendent. It's one undivided whole. The leaf falling in New Jersey is integral to the hurricane that forms in the ocean on the other side of the world. Everything is the cause and the effect of everything else.

On the relative level of ordinary reality, the starving child really *does* need food to survive, and the hunger pains really *do* hurt, and the mother's grief really *is* agonizing, and each of us will do whatever life moves us to do when faced with this reality. But from the cosmic perspective, whether the child survives or not, whether being hungry hurts or doesn't, whether we join an aid organization or turn away, is all simply another momentary appearance in the seamless totality that includes everything. In that larger sense, it is one undivided energy, endlessly reshaping itself. It only *appears* to be a child or a famine or a sensation we call hunger or a feeling we call compassion.

One moment our life drama and the world drama seem totally real and important, and in another moment, they seem no more substantial than last night's dream. Children love to build sandcastles and then smoosh them. We love to go to the movies and then come out again after it ends. Tibetan monks sometimes spend days creating intricate mandalas with grains of colored sand, and then when they've finished, they enjoy it for a moment, and then they wreck it. Maybe the entire universe as we know it is like one of those mandalas, a beautiful painting in emptiness. Perhaps all these examples are microcosms of how consciousness likes to create things and then gleefully destroy them. Maybe every moment is a painting in emptiness. Maybe the whole history of planet Earth and human development is like one of those sandcastles on the beach, and at some moment, consciousness or God or the universe will wipe it out with climate change or a nuclear holocaust or an asteroid. Maybe a lifetime is a mandala, and at death, it is gleefully wiped out.

Maybe this whole manifestation that we call "the world" or "the movie of waking life" is a neverending look into the mirror. Everything I see "out there" is myself. One moment Buddha, the next moment Hitler. The One Self—aka, no self at all—is playing all the parts, dreaming all the dreams, exploring every possibility.

But rather than getting tied up in knots trying to figure out how the whole universe works, or trying to nail down the right metaphysical formulation or the best philosophy, or trying to figure out once and for all what happens after death, I find it much more helpful to drop *all* our ideas, concepts and beliefs and return again and again to the openness of not knowing and the immediacy and simplicity of this moment, this living presence Here-Now.

The Freedom of the Elbow Not Bending Backwards

I found that things became a lot easier when I no longer expected to win. You abandon your masterpiece and you sink into the real Masterpiece.

—Leonard Cohen

As I age, life has gotten simpler and quieter. I'm content with less. I appreciate ever more deeply the beauty of nothing, the beauty of not doing, the beauty of silence, stillness and emptiness. I get great joy from simple, ordinary, everyday things—the view out my window, the sounds of rain, the glowing light on a tree at sunrise or sunset, the pleasure of being with a friend, the enjoyment of a cup of coffee, sitting quietly doing nothing. I am more able to relax with the natural movements of life that bring an ever-changing mix of war and peace, sadness and joy, birth and death. This is the freedom of realizing that "nothing really matters," as my mother so joyously expressed it, and the wonder of "everything falling away" that my first lover found so irresistibly interesting.

Again and again, I find liberation in the very places I thought it was not—in brokenness and imperfection, disappointment and disillusionment, limitation and death, failure and darkness, unresolvability and uncertainty, groundlessness and everything falling apart. This is "the freedom of the elbow not bending backwards," as they say in Zen. Of course, the elbow can't bend backwards without breaking. So this is not the freedom to do what I want, but the freedom to be as I am, and the freedom for everything to be as it is, which is no way and every way, and never the same way twice. This is the freedom of nothing to grasp.

There's no one-size-fits-all path through life. Every one of us is unique. Each of us is a jewel with a particular gift to give that no one else can offer. Slowly, I am learning to be who I am in every sense—to be Joan and not somebody else, and to be no-thing at all—the open space of awareness, the undivided presence, the light, the germinal darkness, the unconditional love that is our essential nature. In one sense, I can't possibly fail at either but, in another sense, I fail again and again. And yet, I feel deeply that there are no mistakes. We live in extraordinary times, facing the probable collapse of the civilization we've so innocently built on sand, with all the chaos and suffering this will likely entail, ending perhaps in the extinction of life on Earth. But whatever happens, I feel certain that there is something at the Heart of everything that cannot be destroyed; and that the deepest truth is love, not hate.

For me, the never-ending, always Now, pathless path of awakening boils down to simply being awake, being present, being truly alive—seeing the beauty in everything, living in gratitude and devotion, enjoying the dance of life, being just this moment, not knowing what anything is, clinging to nothing, recognizing—not in the head, but in the heart—that *everything belongs*, that nothing persists, that every moment is fresh and new.

The spiritual journey is about waking up again and again (Now) from the hypnotic trance of thought and belief. When upsets come, when there is a storm of me-centered emotion-thought, it is the willingness to allow the heart to break open—to see and feel those powerful urges to control, to defend, to win, to be right, to make myself and the world and everyone in it behave in the ways I think we all should—and to allow those hardened walls to melt and dissolve. This is both incredibly challenging and incredibly easy. The challenging part is getting to the place where there is the willingness to let go. Sometimes that takes a while. In the meantime, it is the willingness to simply *be* that tight, contracted energy, to feel the pain of it. The letting go is effortless and always such a huge relief once it happens. As Leonard says, you abandon your masterpiece, and you sink into the real Masterpiece, which is actually where you've always been and all there is.

May we all cherish the gift of life and, when the time comes, welcome the gift of death. If we're lucky enough to reach old age, may we enjoy the adventure of falling apart and losing everything. May we meet this *Kali Yuga*, this planetary time of darkness and collapse, with an open heart, with tenderness, with love for all beings, with joy and not despair. May we discover the Holy Reality everywhere, in every breath, in every moment, even in the pain and the darkness. May we find the wisdom in no escape. That is my prayer for all of us, the One appearing as many in this dance of birth and death, coming and going, arriving and departing, always Here-Now.

Acknowledgements

Infinite gratitude to my parents, Dorothy and Wallace, my first teachers and greatest supporters, always in my heart.

A deep bow to Judith Cope and Ann Strauss for your friendship and support, especially during my journey with cancer. You are my heroes.

Thank you to Karen Dodson for your very generous support and friendship in the wake of my mother's death. You made joyful and easy what would otherwise have been daunting.

Thank you to Crystal Chubb, Amalia Durham and Lola Moonfrog for being there for Mom and me during her life and in her dying. Thank you also to Michael Jones, Sarah Nevin, all my Chicago friends and my mother's many friends for your loving support of her and me.

Thank you to those Chicago friends who so generously and tirelessly helped me pack up to leave for Oregon, especially Tom Fleming, Diana Warren, Linda Grossman, Dan DeLorenzo and Allen Baker.

Thank you to all the friends who supported me in so many different ways when I had cancer, especially Paula Kimbro, Micky Duxbury, Carl Miskell, Lisa Schwartz, Susan McCallum, Ajana Miki, Susan Bartholomew, Russell Graves, Zaya Benazzo, Arida Emrys, Frank Connors, Jill Limerick, Molly Jones, Holly McCormack, Jane Barber, Loretta Callahan, Les Collins, Betsy Wessler, Sharry Teague, Jon Bernie, d Allen, Dennis Peak, Grace Bubeck, Lynn Fraser, Lenore Friedman, Layena Camhi, Dami Roelse, Canela Michelle Meyers, Lynne VandeBunte, and so many other friends and people on Facebook who sent their love, prayers and support in many different ways.

Thank you to the remarkable medical team who saved my life, especially Dr. Mark Mason, my surgeon; Dr. Kenneth Haugen, my radiation oncologist; Dr. Mujahid Rizvi, my chemo oncologist; Jessica Luckman and Dr. Brooks at urogynecology; the marvelous wound-ostomy nurses Bev and Jeannette; all the nurses who cared for me in the hospital; the wonderful radiation techs with whom I had such a great time while burning my private parts and dissolving my tumor; my home health nurses; and all the PAs, NPs, nurses, phlebotomists, medical assistants and clerical workers at the cancer centers. I received such excellent and loving care from all of you, for which I remain profoundly grateful.

A deep bow to the world's greatest therapist, Fern Snogren.

Deep gratitude to Ken James, Susan Bartholomew, d Allen, and Catherine Noyce for very helpful feedback on an initial draft of this book; to Nancy Parker for editing the final draft; and to Rose Youd for final proofing.

Huge thanks to Julian and Catherine Noyce for publishing my books and doing such a beautiful job—and for your friendship, your devotion to animal welfare, and all the great books you've delivered to the world.

Very deep appreciation to Zaya and Maurizio Benazzo, Lisa Breschi and the whole SAND team for your extraordinary generosity to me and for all the truly remarkable work you do in fostering open-minded, openhearted exploration and dialog among many diverse perspectives, spiritual and scientific, in a spirit of love, joy, wonder and delight.

Immense gratitude for all the teachers, colleagues, friends and fellow travelers who have been helpful to me on the pathless path. Special thanks to Toni Packer, Springwater Center, Steve Hagen, Anam Thubten, Joko Beck, Gangaji, Francis Lucille, Rupert Spira, Mooji, John Butler, Richard Witteman, Mark Bryant, Sandra Gonzalez, d Allen, Darryl Bailey, Jon Bernie, Mel Weitsman, Joyce Lichenstein, and John Tarrant.

Finally, thank you to everyone I've been blessed to meet with individually or in groups, to all my readers, to all the generous people who have sent in donations, to the many friends and teachers I haven't named, and to anyone I would surely have wanted to mention but have inadvertently, in my ever-increasing senility, left out. Thank you all.

Books in print from New Sarum Press

Real World Nonduality—Reports From The Field;
Various authors

The Ten Thousand Things by Robert Saltzman

Depending on No-Thing by Robert Saltzman

The Joy of True Meditation by Jeff Foster

'What the...' A Conversation About Living by Darryl Bailey

The Freedom to Love—The Life and Vision of Catherine Harding
by Karin Visser

Coming in Winter 2019

Glorious Alchemy—Living the Lalitā Sahasranāma by
Kavitha Chinnaiyan

Collision with the Infinite by Suzanne Segal

Open to the Unknown by Jean Klein

Transmission of the Flame by Jean Klein

Yoga in The Kashmir Tradition (2nd Edition) by Billy Doyle

The Mirage of Separation by Billy Doyle

Conversations on Non-Duality
Twenty-six Awakenings

Interviews by Iain and Renate McNay for conscious.tv

Self-realisation, awakening or enlightenment has been the goal of spiritual
seeking since time immemorial. Another
way of saying this is that everyone is
searching for happiness. What is the
nature of this happiness? What is the
self that is to be realised? What is meant
by 'awakening' or 'enlightenment'? Can
it be brought about by effort? To whom
does it occur? How is it expressed in life?

Everybody seeks happiness although
it is not often noticed that seeking itself is
precisely the activity that veils the very
happiness that is being sought. When it
is seen very clearly that happiness is not to be found in any particular
object, state of circumstance, a deep relaxation takes place. This relaxation leaves us at the threshold of another possibility. This possibility is
felt as an invitation from an unknown and yet strangely familiar direction. It is a call to return to our true home, the source of happiness.

Conversations on Non-Duality gives twenty-six expressions of
liberation which have been shaped by different life experiences, each
offering a unique perspective.

David Bingham, Daniel Brown, Sundance Burke, Katie Davis,
Peter Fenner, Steve Ford, Jeff Foster, Suzanne Foxton, Gangaji, Richard
Lang, Roger Linden, Wayne Liquorman, Francis Lucille, Mooji,
Catherine Noyce, Jac O'Keeffe, Tony Parsons, Bernie Prior, Halina
Pytlasinska, Genpo Roshi, Florian Schlosser, Mandi Solk, Rupert
Spira, James Swartz, Richard Sylvester and Pamela Wilson.

www.conscious.tv

Made in the USA
Columbia, SC
21 February 2020

88240877R00171